Energy Investing

FOR

DUMMIES®

A Wiley Brand

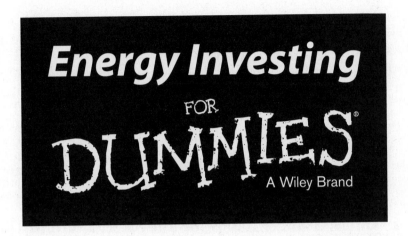

Energy Investing

FOR

DUMMIES

A Wiley Brand

by Nick Hodge
with Jeff Siegel, Christian DeHaemer,
and Keith Kohl

Energy Investing For Dummies®

Published by: **John Wiley & Sons, Inc.,** 111 River Street, Hoboken, NJ 07030-5774, www.wiley.com

Copyright © 2013 by John Wiley & Sons, Inc., Hoboken, New Jersey

Published simultaneously in Canada

For general information on our other products and services, please contact our Customer Care Department within the U.S. at 877-762-2974, outside the U.S. at 317-572-3993, or fax 317-572-4002. For technical support, please visit www.wiley.com/techsupport.

Wiley publishes in a variety of print and electronic formats and by print-on-demand. Some material included with standard print versions of this book may not be included in e-books or in print-on-demand. If this book refers to media such as a CD or DVD that is not included in the version you purchased, you may download this material at http://booksupport.wiley.com. For more information about Wiley products, visit www.wiley.com.

Library of Congress Control Number: 2013942774

ISBN 978-1-118-11641-8 (pbk); ISBN 978-1-118-22430-4 (ebk); ISBN 978-1-118-26254-2 (ebk); ISBN 978-1-118-23323-8 (ebk)

Manufactured in the United States of America

10 9 8 7 6 5 4 3 2

Contents at a Glance

Table of Contents

Part V: Investing in the Future: Modern Energy........... 235

Chapter 17: Solar Investing: It's Raining Electrons 237

Chapter 18: When the Winds Change Direction 249

Chapter 19: Geothermal: The Devil's Hot Tub 259

Introduction

Energy affects every single human endeavor. It's at the heart of everything people do. From wood to whale oil to the modern forms of energy you see today, each generation has needed more energy and looked for new ways to get it. Today, supplying energy to a growing global population is one of the largest and most valuable industries in the world. Valued at around $7 trillion, the global energy industry is responsible for 10 percent of the world's annual gross domestic product (GDP).

Energy powers your car, your house, and your phone. It moves people and goods across oceans and continents. It has created cartels, started wars, and produced family fortunes. No person or company is isolated from energy implications.

Because of constant and growing demand, energy makes for a great investment. It historically outperforms the market. Over the past 15 years, for example, a well-managed, broad-based energy fund returned 400 percent more than the Dow Jones Industrial Average. Energy prices haven't slouched, either, as you undoubtedly see at every gas station marquee. For these reasons, retail investors have taken an extremely strong interest in energy investing.

But the energy market is complex and has many levels. It encompasses multiple fuel sources, commodities, companies, and funds. The goal of *Energy Investing For Dummies* is to help you understand and successfully invest in all the various parts of this market.

According to the International Energy Agency, the world needs to cumulatively invest $37 trillion in the global energy supply system to replace aging infrastructure and keep pace with rapidly growing energy demands. Using this book, you'll prepare yourself to maximize the investment potential of this massive industry while avoiding its pitfalls and discovering how all its parts work together.

About This Book

My goal in writing *Energy Investing For Dummies* is to present you with an all-encompassing guide to the world's energy markets and to give you the data and tools you need to profitably invest in them. You don't have to speculate on crude oil prices to be an energy investor. Today, thanks to easy retail access to the market and exchange-traded funds (ETFs), investing in niche sectors of the energy market is easier than ever. You can buy individual companies, funds that hold groups of companies, or tradable instruments that represent a commodity's price. And you can do this across multiple types of energy sources, from oil and gas to solar and wind, and everything in between. My aim is to give you a foundation of knowledge to feel confident investing in all of them while using simple language and real-world examples to demystify what can certainly be viewed as a mystifying topic.

Anyone who has tried to deconstruct the energy industry on his own realizes how many variables there are. Terms like *barrels, therms, kilowatt-hours, reserves, capacities,* and more can frighten off or confuse even seasoned investors. This book explains all these terms and more in simple language so you can feel confident in your understanding and ability to invest in all energy sectors.

Here are some of the energy investment concepts, techniques, and strategies you find in this book:

- ✔ **Getting in tune with the crude oil market:** Oil prices have vast implications for everyone. But what drives them? Knowing where the world's oil comes from, which countries use the most of it, how to get it, and how the industry is adapting to continually harder-to-get resources is critical to being able to gauge what makes oil prices tick and how to know when they're over- or undervalued. See how all these pieces come together in Chapter 6.

- ✔ **Capitalizing on commodities without contracts:** You no longer need a broker to profit from moves in commodity prices. Until recently, the only way to invest in commodity prices directly was to buy contracts on a futures exchange. For oil, this requires buying at least 1,000 barrels at a time. Today, exchange-traded funds (ETFs) track the price of commodities. You can buy and sell these funds just like a stock to profit from moves in the price of crude oil. I cover how it's done in Chapter 10.

- ✔ **Realizing that traditional fuels encompass a global market:** You've probably heard that there's a "war on coal," but this really only applies to the developed nations of North America and Europe. Emerging markets, especially in Asia, will continue to rely on coal as a primary energy source for decades to come. In 2035, the world will still be getting one-third of its energy from coal, though there will be a shift in which countries use the most of it. You can find out how to use coal's continued dominance and shifting demographics for profit in Chapter 13.

This book has a few typographical conventions you should be aware of:

- *Italic* is used for emphasis and to highlight new words or terms.
- **Boldface text** is used to indicate key words in bulleted lists or the action parts of numbered steps.
- `Monofont` is used to make web addresses stand out.

Foolish Assumptions

To avoid writing a how-to guide in basic investing, I had to assume certain things about you. Rest assured, I explain all jargon and adequately define all necessary terms, but I don't provide entry-level investing information (although I do support and reinforce it). Here's what I've assumed about you:

- You're not brand-new to investing. You've bought and sold stocks, and maybe even a few funds. You understand basic concepts like being long or being short. And you know stocks and funds trade on various exchanges and that each stock or fund has a ticker.
- You're looking to expand this basic investment knowledge to capitalize on different sectors of the market.
- You understand that energy is a far-reaching and complex topic, and you want to gain a better understanding of its inner-workings.
- You're aware that more than just supply and demand determine energy prices. Weather, politics, macroeconomics, and random one-time events all have an impact. You want to know how to successfully incorporate these things into your investment strategy.
- You know that emerging economies like those in Brazil, China, and India will require vast amounts of energy. You want to see how this is affecting and will affect the global energy picture and put that knowledge to use in your portfolio.
- You've noticed that gasoline prices have averaged more than $3 per gallon for the past few years, and you want to know what is causing this or how you can benefit from it.
- You're aware that renewable energy is becoming a more important source of global energy. You want to see what types of renewables there are and what ways you can invest in them.
- You've come across bits and pieces of information regarding a certain energy sector and want to know more about it.

- ✔ You've seen sensationalized stories about energy relating to things like peak oil, fracking, or nuclear disasters, and you want some straightforward information on these topics and what they mean for your investments.

- ✔ You know that a book like this is the perfect place to gain broad-based knowledge and trading skills for the energy market, but you're also aware that a constantly evolving market like energy requires further reading and changes to your investment strategy to remain up-do-date and successful.

Icons Used in This Book

All *For Dummies* books use special icons to flag important pieces of information and make them easy to find. Here are the icons used in this book.

I use this icon to highlight information you'll need to frequently recall when investing in energy or info that's important to remember because it's referenced in other parts of the book.

Whenever you see the bull's-eye, pay special attention to the related text, as it offers actionable investment advice or explains how to execute a particular strategy.

Jargon inevitably appears when discussing investments in global energy markets. This icon denotes paragraphs you can skip over if you're simply looking for an overview of energy investing. But be sure to read them for a deeper understanding of the industry or before you make any serious investments.

All investments carry risks. Make sure you fully understand them as they relate to energy investing by reading the paragraphs accompanied by this icon.

Beyond the Book

You got more than you bargained for when you bought this book. To accompany this fine text, additional information is hosted on Dummies.com:

- ✔ You can download the book's Cheat Sheet at www.dummies.com/cheatsheet/energyinvesting. It's a handy resource to keep on your computer, tablet, or smartphone.

- ✔ You can read interesting companion articles that supplement the book's content at www.dummies.com/extras/energyinvesting. I've even written an extra top-ten list, which *For Dummies* readers seem to love.

Where to Go from Here

For Dummies books are organized to be modular in nature, meaning that though you can read this book from front to back like any other, doing so isn't entirely necessary. If you're looking for information about one energy sector in particular, you can simply skip directly to that section. However, if you're a true beginner, I recommend reading Part I carefully before skipping ahead.

Part I
Getting Started with Energy Investing

getting started
with
energy
investing

In this part . . .

✔ Get a brief history of energy development and investments.

✔ Examine the data to see how the need for energy is constantly growing.

✔ Discover how energy is used, even in hidden ways, all around you.

✔ Learn what you need to make your first energy investment.

✔ Identify the risks and rewards of energy investing.

Chapter 1

Powering Your Portfolio: Energy in Brief

In This Chapter

▶ Defining energy

▶ Understanding why energy makes for a great investment

▶ Knowing the risks

▶ Identifying the various ways to invest in energy

*E*nergy is the most vital industry the world has ever seen. It generates the most revenue and it's a foundational requirement for all other industries. Apple needs energy to make its computers and run its warehouses full of servers. Walmart needs energy to transport its goods and keep the lights on at its thousands of retail locations. As such, the energy market is fertile ground for investment.

But where does one start? With so many sources of energy and companies to choose from, a beginner can become overwhelmed very quickly. Unlike other sectors of the market, like restaurants or retail, for example, investing in energy is about much more than just individual companies with a singular goal. Energy crosses borders, both geographically and in the way it upends the traditional approach of categorizing companies with neat and tidy labels.

Apple is a technology company; Walmart is a retail company. That's pretty straightforward. But what is Exxon, which trades on the New York Stock Exchange (NYSE) under the ticker XOM (written as NYSE: XOM)?

Is it an oil company? A natural gas company? A refiner? A retail gasoline company? A commodity trader? You get the idea. The point is that it and many other so-called major integrated oil and gas companies, or majors, is all of the above, and sometimes more. BP (NYSE: BP) and Shell (NYSE: RDS-A), for example, are also solar, wind, and biofuel companies, which also makes them technology and agriculture companies.

This diversity is what makes the energy market so unique and such a great place to invest in. The energy market involves exploration, mining, processing, refining, retail, shipping, pipelines, technology, and more. And you can invest in companies at every step of the process, whether they do it all or specialize in one or two parts of the chain.

What Is Energy?

Before simply jumping in, I'd like to define energy as I cover it in this book. It's important to know the nature and scope of a market you'll be putting your hard-earned dollars into. The *Merriam-Webster Dictionary* definition of energy breaks it down into several parts.

Energy

✔ Has a dynamic quality

✔ Is a vigorous exertion of power

✔ Is a fundamental entity of nature that is transferred between parts of a system in the production of physical change within the system, and is usually regarded as the capacity for doing work

✔ Is usable power (such as heat or electricity) or the resources for producing such power

For investment purposes, I like a combination of the third and fourth definitions. To put a finer point on it, the two types of energy are *primary energy* and *secondary energy*.

For an energy source to be primary, it must naturally exist in nature. Primary energy sources can't be man-made. Primary energy is the primary focus of this book and includes

✔ **Crude oil:** The most widely traded commodity on the planet, oil fulfills one-third of the world's energy needs. From exploration and drilling to refining and distribution, oil presents myriad investment opportunities. I cover the crude basics in Chapter 6, futures trading in Chapter 8, producers in Chapter 9, and funds in Chapter 10.

✔ **Natural gas:** This was once considered a waste fuel, as companies routinely burned it off just to get rid of it. Today, thanks to new drilling technologies and concerns about oil depletion, natural gas is being looked to as the fossil fuel of the future. I spell out what you need to know in Chapter 7.

- ✔ **Coal:** No other fuel provides more electricity than coal. Forecasts show that coal will surpass oil as the world's top fuel source by 2022. It's cheap and abundant, but it's also dirty. I give you coal fundamentals in Chapter 11, analyze coal's future in Chapter 12, and chronicle investment opportunities in Chapter 13.

- ✔ **Uranium:** Many countries are looking to provide emission-free electricity with nuclear reactors, especially in Asia. China alone has plans to build more than 150 new reactors. But even though nuclear has been proven safer than other fuels, high-profile incidents make nuclear the most contentious of all energy sources. You can find a nuclear overview in Chapter 14, uranium life cycle and mining info in Chapter 15, and the best ways to invest in Chapter 16.

- ✔ **Solar energy:** In a single second, the sun produces enough energy to meet current global needs for 500,000 years. The world just hasn't quite figured out how to efficiently harvest it yet. But the process of doing so is now big business. I shine light on solar investments in Chapter 17.

- ✔ **Wind energy:** Already cheaper than coal and nuclear for electricity production in certain areas, wind has attracted the attention of countries and companies worldwide. Wind is a very young market with much room to grow; the United States, for example, still hasn't erected its first offshore wind farm. I get you in position to profit on wind in Chapter 18.

- ✔ **Geothermal energy:** The only renewable resource capable of providing constant energy, geothermal has been used as an energy source for more than a century. I outline geothermal opportunities in Chapter 19.

- ✔ **Biomass (organic material):** This can be burned to create electricity or processed into liquid fuels for transportation. Though it has been criticized for displacing food from hungry mouths, plant-based fuel is finding success in various locales. You can find a discussion of biofuel investments in Chapter 20.

Some sources of primary energy are transformed into more usable forms of energy. Electricity, for example, is a form of secondary energy because it's produced from primary sources. Gasoline is also a secondary energy source because it's refined from oil.

Why Energy Investing?

Just because various energy sources exist doesn't mean that they're easy to get or that they can provide enough reliable, affordable energy for the entire global population. More than 1.2 billion people worldwide still lack access to electricity, and more than 2.5 billion still use wood, charcoal, and dung for the energy to cook and heat. The fact that demand is this much greater than supply inherently makes energy a prime market for growth. As those billions of people in Africa, Asia, and South America begin to embrace the comforts of the developed world, the already record-breaking revenues of energy companies are going to expand even more. And the developed world isn't using any less, either.

This constant need for more energy is what sends prices ever higher. Average retail prices for gasoline set a record in 2011 and then set another record in 2012. Retail prices for electricity are climbing as well. My view is that if energy prices are constantly rising because of incessant demand and limited supply, why not invest in energy to profit?

Between now and 2035, the International Energy Agency has forecast that "global energy demand will push ever higher, growing by more than one-third," and to meet those growing energy needs, "cumulative investment of $37 trillion is needed in the world's energy supply system." That is the kind of environment I want to invest in.

Investing in energy companies

Need more reasons to get started investing in energy? Here you find a list of the world's largest companies in order of the revenue they generated in the most recent fiscal year. Finding the pattern isn't hard: Nine of the ten companies in the world with the highest sales are energy companies. If the list kept going, you'd also find energy companies in spots 11 and 13.

Every other industry needs energy. That's why when I look to invest, energy is always the first place I start. It's like the guy who sold picks and shovels during the California gold rush. He made money whether or not the prospectors found gold. Energy is the picks and shovels for everything in the modern world, from food production to construction to transportation to computers.

Company	Industry	Annual Revenue (Billions of Dollars)
Exxon Mobil	Oil and gas	$482.3
Royal Dutch Shell	Oil and gas	$481.7
Walmart	Retail	$469.2
Sinopec Group	Oil and gas	$441.4
BP	Oil and gas	$388.3
China National Petroleum Corp.	Oil and gas	$378.0
Saudi Aramco	Oil and gas	$356.0
Vitol	Energy commodities	$297.0
State Grid Corporation of China	Electric utility	$265.9
Chevron	Oil and gas	$253.7

I also think energy makes for a great investment because the industry is constantly innovating. Whether it's the perfection of fracking technology to economically harvest once uneconomic shale gas reserves, or the constant improvement in how much light a solar panel can turn into electricity, or the advent of using Internet technology to reduce how much energy people use in their homes and offices, new advances are always being made — and monetized — in the energy sector. I outline many more reasons to invest in energy in Chapter 3.

Fears, Risks, and Politics

Energy, like all other investments, carries risks. Policy is always changing. Improved technology can quickly make an entrenched technology obsolete. Geopolitical rifts can happen overnight. But if you identify and properly manage the risks, energy can provide above-average returns that many other sectors can't.

Many countries publish multiyear plans that outline the direction they want to take when it comes to procuring energy. In the United States, you can read bills being proposed in Congress. The more you read about energy and follow the news, the easier it is to spot potential shifts or disruptions on the horizon. Some things, however, you can't control. A tsunami that knocks out nuclear reactors, a blown-out well at the bottom of the ocean, an overthrown dictator in Libya — all these things are out of your control, and you should accept that fact before you put any money on the line.

If you manage the risks you can control and make peace with the ones you can't, energy investing offers a bevy of benefits. Not only can you beat the returns of the broader market, such as the Dow Jones Industrial Average or the S&P 500, but you can also attain a greater sense of self-worth by investing in the types of energy you believe in. You can get an education by following and reading about all the things that affect and relate to the global energy industry. I devote all of Chapter 5 to the risks and rewards of energy investing.

Ways to Play

One way to play is by buying shares of, say, Exxon or Shell and holding them forever. And many people do just that. But you have many more ways to invest in energy besides the company names on your corner gas station. For starters, hundreds of publicly traded companies explore and drill for gas on their own. And other companies specialize in a niche part of the energy market — leasing oil rigs, for example, or operating a pipeline.

And when you move past oil and gas, you have still hundreds more companies to choose from: coal and uranium miners and processors, companies that build nuclear plants, solar panel producers, and wind turbine manufacturers, just to name a few.

Your options aren't restricted to just companies, either. Commodities are a huge part of the energy game. You can trade oil, gas, coal, uranium, and even electricity on exchanges with futures contracts, although, as Chapter 8 points out, doing so can be risky and requires large amounts of capital. You also have an entire universe of mutual and exchange-traded funds (ETFs) that you can use to invest in energy. Some focus on a specific energy source and the companies that produce it; others focus on the price of certain energy commodities; and some blend the two. And like most investments, you can deploy various strategies like shorting and leverage.

You can find a detailed discussion of all the various energy investment vehicles in Chapter 4. You can find specific investment options for various energy sectors in their respective chapters throughout the rest of the book.

Chapter 2

Making a Connection

*E*nergy is all around us. It always has been. It always will be. But the ways that people harness and use it are constantly changing. Knowing energy's past, and seeing how it evolved and grew, is vital for investing in the energy of today and tomorrow. In the earliest days, humankind relied solely on muscular and biomass sources of energy. People needed to fuel only themselves, their animals, and their fires. They did work manually or with domesticated livestock. They fueled their heating and cooking needs with wood; some still do.

Before barrels and British thermal units (BTUs), the world had *calories,* or the amount of energy needed to raise the temperature of one gram of water by one degree Celsius. Energy is required for all human tasks, from flipping a page in this book to flying a 747 across an ocean. Effectively using energy is all about harnessing a fuel source to make it do something else, usually to make heat or drive motion. For literally thousands of years, the only way people knew how to do this was by turning chemical (caloric) energy into mechanical (kinetic) energy. I tell you this not for the historic value but to convey that energy is energy is energy, whether you're filling your stomach or your gas tank.

In this chapter, I cover the various ways humans have invested in energy throughout history. I also take a look at energy innovations that have gotten the world where it is today, and I show how even your everyday activities are dependent on energy and can serve as a muse for potential investments.

Early Energy Sources

Energy is the key to the advancement of civilization. This notion is commonly represented by the simple formula: energy = progress = civilization. Humans are the only species that have overcome physical limitations to harness energies outside their own bodies.

Water and wind

Long before humans were able to master the power of combustion, they relied on naturally occurring sources of energy to help them advance, most notably water and wind. Using simple tools like axes and plows, along with early power plants run with water wheels and windmills, humans transformed themselves from wandering hunter-gatherers into sprawling civilized societies. People used these rudimentary sources of energy to establish agriculture and commercial woodlots, to power the first iron mines, and to build the earliest transportation networks.

Thousands of years ago, humans developed the water wheel, using it to crush grain, make cloth, tan leather, smelt iron, and saw wood. Access to yesteryear's prime water resources was the equivalent of living on top of an oil field today. Energy investment has always been a part of the human experience, though returns then can be measured in societal progress rather than dollars. As people used energy to increase productivity, reliance on human and animal power began to decline, and the societies that best harnessed water's power advanced the fastest and became the first centers of commerce. Then as now, energy was central to civilization.

The use of water as energy spread very quickly thanks in part to another source of energy — wind — which humans used to sail ships around the globe. The ability to store and direct water pressure evolved from mills into hydropower dams. By the 15th century, large milling complexes were centered on advanced forms of water power. This led to the invention of camshafts and crankshafts used for reciprocating motion, which transformed the iron industry. For 200 years, people perfected this technique, eventually using it to power textile factories and industrial expansion in Europe and the New World.

Full steam ahead

Clear through to the 1800s, humankind's primary sources of energy were animals, biomass, and water. It wasn't until then, with the introduction of steam power, that today's modern energy infrastructure began to take shape. Figure 2-1 shows how reliance on different energy sources changed from the 15th century into the 21st.

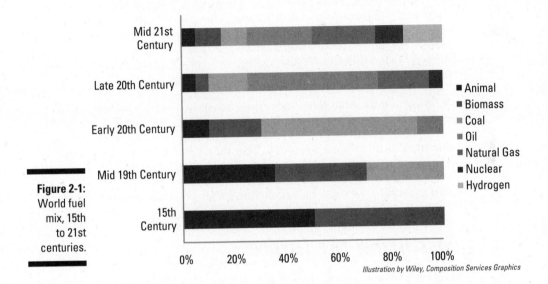

Figure 2-1: World fuel mix, 15th to 21st centuries.

Illustration by Wiley, Composition Services Graphics

Thomas Savery patented the first steam engine in England in 1698. He described it in a 1702 book, *The Miner's Friend; or, An Engine to Raise Water by Fire.* The patenting of a device to improve an industrial process is one of the earliest modern energy investments. Both Savery and the miners who wanted his device to increase productivity were fully embracing capitalism. Thomas Newcomen improved Savery's invention a few years later by adding a piston. This addition made it the first practical device to use the power of steam to do mechanical work, and the design is still recognizable today.

Born twenty-some years after Newcomen invented his engine, James Watt is the man who turned the engine into the device that kicked off the Industrial Revolution. Watt improved the efficiency of the steam engine by eliminating the constant need for cooling and reheating. His addition of a separate condenser allowed for greater power, efficiency, and cost-effectiveness. He also changed the design to produce rotary motion, which allowed the engine to complete a much wider variety of tasks than simply pumping water, the most important of which was powering the locomotive. For helping usher in the Industrial Revolution and allowing millions of people to easily move across continents, Watt is often considered one of the most influential people in human history.

Leaving the horse behind

The goal of energy investing is always to do more with less — to get more energy returned than energy invested. James Watt's perfection of the steam engine is a prime example of this principle. His quantification of energy allowed humankind to start measuring this metric and to start deciding whether certain endeavors were worthwhile based on the energy returned on energy invested (EROEI). He introduced the concept of horsepower and lent his name to a unit of power measurement — the *watt.*

It's fitting that the first Watt engines were installed for commercial enterprises in 1776, as they gave all of humanity independence from antiquated energy sources. The Watt engine also kicked off the age of energy entrepreneurship that still flourishes today. Watt didn't make all the engines that were being installed at the time; others constructed them by licensing Watt's design. He continued to make improvements and file patents over the next quarter century. As such, he's really the father of modern energy investing.

Fossilizing the future

In an early form of market-based competition, the steam engine began to vie with water wheels for the bulk of industrial business. Because of its flexible utility and economic efficiency, the steam engine won out and began to be more widely adopted and improved. As the 19th century approached, thanks to improvements in ironworking, the engine was able to use high-pressure steam instead of steam at atmospheric pressure, and its use exploded from there. By the early 1800s, horses that had been used for land transportation for centuries were giving way to steam-powered carriages. Steam now powered textile factories and giant cotton and grain mills. Riverboats and railroads kicked off a revolution in transportation. And the race to fuel it all was on.

European countries began switching from wood to coal for steam generation around 1800. By the mid-19th century, Appalachian coal surpassed wood as the primary steam fuel in the eastern United States. On the Pacific coast, coal was imported from as far away as Australia — an early glance at international energy trade and America's still-going battle with energy independence. The bond between industrial expansion and reliance on fossil fuels was being permanently sealed.

Past influences present

James Watt, Alessandro Volta, and Michael Faraday left lasting impressions on energy and the world. Watt adopted the term *horsepower* to compare the water-pumping power of steam engines to draft horses. This was his marketing strategy for showing miners that they could replace a large team of horses with one engine. Modern pumps and engines are still rated by horsepower to show the rate at which work is done. Watt's name was posthumously adopted for a unit of power that measures energy conversion — the *watt*. Similarly, Alessandro Volta, who pioneered one of the first chemical batteries, lent his name to the *volt,* the unit that measures electric potential, or the energy required to move an electric charge along a desired path. Michael Faraday made such great contributions to electricity that Albert Einstein kept a picture of him on his study wall. Faraday formed the foundation of modern electric motors, discovered electromagnetic induction and the laws of electrolysis, and popularized terms still in use today, like *anode, cathode, electrode,* and *ion.* Understanding and measuring modern energy wouldn't be possible without these men's contributions.

A Light Bulb Goes Off

One of the major challenges of steam engines was the transmission of power. A steam engine needed to be directly attached to the factory or locomotive it was powering via gears, drive shafts, or belts. A solution to this problem began to emerge in the early 1800s with electrical experiments. The first big leap forward came with Alessandro Volta's invention of the *voltaic pile,* the first battery that could provide a constant current to a circuit. The voltaic pile accomplished this by stacking several layers of copper and zinc discs, separated by cloth or cardboard, and connecting the top and bottom contacts with a wire. After the wire was connected, an electric current flowed through the device. Batteries derived from the voltaic pile powered the entire 19th-century electric industry until the electric generator was perfected in the 1870s.

Harnessing electricity

The era of electricity generation as it's known today began with Michael Faraday's invention of the electric motor in 1821. Faraday also, through his work with magnetic fields, conductors, and direct current, established the concept of *electromagnetism,* which deals with how charged particles and magnetic fields interact. His discovery of electromagnetic induction and the laws of electrolysis are largely responsible for electricity having practical uses with technology. Today's power plants bear little resemblance to Faraday's 1831 *homopolar disc generator,* but they continue to rely on the same electromagnetic principles he discovered.

Electricity is still generated by the movement of a loop of wire or disc of copper between magnetic poles. This is called *electromechanical generation.* The generators operate the same way whether they're driven by heat engines fueled by the combustion of coal or natural gas, by nuclear fission, or by the kinetic energy of water (hydropower) and wind. People use and invest in all these methods of turning energy into electricity, but their roots reach back more than 180 years.

The first utility

After electricity could be reliably produced, the search was on for ways to control, transmit, and use it. At this juncture, energy investing in its modern form really begins to take shape. The light bulb had been around since the early 1800s, but not until Thomas Edison perfected it in 1879 did it become viable for widespread home use. Edison's real genius, however, wasn't the light bulb but a system for electricity distribution. The electric lamp, as it was called then, was worthless without a steady supply of electricity. With financiers that included J. P. Morgan and the Vanderbilt family, Edison formed the Edison Electric Light Company in 1878 and then the first investor-owned utility, the Edison Illuminating Company, in 1880.

Profit was a core motivator from the earliest days of distributed energy. Edison didn't invent the light bulb, but he did invent the electric meter. He used this meter to bill customers for the electricity they consumed. In true American fashion, Edison sold people light bulbs from his Light Company and created a recurring revenue stream by continually charging them for the necessary electricity, provided by his Illuminating Company. People still use that model today. The Edison Electric Light Company is now known as General Electric (ticker symbol GE on the New York Stock Exchange, or NYSE). Perhaps you've heard of it. The Edison Illuminating Company is still around, too. It's doing business as Consolidated Edison (NYSE: ED) and provides electricity to more than 3 million customers.

War of the currents

Edison's system (see the preceding section) had a detrimental flaw — it worked only with *direct current* (DC), which could be transmitted only short distances because of voltage loss during transmission. As a result, power plants had to be located within a mile of the electricity's final destination.

Just four years after Edison began selling electricity, competition emerged in the form of *alternating current* (AC). Thanks to the invention of the transformer in 1884, alternating current could be transmitted at much higher voltages and, therefore, distances. Because electricity could travel farther with the AC system, fewer generating plants were necessary to power a given area.

Alternating current was the clear winner. The only problem was that all the world's motors at the time were designed to work with direct current. What tipped the scale was Nikola Tesla's 1887 invention of the *AC induction motor.* Simultaneously, George Westinghouse and his Westinghouse Electric & Manufacturing Company were already believers in AC's superiority and had already invented a meter for it. After Edison rejected him, and he struck out on his own, Tesla eventually signed a licensing deal with Westinghouse in 1888, getting $60,000 in cash and stock and a $2.50 royalty per AC horsepower produced by each motor.

Though he fought tooth and nail, Edison's DC system was inferior and ultimately lost out to Tesla's AC system. The future of electricity was sealed in 1893, when the Niagara Falls Power Company rejected General Electric and chose Westinghouse to build hydroelectric generators based on Tesla's AC patent. General Electric was chosen to build the transmission lines, and the electric grid as it is today began to take shape. The "war of the currents" was more than a battle of ideas and egos; it involved heavy investments by many companies that were positioning for a lion's share of the revenue in what would become one of the biggest industries on earth.

Barons to Barrels

Electric motors had a several-decade head start on internal combustion engines, early designs of which began floating around between 1820 and 1860 in Europe. The first person to build and sell the engine was German inventor Nikolaus Otto in 1862. His free-piston engine beat out the competition because of its efficiency and reliability. Working with Gottlieb Daimler and Wilhelm Maybach, Otto pioneered the four-stroke engine in 1876, but a German court ruling on its patent allowed the design to be open to everyone, and in-cylinder compression became universal. Karl Benz patented a two-stroke version in 1879 and later built a four-stroke engine that he used in the first production automobiles in 1886. Rudolf Diesel unveiled the diesel engine in 1900, which actually ran on peanut oil instead of petroleum-based fuel.

To this day, you can run a diesel engine on vegetable oil, but the market for fuels derived from crude oil is exponentially larger. I cover oil investments in Part II of this book and examine biofuel investments in Chapter 20. In the next few sections, I present a historical road map of oil investments before showing you how to identify energy investments all around you.

Oil investment past to present

The perfection of the internal combustion engine provided the fuel demand that has sustained the oil industry to this day. Used for thousands of years by many civilizations because of its medicinal and sealing properties, oil began to be used as an energy source for lamps when it was distilled into kerosene in ninth-century Persia. But the real advancement didn't come until centuries later, when petroleum was first fractionated at Yale University in 1854, and the ability to refine fuels from oil spread around the world. The first modern refinery was built at the Pechelbronn oil field in 1857 — a field that was active until 1970 and was the birthplace of oil service companies like Schlumberger (NYSE: SLB) and Antar, now a unit of UGI Corporation (NYSE: UGI) that you can still invest in today.

Though many oil fields existed at the time, because it was drilled and not dug, used a steam engine, and was backed by a company, the first commercial oil well is considered to be Edwin Drake's 1859 project in Titusville, Pennsylvania. Drilled wells were popping up in Canada, Poland, Romania, and Azerbaijan around the same time. Seeing the potential, John D. Rockefeller founded Standard Oil, the largest corporation in the United States, with $1 million in capital in 1870.

In an example of efficient markets at work, demand for oil all but disappeared in 1878 with Edison's perfection of the light bulb, and that demand wouldn't fully return until the automobile started gaining popularity a few years later. During this time, Rockefeller and his Standard Oil cemented their hold on the young oil industry.

Delegating tasks and setting up committees while remaining the largest shareholder, Rockefeller laid the foundation for what became one of the world's first and largest multinational corporations, embracing capitalism to out-compete his rivals with lower costs and greater efficiencies in production and logistics. Many industries today still use pieces of the template he created, such as using trustees to manage large entities and growing through acquisitions. Rockefeller and other trustees used the dividends paid by Standard Oil, which totaled $548.5 million between 1882 and 1906, to make large share purchases in related industries like railroads, steel, copper, agriculture, and electric utilities that still exist today. Rockefeller and other trustees invested in

- U.S. Steel (NYSE: X)
- Amalgamated Copper, today a U.S. superfund site controlled by BP (NYSE: BP)
- Corn Products Refining Company, today called Ingredion (NYSE: INGR)
- Consolidated Gas Company of New York, today called Consolidated Edison (NYSE: ED)

Carving up the future: The breakup of Standard Oil

By 1890, Standard Oil was producing 88 percent of the refined oil in the United States. It controlled 91 percent of the market in 1904 after turning from a trust into a holding company that held stock in 41 other companies. Standard Oil had a full-fledged monopoly on the oil business. The U.S. Department of Justice sued Standard Oil in 1909 under the Sherman Antitrust Act, and in 1911 it was ordered to break up into separate companies, with autonomous boards of directors. In Table 2-1, you can see the major companies and what they're called today, after more than a century of mergers and acquisitions.

Table 2-1	Standard Oil Successor Companies		
After Breakup	*Bought by/ Merged with*	*Then Became*	*Now Called*
Standard Oil of New Jersey, or Esso (S.O.)	Humble Oil	Exxon	ExxonMobil
Standard Oil of New York	Vacuum Oil	Mobil	ExxonMobil
Standard Oil of California			Chevron
Standard Oil of Indiana		Amoco	BP
Standard Atlantic	Richfield Oil	Atlantic Richfield (ARCO)	Sunoco
Standard Oil of Kentucky (Kyso)	Standard Oil of California		Chevron
Continental Oil Company (Conoco)	Marland Oil Company	Part of DuPont	Conoco-Phillips
Standard Oil of Ohio	BP		BP
The Ohio Oil Company	United States Steel	Marathon Oil	Marathon Oil
Buckeye Pipe Line		Buckeye Partners	Buckeye Partners
Chesebrough Manufacturing Company	Unilever		Unilever
South Penn Oil	Pennzoil	Pennzoil-Quaker State	Royal Dutch Shell
Anglo-American	Standard Oil of New Jersey	Esso UK	ExxonMobil

Many oil companies not owned by Standard Oil also began to thrive and compete internationally. They all still exist, though like the Standard Oil successor companies, many of the names have changed over time. Table 2-2 identifies these companies and their path to modern day.

Table 2-2	Early Oil Companies	
Originally Called	*What Happened?*	*Now Called*
Union Oil Company (Unocal), founded 1890	Merged with Chevron, 2005	Chevron
Texaco, founded 1901	Merged with Chevron, 2001	Chevron
Gulf Oil, founded 1901	Merged with Chevron, 1985	Split among Chevron, BP, Cumberland Farms
Sun Company, incorporated 1901	Changed name to Sunoco in 2011	Merged with Energy Transfer Partners
Cities Services Company, founded 1910	Acquired by Occidental Petroleum	Drilling and exploration owned by Occidental; refining and retail became Citgo
Pure Oil, founded 1914	Merged with Union Oil Company of California (Unocal), 1965	Chevron

It's not a coincidence that a few of these companies were founded in 1901. Oil was struck in the legendary Spindletop oil field that year. It produced more than 100,000 barrels per day within a year, more than any field in the world to that point. It kicked off the Texas oil boom and soon made the United States the world's largest oil producer. The global oil industry, from North America to the Middle East, has been continually looking for the next gusher ever since.

Everyday Energy

For the past 150 years, the entire world has slowly grown addicted to cheap and abundant energy. Machine labor has largely supplanted human labor, dramatically increasing humankind's per capita energy consumption.

Everyone today uses what would've taken the energy of many servants to achieve in the past: hot water at the turn of a handle, a cooler house at the touch of a button, clothes dried with the flip of a switch. All these tasks, and thousands more, have been exported to machines that consume much more energy than the humans previously doing the jobs. As you can see in Figure 2-2, world per capita energy consumption has grown 300 percent since 1820.

World per Capita Energy Consumption

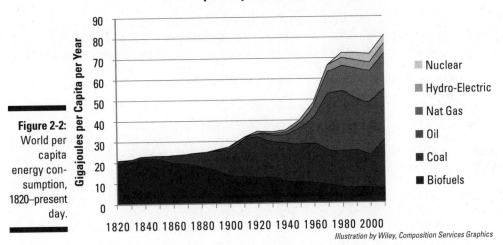

Figure 2-2: World per capita energy consumption, 1820–present day.

Illustration by Wiley, Composition Services Graphics

This constantly growing need for energy is what makes the sector such a good place to invest, especially as developing nations continue to mature. Citizens in the United States and Australia, for example, use seven to ten times more energy per person than those in China, India, and Brazil. The energy demand that these developing nations create as they seek a more modern way of life based on exporting tasks to machines run on energy will create a bullish investment environment for decades to come.

Cheap energy: The key to modern life

It's easy to think of energy as simply fuel for your car and electricity for your home, but energy's reach stretches much farther than that. Understanding how pervasive energy is in modern life is an important insight for energy investing. Energy is found in every product you buy, own, and use, be it your shoes, your coffee cup, or this very book. Companies don't just use energy to transport these goods from production sites to retail sites; they use it to make the products themselves. Consider these hidden ways that energy is consumed:

- Constructing the average car requires up to 1,700 gallons of oil.
- Making the average computer requires more than ten times its weight in fossil fuels.
- Every calorie of food eaten in the United States requires roughly ten calories of fossil fuels.

The comforts of modern life wouldn't be possible without cheap energy. To see how advanced a civilization would be without the use of cheap energy, all you have to do is look at the lives led by the Amish, living in suspended animation at the peak of their own society, before cheap energy was successfully harnessed: no electricity, no plastic, no cars, no cellphones, no computers, no television.

 Constant demand for creature comforts, and the need for cheap and abundant energy to make them possible, is largely responsible for driving the energy market. These microeconomic factors have much sway on larger macro trends, and you need to keep tabs on them when investing in all forms of energy. During times of high unemployment and recession, like the past half decade, decreased demand for energy typically leads to a decrease in prices. Between 2007 and 2009, for example, as the world entered the most recent recession, global demand for oil eroded by some 2 million barrels per day. After peaking at more than $140 per barrel in 2008, oil prices plummeted to less than $40 per barrel as a result. Conversely, in good economic times, people are more willing to travel, to buy goods, and to raise or lower the thermostat in their homes by a few more degrees, all of which increases demand and prices for energy.

Don't touch the thermostat

When I was younger, in response to leaving a light on or wanting to adjust the temperature of the house, my parents often asked whether I thought we owned the electric company. And while that's partially possible by owning shares in any of the hundreds of publicly traded utilities out there, their point was that you can keep more dollars in your pocket by being conscious of your energy decisions. Today, I view this as an energy hedge. Investments in energy don't always mean buying a stock or commodity.

Investing in a programmable thermostat, for example, can save you hundreds of dollars per year. Setting it to change 10 to 15 degrees when you're out of the house or asleep can shave 10 percent off your utility bills annually — a respectable return for any investor. Because the water heater can account for up to 25 percent of the energy consumed in your home, reducing its temperature also has a positive impact on your bottom line.

Check out sites like www.energy.gov/public-services and www.consumer energycenter.org to see the best quantification strategies for this type of alternative energy investing.

Food production

In the United States, food travels on average 1,500 miles to reach your table. More than seven units of fossil fuel energy are necessary to generate one unit of food energy, including petrochemical pesticides and herbicides, petroleum fuels to run farm machinery and refrigerated transport vehicles, natural gas for fertilizer, drying and processing, and so on.

The modern food production system is essentially a process of converting fossil fuels into food. Rising energy prices almost instantly translate into higher food costs and even shortages. Thanks to a wealthier and growing global population, food demand is only heading higher. And because the energy inputs for agriculture are higher than the energy outputs of the food, the already tight energy supply and demand balance will be exacerbated going forward. Figure 2-3 breaks down the energy flows of the current food system.

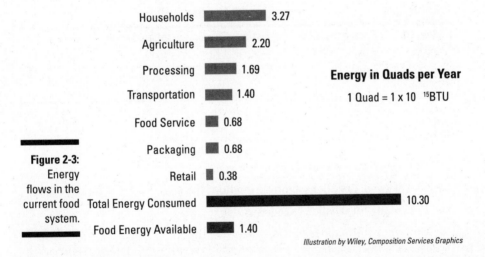

	Energy in Quads per Year
Households	3.27
Agriculture	2.20
Processing	1.69
Transportation	1.40
Food Service	0.68
Packaging	0.68
Retail	0.38
Total Energy Consumed	10.30
Food Energy Available	1.40

Energy in Quads per Year

1 Quad = 1 x 10 ^{15} BTU

Figure 2-3: Energy flows in the current food system.

Illustration by Wiley, Composition Services Graphics

Consider that China's consumption of soybeans has risen fivefold since 1995. Its per capita beef consumption is up 150 percent over the past three decades. And already-developed nations aren't consuming any less for balance. The net effect is increased food demand and, by default, an increase in the energy needed to produce it.

You can leverage this trend into a tangential energy investment, either by purchasing shares of companies that make agriculture more efficient or by investing in the commodities whose prices will be higher as a result.

Tracking Trends in Energy Use

I often use experiences in my own life to identify larger energy trends that allow me to more successfully invest. Knowing energy's past (covered earlier in this chapter) and taking notice of its present is the springboard to investing successfully in its future.

Watching your own energy use

Tracking your personal energy use allows you to get in tune with your consumption and prices. Keep a spreadsheet that tracks how many miles you drive, how many gallons of gas you buy, and how much it costs. You can see a template for such a spreadsheet in Table 2-3.

Table 2-3		Tracking Miles per Gallon		
Amount	*Price per Gallon*	*Gallons Bought*	*Miles Driven*	*Date*
$87.04	$3.40	25.6	300	January 1
$88.02	$3.38	26.0	315	January 24

By tracking all this information, you know

✔ How much you spend on gas each year

✔ The average cost per gallon throughout the year

✔ How many total gallons you consume

✔ How many total miles you drive

By dividing miles driven by gallons purchased, you can find your average miles per gallon. You can do the same thing with utility bills to analyze how many kilowatt-hours of electricity or therms of natural gas you consume relative to daily temperatures.

Then the key is translating what you see in personal habits into potential energy investments. If you notice rising gas or utility prices, you can go long in a fund that tracks either. Conversely, if you notice falling prices or other signs of economic weakness, you can easily get on the short side. The idea is to make a connection between the market and your real-world experience. You don't have to complain about rising gas prices; you can profit from them.

Keeping an eye on prices

In addition to tracking your personal energy consumption (see the preceding section), you want to examine other aspects of the energy industry you come across in your daily routine. The most obvious thing you should notice is that gasoline prices haven't averaged less than $2 per gallon for almost a decade now. The only thing that could push them below that level is a widespread global economic calamity that would cause much less fuel to be needed, like what happened briefly in late 2008.

Gas prices, of course, are driven by crude oil prices, which have gone from $30 per barrel to $100 per barrel in the same time (see Figure 2-4). This increase has led to profit for investors wise enough to put the trend to use in their portfolios, but it has also led to market-based changes in the energy and transportation sectors that you can still invest in today.

Price of Gasoline, 2001-2011
*Unleaded regular gasoline, U.S. city
average retail price*

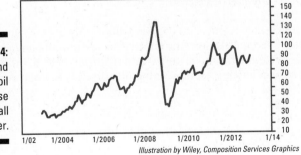

Spot Oil Price: West Texas Intermediate — 10 Year Chart

Figure 2-4:
Gas and crude oil prices rise and fall together.

Illustration by Wiley, Composition Services Graphics

Looking for new energy uses

Have you noticed that the buses and taxis you see in major cities now run on natural gas instead of diesel? Natural gas trading at $3 per million BTU translates into 38 cents per gallon of gasoline equivalent. With gasoline prices averaging well over $3 per gallon, switching vehicles to run on natural gas makes sense, even if prices double to $6 per million BTU. A Class A truck that uses 20,000 gallons of fuel per year could save $40,000 per year. That's why more than 50 percent of transit buses and garbage trucks sold in 2012 run on natural gas and not diesel. Companies betting on this approach include

- Clean Energy Fuels (NASDAQ: CLNE), which is committed to building 150 natural gas filling stations in two years as part of "America's Natural Gas Highway"
- Shell (NYSE: RDS-A), which is building 100 filling stations
- Loves Travel Stops, On Cue Express, and Kwik Trip, which are all adding natural gas to their stations
- Westport Innovations (NASDADQ: WPRT), which is making natural gas engines for big rig trucks; many automotive manufacturers are beginning to offer passenger vehicles in natural gas versions as well

A future electric

You should also notice the growing use of electric vehicles in response to rising oil prices, sales of which are expected to triple by 2015 (see Figure 2-5). You've undoubtedly seen increasing numbers of Toyota Priuses, Chevy Volts, and various Tesla models in the lanes beside you on the highway while the Hummers continue to disappear. This is a logical, market-based reaction to continually high oil and gas prices.

It's also a very investable trend. You can invest not only in the manufacturers that are taking the lead in this new automotive sector but also in the outfits that provide the next-generation batteries and materials that allow for farther ranges and higher efficiencies, all of which I fully discuss in Chapter 20.

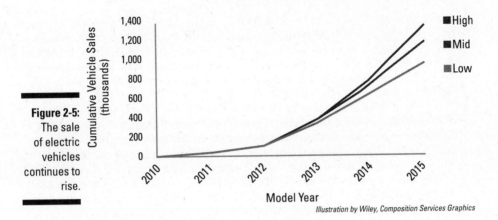

Forecast of Plug-In Electric Vehicles (U.S.)

Figure 2-5:
The sale of electric vehicles continues to rise.

Global green movement

Partly in response to climate fears and partly in response to record energy prices, a movement is solidifying around all things sustainable and efficient. Sustainability as it relates to energy involves generating electricity using renewable resources. Instead of combusting a fuel like coal, oil, or gas, energy is harnessed from sources that can't be depleted, like the sun, wind, or ocean movements. But the clean side of the energy equation doesn't just include creating energy.

Energy efficiency isn't as sexy as erecting a massive wind farm or commissioning a new nuclear reactor — and it certainly offers far fewer photo ops — but businesses and decision-makers the world over are quickly starting to realize its power. Forbes has noted that energy efficiency is the "largest, cheapest, safest, cleanest, fastest, most diverse, least visible, least understood and most neglected way to provide energy services." Walmart has added billions to its bottom line by making its stores and supply chain more efficient. Boeing has outdone Airbus with its 20 percent more efficient Dreamliner plane that costs the same to produce.

Sneaky sustainability

Many examples of a move toward corporate sustainability aren't immediately viewed as such or are dismissed as wantonly green, meant to make consumers feel good but not necessarily to improve the bottom line. This couldn't be further from the truth. Plastic shopping bags are made with and transported by oil. The reduction or elimination of them by grocery chains minimizes a variable cost.

You can see the same principle in ever-thinner plastic water bottles, maximization of recycled content in packaging, and relocation of production facilities closer to where the product is used. Toyota not only locates its manufacturing facilities in the United States but also designates them as zero-waste, meaning that all waste is either recycled or reused, with nothing sent to the landfill. PepsiCo has done the same thing with many of these plants. These aren't feel-good actions; they're energy investments by another name, and I cover the related opportunities in Chapter 21.

Bloated with natural gas

"We have a supply of natural gas that can last America nearly 100 years," declared President Barack Obama in his 2012 State of the Union address. The statement was made possible by hydraulic fracturing, or *fracking,* a new drilling technique pioneered in the United States that allows energy companies to access natural gas and oil in deep rock formations once thought off-limits. In 1997, the Energy Information Administration estimated U.S. proven natural gas reserves at 167 trillion cubic feet. Today, thanks to advancements in fracking, that estimate is closer to 300 tcf, and production is booming.

You've seen and heard about the implications of this as it has played out. North Dakota is hosting fracking boomtowns, attracting so many jobs that people are living in trailers in Walmart parking lots. Natural gas prices in 2012 were at decade lows as a result. Matt Damon even made a movie about farmers selling their land to energy companies desperate to frack it. Chinese companies have made several multibillion-dollar purchases of U.S. drilling companies to gain knowledge about the technology. It's one of the biggest energy stories of our time.

Chapter 3

A Bright Investment: Running the World Takes a Lot of Energy

*P*owering the world in 2011 took 12.3 billion tonnes of oil equivalent. Except for 2009 because of a global recession, the world has used progressively more energy every year since 1983, when primary energy demand was 6.7 billion tonnes of oil equivalent. World energy use has doubled over the past 30 years, but population has grown only 40 percent. People consistently consume more energy each year, with per capita use in developing nations growing much faster than use in developed nations.

A *tonne* is a metric ton, or 1,000 kilograms (kg). The United States commonly uses *short tons*. A tonne contains 1.1 short tons, or just over 2,200 pounds. So the units are similar, but not exact.

The world doesn't run on just oil, of course. Using *million tonnes of oil equivalent* (mtoe) is an easy way to measure all forms of energy consumption using one unit, making it easier to see the bigger picture. A tonne contains roughly 7.1 barrels of oil. Table 3-1 shows how much of each primary source of energy the world uses based on this unit. In this chapter, I cover the most widely used and invested in sources of energy, how much the world uses, and why that makes it a great sector in which to invest.

Table 3-1	2011 Primary World Energy Use by Source, Million Tonnes of Oil Equivalent					
Oil	Natural Gas	Coal	Nuclear	Hydro-electricity	Renewables	Total
4,059.1	2,905.6	3,724.3	599.3	791.5	194.8	12,274.6
33.0%	23.7%	30.3%	4.9%	6.5%	1.6%	100%

Energy Sectors and Markets

For investment purposes, each source of energy is considered its own market sector. Fossil fuels — or, more precisely, nonrenewable fuels like oil, natural gas, coal, and nuclear — dominate global energy consumption, with a 92 percent market share. Renewable fuels like hydroelectricity, solar, wind, and biofuels account for just 8 percent. But because they account for such a small percentage, renewables are growing much faster on a market-share basis. Oil, for example, has lost market share for the past 12 years, going from 38 percent of primary energy consumption in 2001 to 33 percent in 2011, while renewables have grown from 0.5 percent to 1.5 percent — a 300 percent increase in market share — in the same time period.

In this section, I examine each energy sector in a little more detail.

Oil

Oil in all its forms accounts for one third of global energy consumption. This includes crude oil, shale oil, oil sands, and the liquid content of natural gas, called *natural gas liquids,* or NGLs. As a result of including these different forms, you sometimes see different numbers depending on the source and whether it's reporting just crude oil or total liquids. Oil is traded by the barrel, which contains 42 gallons. The common unit used for oil is thousand barrels per day, abbreviated tb/d. Table 3-2 shows world oil consumption and production in multiple units.

Table 3-2	2011 World Oil Consumption and Production in Various Units	
Unit	Consumption	Production
Thousand barrels per day	88,034	83,576
Million barrels per day	88.034	83.576
Million tonnes per year	4,059.1	3,995.6

Natural gas

Natural gas accounts for just under one-quarter of global energy consumption. You can measure natural gas by volume, usually in cubic meters or feet, or by the amount of heat it can produce in *therms,* or British thermal units (Btus). Table 3-3 shows how these units relate to each other.

Table 3-3	Relationship of Natural Gas Units	
Cubic Feet	*Btus*	*Therms*
1	1,000	0.01
0.001	1	0.00001
100	100,000	1

Because such large quantities of natural gas are needed and produced, you commonly come across units for thousands, millions, or billions of cubic feet and Btus. You can simplify them like this:

- 1,000 cubic feet (cf) = 1 Mcf
- 1 million Mcf = 1 billion cubic feet (Bcf)
- 1,000 bcf = 1 trillion cubic feet (Tcf)
- 1 million Btu = 1,000 MBtu = 1 MMBtu

In 2011, the world produced 115.7 trillion cubic feet of natural gas and consumed 113.8 Tcf. Unlike oil, more natural gas was produced than consumed, which is why natural gas prices were near-record lows in 2011 and 2012, while oil prices hovered near all-time highs. Natural gas is traded in million British thermal units (MMBtu).

Coal

Coal provides 30 percent of global energy needs, and in 2011, it was the fastest-growing form of fossil fuel energy. The world produced 7,678 million tonnes (Mt) of coal and consumed 7,217 Mt.

In the United States, coal is traded in contracts of 1,550 short tons. In Europe, coal is traded in contracts of 5,000 tonnes. Because of carbon emission restrictions in many countries, coupled with sharply rising demand in developing nations, the price of coal has increased from around $30 per short ton in 2000 to around $65 in 2013. Not all coal is created equal. The most common type, *bituminous coal,* provides between 10,000 Btus and 15,000 Btus per pound. Coal that generates more heat per pound fetches higher prices.

Nuclear

Instead of burning fuel to produce steam, nuclear energy produces heat to create steam by controlling the continuous fission of uranium atoms. In 2011, nuclear energy generated more than 2,600 billion kilowatt-hours of electricity, or 4.9 percent of global primary energy production, requiring nearly 68,000 tonnes of uranium. As of 2013, 435 nuclear reactors were operating in the world, with 65 under construction and 167 planned.

Uranium is traded in contracts of 250 pounds. Prices ranged from $10 to $135 per pound between 2003 and 2013. As with all nonrenewable fuels, you can trade the commodity directly or invest in companies that produce it.

Hydroelectricity and other renewables

Renewable resources don't require a finite source of fuel to produce energy. Instead, naturally occurring sources are captured and converted into usable forms of energy. The power of rivers and wind can spin turbines, heat from the earth's core can make steam, and the sun's rays can be converted into electricity.

Combined, hydroelectricity and other renewables accounted for almost 8 percent of global energy use in 2011, with hydro producing 3,500 billion kilowatt-hours and the others generating 860 billion kilowatt-hours. Because these renewables generate a much smaller percentage of total generation, they're growing much faster than traditional sources of energy. Global oil use, for example, grew by 0.7 percent in 2011, while wind energy grew 25.8 percent and solar grew 86.3 percent. Renewables' growth when it comes to percentage of global generation is even faster, up 130 percent from 2001 to 2011, from 0.7 percent of generation to 1.6 percent of generation.

You can invest in this type of energy by buying the companies that make the necessary equipment, like solar panels and wind turbines, or the utilities that use them.

Major markets

As of 2011, China passed the United States in terms of total energy consumed. On a per capita basis, however, the United States is far and away the world leader, consuming nearly twice as much per person as the nearest competitor, France. Figure 3-1 shows the top total energy-consuming nations and how their consumption changed from 2001 to 2011.

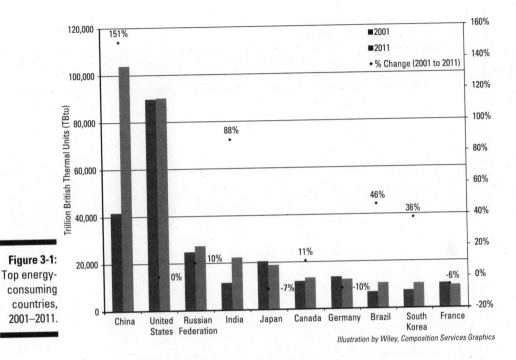

Figure 3-1:
Top energy-
consuming
countries,
2001–2011.

Illustration by Wiley, Composition Services Graphics

Currently, all net growth in energy consumption is coming from emerging economies. Consumption in developed nations has actually declined over these past few recessionary years. China alone accounted for 71 percent of global energy consumption growth in 2011. Table 3-4 shows regional markets for all sources of energy.

Table 3-4   **2011 Regional Consumption Markets for All Energy Sources**

	Oil (Thousand Barrels per Day)	Natural Gas (Bcf/ Day)	Coal (Thousand Short Tons)	Nuclear (Billion Kilowatt-hours)	Hydro (Billion Kilowatt-hours)	Renew-ables (Billion Kilowatt-hours)
North America	23,156	83.6	1,071,818	936.7	740.7	227.1
South and Central America	6,241	15.0	49,568	21.9	743.5	50.1

continued

Table 3-4 *(continued)*

	Oil (Thousand Barrels per Day)	Natural Gas (Bcf/ Day)	Coal (Thousand Short Tons)	Nuclear (Billion Kilowatt-hours)	Hydro (Billion Kilowatt-hours)	Renew-ables (Billion Kilowatt-hours)
Europe/ Eurasia	18,924	106.5	1,452,169	1,200	791.6	372.7
Middle East	8,076	39.0	16,811	0.1	21.9	0.4
Africa	3,336	10.6	214,972	12.7	103.6	5.5
Asia Pacific	28,301	57.1	5,338,369	477.3	1,096.5	205.0

Table 3-5 shows regional production markets for nonrenewable resources. Renewables aren't included because they're consumed where they're produced.

Table 3-5 — **2011 Regional Production Markets for All Energy Sources**

Region	Oil (Thousand Barrels per Day)	Natural Gas (Bcf/Day)	Coal (Thousand Short Tons)	Nuclear (Tonnes of Uranium)
North America	14,301	83.6	1,181,967	10,682
South and Central America	7,381	16.2	104,009	265
Europe/ Eurasia	17,314	100.3	1,362,013	26,698
Middle East	27,690	50.9	1,294	0
Africa	8,804	19.6	284,279	9,037
Asia Pacific	8,086	46.4	5,527,345	7,928
Total	83,576	317.0	8,460,907	54,610

Demand: The World Always Needs More

More and more energy is needed with every new person, device, and machine. Figure 3-2 shows historic world energy demand aligned with population growth. The two track almost identically. Unless per capita use decreases through efficiency measures or behavior modifications, you can expect demand for energy to keep on growing, creating favorable conditions for investing in energy.

Global Primary Energy Consumption 1830 – 2010

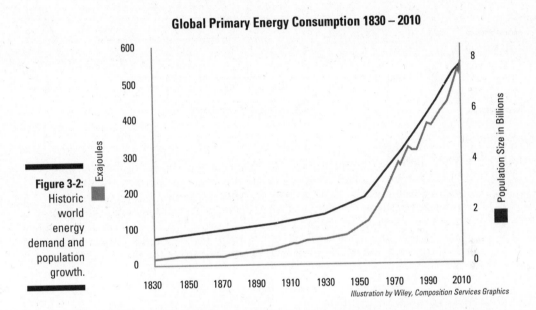

Figure 3-2: Historic world energy demand and population growth.

Illustration by Wiley, Composition Services Graphics

After a nation is developed, its per-person energy use begins to level off. You can see this in North America and Europe, where energy demand has remained flat, or fallen slightly, in each of the past few years. But the 1.3 billion people on those two continents are far outweighed by the 5 billion people in Asia and Africa, who currently have an insatiable appetite for easily accessible energy, ensuring that overall energy demand will rise for years to come.

Historic performance

Prices for crude oil in 2010 dollars remained less than $30 per barrel for nearly a century. When U.S. oil production peaked in 1970, the established oil companies at the time were no longer able to satiate demand and control prices, and the cost of crude began rising dramatically. Upward pressure has been the trend ever since, with periods of recession offering the only relief. Figure 3-3 shows the non-inflation-adjusted purchase price of crude oil for the past 150 years.

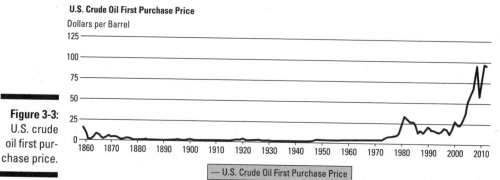

U.S. Crude Oil First Purchase Price

Figure 3-3: U.S. crude oil first purchase price.

Illustration by Wiley, Composition Services Graphics

The rapidly increasing price of crude has allowed the energy sector to be one of the historically best-performing sectors in the market. Over the years, you've undoubtedly seen this play out with gas prices, but it has also been reflected in the performance of related stocks. Figure 3-4 shows the performance of ExxonMobil (NYSE: XOM) and Chevron (NYSE: CVX) relative to the Standard & Poor's 500 (S&P 500) since 1970. The oil majors returned between 4,000 percent and 5,000 percent, or two to four times the return of the broad market index.

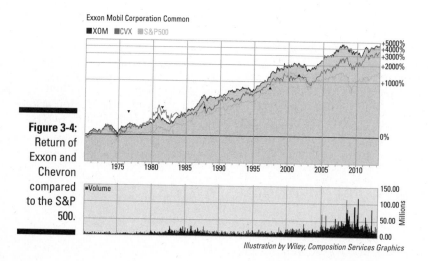

Figure 3-4: Return of Exxon and Chevron compared to the S&P 500.

Illustration by Wiley, Composition Services Graphics

Other sectors responsible for providing a lesser percentage of global energy have had more mixed results, but with the exception of renewable energy, they've still outperformed the broad market over the past decade, as seen in Table 3-6.

Table 3-6	Ten-Year Performance of Leading Energy Indexes Relative to the S&P 500		
Index	Value on January 1, 2002	Value on December 31, 2012	Change
S&P 500	1,172.5	1,466.5	25.1%
World Nuclear Energy Index	1,000.4	2,328.5	132.8%
Dow Jones U.S. Coal Index	92.0	164.8	79.1%
Dow Jones Utility Average	290.4	464.6	60.0%
RENIXX Renewable Energy Industrial Index	1,128.5	183.0	−83.8%

The collapse of global markets in 2008, resulting in strict access to capital and falling energy demand, took all the momentum out of a nascent clean energy industry. After oil prices nearly reached $150 per barrel in mid-2008, they crashed to less than $40 by early 2009, taking away the urgency to invest in renewables — a depression from which the industry is still recovering today.

Demand in the future

According to the International Energy Agency's (IEA's) World Energy Outlook 2012, global energy demand will grow more than 33 percent through 2035, with China, India, and the Middle East accounting for 60 percent of the increase. Demand in developed nations will rise only marginally, with a noticeable shift away from oil and coal and toward low-carbon sources like natural gas and renewables. Figure 3-5 shows projected growth in primary energy demand and where it comes from through 2035.

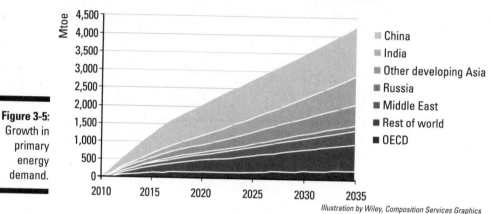

Figure 3-5:
Growth in primary energy demand.

Illustration by Wiley, Composition Services Graphics

Other trends to watch during this period include:

- ✔ The revival of Iraq's oil sector
- ✔ The overtaking of Saudi Arabia by the United States as the largest oil producer by 2020
- ✔ Global measures to reduce energy intensity
- ✔ Oil demand approaching 100 million barrels per day, up from 87.4 in 2011
- ✔ Coal use growing through 2020 because of India and China
- ✔ Electricity demand growing twice as fast as total energy demand
- ✔ Renewables approaching coal as a primary source of electricity
- ✔ Water needs for energy production growing at twice the rate of energy demand

Figure 3-6 shows projections for world energy consumption by fuel through 2035.

The projected 33 percent growth in world energy demand over the next two decades will put a strain on the system like it has never experienced before. Use of every single source of fuel is anticipated to reach levels never before seen.

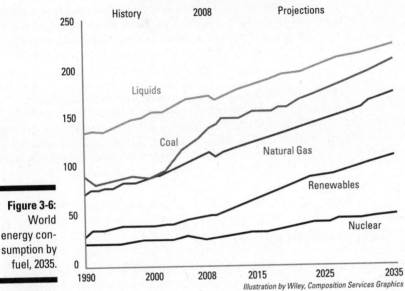

World Energy Consumption by Fuel
1990 – 2035 (Quadrillion Btu)

Figure 3-6:
World
energy con-
sumption by
fuel, 2035.

Illustration by Wiley, Composition Services Graphics

To stay up-to-date on energy demand forecasts and scenarios, be sure to check out these sources:

✔ The International Energy Agency's World Energy Outlook: www. worldenergyoutlook.com

✔ The Energy Information Administration's International Energy Outlook: www.eia.gov/forecasts/ieo

Trillions of Reasons to Invest

Energy is the largest market in the world, accumulating more annual expenditures than the agriculture, telecom, automotive, chemicals, or pharmaceuticals market. The energy market is expected to remain this way for the foreseeable future, growing to $10.4 trillion per year by 2020.

A huge global investment opportunity

To meet growing energy demand and replace aging supply capacity, cumulative global investment of $37 trillion is needed by 2035, which equates to 1.5 percent of annual global gross domestic product (GDP) during that period. Securing oil and gas supply accounts for $19 trillion, and $17 trillion goes toward electricity generation, transmission, and distribution.

Other industries have offered their own projections for how much future investment is required to meet demand. The Organisation for Economic Co-operation and Development's Nuclear Energy Agency estimates almost $4 trillion is needed for that sector by 2050, including $893 billion in China and $883 billion in the United States and Canada. Bloomberg New Energy Finance projects $7 trillion will be invested in renewables by 2030, rising to $460 billion per year.

The water-energy nexus

A discussion of future energy needs and required investment isn't complete without discussing water. Water is critical in all stages of energy production, from cooling power plants to oil and gas well injection to irrigation for biofuels. Water needs for energy production in 2010 totaled 583 billion cubic meters — enough to fill more than 233 million Olympic-sized swimming pools. The need for water is expected to rise 85 percent by 2035, twice the rate of energy demand growth. This codependence, called the *water-energy nexus,* will create new problems, leading to new types of energy investment to overcome them.

Most energy solutions fail without water, but all water solutions fail without energy. At its core, the energy-water problem stems from the fact that the world has a finite supply of each, and neither can be created nor destroyed — only harnessed in different ways. So humankind has to find novel and efficient ways to use each of these precious resources. Here are a few examples of this growing interdependence:

- ✔ Producing just one barrel of oil requires four barrels of water. This may be water used for well injection, cooling, or a variety of other applications.

- ✔ The Canadian tar sands use more water than does the entire population of Alberta (where they're located) on an annual basis.

✔ In the United States, the transportation and purification of water consumes 4 percent of all electricity.

✔ In California, water consumes 19 percent of the state's electricity and 31 percent of its natural gas.

✔ 50 to 80 percent of desalination costs are for energy.

As a result, energy investors need to pay attention to water infrastructure, which has been given a grade of D– by the American Society of Civil Engineers. Booz Allen Hamilton, a private government consulting firm, estimates that $22.6 trillion needs to be invested in water and related infrastructure to quell a large portion of the problems. Add to that the fact that water is undervalued by 300 to 500 percent (just compare the price of a gallon of Deer Park spring water to a gallon of gas), and you're looking at an overlooked energy investment opportunity ready to be exploited. Indeed, major energy companies like Shell and ExxonMobil purchasing water rights is already an established and growing theme.

The BRIC path

BRIC is an acronym referring to Brazil, Russia, India, and China — the four countries whose economies are expected to overtake G7 economies in total value by 2027. Unlike North American and European countries that are already developed, these countries are developing now and will be responsible for a large share of future economic and energy demand growth. Combined, these countries have 25 percent of the world's land, 40 percent of the population, and a GDP of $18.8 trillion. Their economies are growing at a rate of 5 to 10 percent annually, compared to flat to 3 percent growth in developed nations.

For perspective, consider that by 2035, India's energy use will more than double, and China's will grow 60 percent. Demand in the United States will rise just 7 percent in the same time, making BRIC and other developing nations the new drivers of global growth. Of the $37 trillion global energy investment needed by 2035, developing nations will require 61 percent, or $22.6 trillion of it.

These nations account for the bulk of the 1.3 billion people without access to electricity and the 2.6 billion people without access to clean cooking facilities. As these people enter the modern era, China will account for 50 percent of increased oil demand through 2035, and China and India combined will account for more than half of global electricity demand growth.

Constant Innovation and Nontraditional Energy

The cheapest unit of energy to produce is the one that doesn't have to be produced at all, making energy efficiency a key investment theme. The IEA estimates that an $11.8 trillion global investment in efficiency through 2035 would be more than offset by the resultant reduced fuel costs and would boost cumulative economic output for that period by $18 trillion. Many countries are taking steps to make this a reality:

- ✔ China is targeting a 16 percent reduction in energy intensity by 2015.
- ✔ The United States has adopted more rigorous automotive fuel economy standards.
- ✔ The European Union has committed to reducing its projected 2020 energy demand by 20 percent.
- ✔ Japan is aiming to shave 10 percent off its electricity consumption by 2030.

These goals, and many others, will result in several nontraditional energy investment opportunities, including technologies that make engines and appliances more efficient, Internet-based programs that allow consumers to monitor and adjust personal energy usage, and materials and systems that allow cars and buildings to use less energy.

Addicted to energy

In many ways, the modern world is addicted to energy. Potentially a problem, this addiction is also the reason energy makes for such a great investment. People always need more of it. Understanding this addiction and the habits it fuels is an important part of investing successfully. The term used to monitor this is *energy intensity,* measured as units of energy consumed per unit of GDP produced (total energy consumed/GDP). As a rule:

- ✔ High-energy intensity indicates a high price or cost of converting energy into GDP.
- ✔ Low-energy intensity indicates a lower price or cost of converting energy into GDP.

For example, the United States consumed 98 quadrillion Btus of total primary energy in 2011 and had a gross domestic product of $13.4 trillion, for an energy intensity of 7,291. In other words, it takes 7,291 units of energy to produce one unit of GDP. By comparison, Germany uses only 4,081 units of energy to create a unit of GDP, showing that it's much more efficient at converting energy into usable products.

Many factors combine to determine a country's energy intensity and per capita energy consumption. Chief among them is the cost of energy, which drives consumption habits. In 2011, when gasoline averaged $3.50 per gallon in the United States, it cost more than $8.30 per gallon in Germany. As a result of high prices, Germans have enacted more efficiency measures: They drive less, use more public transportation, and live in apartments in large numbers. These measures have made the German economy one of the soundest economies in the world. The Germans have found a way to do more with less — to get a higher return on their invested energy.

Cheap energy is necessary for modern life, but using too much of it eats into productivity and profitability. The United States has 5 percent of the global population but uses 25 percent of the world's oil. Americans warm up their cars, leave lights on all night, leave work computers on all weekend, and adjust the thermostat liberally. Now, billions more people are seeking this lifestyle. Feeding this addiction and trying to break it will present myriad investment opportunities.

Fossils get modern

Energy innovation centers on doing more with less or finding ways to extract more energy resources from the earth. The engine in your car is only 40 percent efficient, meaning it wastes 60 percent of the energy as heat. Any fuel that burns wastes energy this way, whether for transportation or for creating electricity. Table 3-7 shows the thermal efficiencies of various fossil fuel engines.

Table 3-7	Thermal Efficiencies of Various Engines
Type of Engine/Plant	*Thermal Efficiency*
Natural gas power plant	50%–60%
Two-stroke diesel	50%
Four-stroke gasoline	43%
Coal power plant	30%

This inefficiency was acceptable when fewer people were demanding more energy, and supply was easy to come by. Today, a more scrupulous eye is being put on this egregious source of waste. More cars, trucks, and buses are being built to run on natural gas, which is much more efficient than gasoline engines. Diesel engines now account for 40 percent of the European automotive market and are quickly making inroads in other countries. More natural gas generation plants are also being built instead of coal. And new coal plants are using advanced combustion technologies to improve efficiency and reduce emissions. A new coal plant owned by DONG Energy in Denmark, for example, converts 49 percent of the coal's energy into electricity and exports the waste heat to help heat buildings and water.

A peak at the future

Attempts to improve efficiency aren't just about cost and emissions. The root of all attempts to do more with less is the fact that all fossil fuels are finite, and when they're gone, they're gone forever. Because oil accounts for 40 percent of total world energy use, declining production rates are of the highest concern. The discussion of oil production decline is called *peak oil theory*, though it applies to all other fossil fuels.

Peak oil is all about production rates, not resource depletion. There are still around a trillion barrels of producible oil beneath the earth's surface. But it's getting harder and more expensive for production rates to keep up with demand. Oil is now being extracted from shale thousands of feet below the surface, and it's being drilled for miles beneath the floor of the ocean. The cheap, easy-to-get oil is gone.

The IEA has already declared that production of conventional crude peaked in 2006. Any gains to oil production will now come from unconventional sources at increasingly higher costs, if they come at all. All oil fields follow a similar production curve of ramp up, peak, and then terminal decline. Peak oil theory suggests total world production will follow the same curve, as first identified by oil geologist M. King Hubbert in the 1950s. You can see the curve and how it relates to individual wells in Figure 3-7. He suggested in 1956 that U.S. oil production would peak between 1965 and 1971. It peaked around 10 million barrels per day in 1971, some 4 million more barrels per day than the United States produces now.

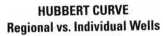

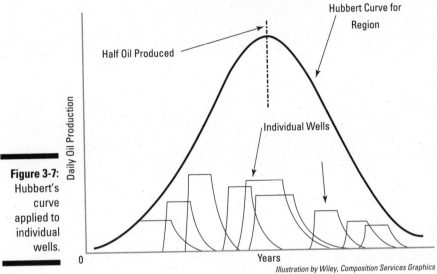

Illustration by Wiley, Composition Services Graphics

Figure 3-7: Hubbert's curve applied to individual wells.

The U.S. Joint Forces Command has warned military leaders to prepare for the consequences of peak oil because "as early as 2015 the shortfall in [oil] output could reach nearly 10 million barrels per day." The U.S. Department of Energy outlined the consequences in a report, *Peaking of World Oil Production: Impacts, Mitigation, & Risk Management:* The peaking of world oil production presents the U.S. and the world with an unprecedented risk management problem. As peaking is approached, liquid fuel prices and price volatility will increase dramatically, and, without timely mitigation, the economic, social, and political costs will be unprecedented. Viable mitigation options exist on both the supply and demand sides, but to have substantial impact, they must be initiated more than a decade in advance of peaking.

Every crisis presents opportunity. The investments in the supply and demand side of energy as a result of this crisis could be the biggest opportunity in human history.

Chapter 4

Getting Ready: The Nuts and Bolts of Energy Investing

You have many ways to invest in energy. You can buy stocks, exchange-traded products, and physical commodities, all of which I discuss in the following chapters. But before you invest, you need to know a few market basics.

A *market* is made when a buyer and a seller agree on a price for a financial instrument. *Financial instruments* represent an agreement involving monetary value. They can include equity in a company (stocks), funds, futures contracts, bonds, and options. All these instruments are listed on exchanges, where the buyer and seller come together to determine a price.

In this chapter, I outline various types of financial instruments, the exchanges on which they trade, and what you need to participate.

Investing with or without a Broker

Whether you invest on your own or with a broker is up to you. A broker can save you time by doing some research and executing trades for you. But that comes with a price in the form of fees and commissions. Trading on your own makes only you responsible for success or failure and can also save you a bundle over the long term.

I'd decide how comfortable you are with investing on your own and how much having someone else do it is worth to you. The next few sections give you guidance no matter your ultimate decision.

Investing on your own

The point of reading a book like this is to be able to invest on your own, of which I'm a huge proponent. Doing your own research and making trades on your own alleviates the need for an expensive broker, whose commissions can quickly eat into your returns.

Investing on your own is about more than just buying and selling. It encompasses the management of all things in your financial life:

- ✔ Budgeting
- ✔ Keeping track of your assets and debt
- ✔ Minimizing tax liability
- ✔ Setting financial goals

If you do all these things, you become the CEO of your life, and achieving investment success becomes much easier.

Starting with a budget

Whether you decide to invest on your own or hire a broker, it's important to keep a budget that tracks your savings, spending, and investments. It should include all bills, debts, incoming cash flow, assets, and home equity, with a dynamic total of your net worth.

Put every single financial transaction in your budget: car payments, cable, phone, utility bills, student loans, IRA, brokerage accounts, savings, credit card, paychecks, and so on.

A budget is a great tool to see a snapshot of your finances on one page so you can identify spending habits, problem debts, cash flow patterns, and more. And then you can start to use that information to make beneficial financial planning decisions, asking yourself:

- ✔ What can I cut out?
- ✔ How can I maximize savings?
- ✔ If I'm not already, how can I get myself debt-free?

An overview of all things in your financial life helps you start answering these questions. I even track the quantity and cost of every gasoline fill-up, as well as the kilowatt-hours of electricity and therms of natural gas I consume at home. You should view this activity as necessary prep work to becoming a successful investor.

Many budgets are downloadable online, or you can download one I created at www.energyandcapital.com/downloads.

Setting up your accounts

To buy stocks, bonds, options, and mutual and exchange-traded funds, you need a brokerage account. This can be a full-service brokerage that offers you investment advice and can fully manage your account, or it can be a discount brokerage that charges you a commission for trades you execute on your own.

To buy commodity futures, like oil, natural gas, uranium, and coal, you need an account with a *futures commission merchant* (FCM), the entity that solicits and accepts commodity orders based on the futures contract market. Alternatively, you can work with an *introducing broker* (IB), who works directly with you to make investment decisions but delegates the trade execution to an FCM. If you'd like a professional to make commodity trading decisions for you, you can select a *commodity trading advisor* (CTA) to manage the account.

You should open a full-service brokerage or managed brokerage account if

- ✔ You don't follow the markets on a routine basis
- ✔ You routinely follow the markets but don't have the confidence or deep knowledge to execute a trading strategy
- ✔ You don't want to allocate the necessary time to managing your own investments
- ✔ You're comfortable allowing someone else make investment decisions for you

Know that ultimately, only you have your best interests in mind, so if you choose a managed account, make sure you investigate the firm by asking about its past performance, current clients, investment philosophy, and fees. No matter which type of account you choose, make sure to read the account agreement and understand which exchanges you'll have access to, what the commissions are, what research tools the account offers, and whether the account has any minimum capital requirements.

You can also employ leverage by using a *margin account,* which allows you to invest with borrowed capital. By using leverage, you can control large positions with little upfront capital. You must be qualified to use a margin account, and though it can lead to larger gains, it can also lead to larger losses. Be sure to check the various margin requirements of brokers and exchanges.

Use these external resources to help choose and evaluate full-service and commodity brokers:

- **Full-service brokers:** Financial Industry Regulatory Authority (FINRA); www.finra.org

- **Futures commission merchants:** National Futures Association (NFA); www.nfa.futures.org

- **Introducing brokers:** National Introducing Brokers Association (NIBA); www.theniba.com

If you want to make all the decisions and execute the trades for stocks, bonds, funds, and options, I suggest going with a discount brokerage. I use an account like this for everything except commodities. Table 4-1 shows the top discount brokers of 2012 as ranked by *The Wall Street Journal.*

Table 4-1	2012 Discount Broker Rankings	
Rank	*Broker*	*Commission on Stock Trade*
1	Fidelity	$7.95
2	Scottrade	$7.00
3	TD Ameritrade	$9.99
4	E-Trade	$9.99
5	Charles Schwab	$8.95
6	TradeKing	$4.95
7	Zecco	$4.95
8	Merrill Edge	$6.95
9	ShareBuilder	$8.95
10	WellsTrade	$8.95

Consider investing in an IRA

Before investing in a standard brokerage account, you should consider investing in an individual retirement account (IRA), which offers multiple tax advantages. Even if you have a 401(k) or SIMPLE IRA through work, you can still contribute $5,500 annually ($6,500 if you're over 50) to an IRA. You don't pay any annual taxes on capital gains, dividends, or other distributions from securities held in this account.

Depending on your income level, you can open either a traditional IRA or a Roth IRA, and you may be able to deduct all or part of your contributions from your taxable income or pay no tax when you make withdrawals in retirement. Because of annual contribution limits, you should place any additional investment funds you have in a regular brokerage account.

Investing beyond stocks

There's much more to energy investing than just buying shares of energy companies. Any successful investment strategy should obviously include stocks but should also incorporate commodities, exchange-traded funds, and master limited partnerships. You can use these non-stock investments to generate income through dividends or income distributions and to help you get access to individual sectors or broad market themes.

Ways to Play

As I go about everyday life, I try to relate the things I see to the market. Are Middle East tensions rising? Time to buy oil. Is it a historically cold winter? Perhaps natural gas is more valuable. Is the White House making a push for clean energy? Maybe it's time to buy solar companies.

With thousands of financial instruments to choose from and infinite data at your fingertips, you usually have more than one way to achieve an investment goal.

Commodities

Commodities are the raw materials that form the foundation of the energy market. The three classes of commodities are

- ✔ Agricultural
- ✔ Energy
- ✔ Metals

Though the price of energy commodities often influences the prices of the other two, I focus solely on energy commodities in this book. These include crude oil, natural gas, coal, uranium, and electricity.

The bulk of these trades are made by consumers and producers of the commodity to manage price risk. A utility that burns natural gas can use the commodities market to hedge against a future rise in price. Conversely, a company that produces natural gas can use the commodity market to hedge against declines in price. You're not a consumer or producer, so you'd simply be trading contracts to profit from price swings, selling the contract before having to take delivery of the natural gas.

Exchanges administer commodities trading in futures markets. Through your futures commission merchant or introducing broker, you can buy contracts for a specific quantity at the determined price to be delivered on a future date. I discuss contract terms for each commodity in later chapters. Table 4-2 lists the exchanges on which energy commodities are traded.

Table 4-2	Exchanges for Energy Commodities
Exchange Name	**Commodities Traded**
Chicago Board of Trade (CBOT)	Ethanol
Intercontinental Exchange (ICE)	Crude oil, electricity, natural gas
Kansas City Board of Trade (KCBT)	Natural gas
New York Board of Trade (NYBOT)	Ethanol
New York Mercantile Exchange (NYMEX)	Crude oil, electricity, gasoline, heating oil, natural gas, propane

The CBOT, KCBT, and NYMEX are all part of the Chicago Mercantile Exchange (CME) Group, which also owns 90 percent of the Dow Jones indexes, including the Dow Jones Industrial Average. The Intercontinental Exchange owns the New York Stock Exchange.

Trading futures is inherently complex because it involves contracts, various units of measurement, hedging, and leverage. Because of this, you can lose more than just the original capital you use to invest. If you don't fully understand the nature of futures contracts or aren't comfortable delegating control of your account to a professional, it's best to invest in energy using the other methods presented in this book.

Equities

Equity is the surplus profit of a company that's distributed among investors after the firm pays off all liabilities. When you buy a company's stock, you're buying a share of this equity. Buying shares of stock means you own a piece of the company. Owning shares gives you a right to a portion of the profits and the firm's assets in case of liquidation, as well as voting rights in the company.

The two main types of stock are

- **Common stock:** When people talk about stocks, this is what they're talking about. The majority of stock is issued in this form. You get one vote per share to elect board members. The firm may offer a dividend, but it's not guaranteed.

- **Preferred stock:** This stock represents owning a piece of the company but usually doesn't come with voting rights. Preferred shareholders are usually guaranteed a fixed dividend forever and are paid off before common shareholders, but after debt holders, in the event of liquidation.

Like commodities, stocks are traded on *exchanges* where buyers and sellers come together to determine price. These can be actual locations where transactions are executed on a trading floor or a virtual network where trades are made electronically. Thanks to the advent of these virtual exchanges, buying and selling stocks on your own is much easier.

When a company issues shares, it does so on the *primary market* by way of an *initial public offering* (IPO), where underwriters determine a price and sell directly to financial institutions. When you and I buy stock, we do so in the *secondary market,* trading shares that have already been issued on an exchange. Table 4-3 lists the major U.S. exchanges.

U.S. exchanges are the largest but still account for only a small portion of all the stocks traded around the world. Other major exchanges include the London Stock Exchange (LSE) and the Hong Kong Stock Exchange (HKSE). Foreign-based companies can list stock on U.S. exchanges provided they adhere to Securities and Exchange Commission (SEC) rules.

Table 4-3	Major U.S. Stock Exchanges
Exchange Name	**Description**
New York Stock Exchange (NYSE)	Founded in 1792 and known as the *Big Board,* the NYSE is the largest equity exchange in the world, home to the majority of the world's largest companies.
Nasdaq	Founded in 1971 as the world's first electronic exchange, Nasdaq has become home to many high-tech stocks.
American Stock Exchange (AMEX)	This exchange is owned by the NYSE and handles about 10 percent of securities traded in the United States, most of them small-cap stocks and exchange-traded funds.
Over-the-counter Bulletin Board (OTCBB)	This is an electronic trading service offered by the National Association of Securities Dealers (NASD), but it's not part of Nasdaq. This exchange has listing requirements, so you find mainly smaller, younger companies here.

Indexes

An *index* is a measure of change in the value of a securities market. Think of it as an imaginary portfolio of securities representing a certain market or specific sector of the market. You're probably already familiar with some indexes, like the Dow Jones Industrial Average or the Standard & Poor's 500 (S&P 500), which are often cited as the broadest measures of the stock market. Table 4-4 shows the four most closely watched stock market indexes in the United States.

Table 4-4	The Four Most-Watched U.S. Indexes	
Index	**Description**	**Owner**
Dow Jones Industrial Average	Tracks 30 large U.S.-based companies	CME Group
Standard & Poor's 500	Tracks 500 leading companies; best representation of overall stock market performance	McGraw-Hill
Nasdaq Composite	Tracks more than 3,000 companies, some foreign, that trade on the Nasdaq exchange	Nasdaq
Russell 2000	Tracks 2,000 small-cap stocks	Northwestern Mutual

The owners of these indexes offer many other indexes that track specific sectors of the market. There are retail indexes, transportation indexes, finance indexes, bond indexes, indexes for specific countries, and more. Of course, there are also energy-specific indexes. You can see the most common energy indexes, along with their annual returns since 2008, in Table 4-5.

Table 4-5	Common Energy Indexes' Annual Performance vs. Dow Jones					
Index	**2008 Return**	**2009 Return**	**2010 Return**	**2011 Return**	**2012 Return**	**Average Return**
Dow Jones Industrial Average	−35%	20%	−11%	6%	6%	−2.8%
Dow Jones U.S. Select Oil Equipment & Services	−62%	66%	29%	7%	−2%	7.6%
Dow Jones U.S. Coal Index	−64%	114%	34%	−48%	−36%	0.0%
Dow Jones Global Utilities Index	−32%	6%	−3%	−8%	0%	−7.4%
World Nuclear Association Nuclear Energy Index	−49%	32%	15%	−25%	1%	−5.2%
Nasdaq Clean Edge Green Energy	−60%	44%	3%	−42%	−5%	−12%

The past few years have obviously been tumultuous for financial markets. As you can see in Table 4-5, oil and gas outperformed the broad market, while utilities, nuclear, and renewable energy underperformed.

Looking at the annual returns of indexes allows you to compare sectors to one another and to the broader market. Indexes are a useful tool to gauge how the market and specific sectors of it are trading. You can't invest directly in indexes. Instead, they form the basis for a variety of mutual funds and exchange-traded funds that track their performance, allowing you to invest in the overall performance of whatever the index is tracking without having to buy shares of every company.

Exchange-traded funds and mutual funds

If you've ever heard people say, "Buy the Dow," they're referring to a fund that tracks the performance of the Dow Jones Industrial Average index. Funds now exist that track almost any aspect of the market you can imagine. You can buy an oil service company fund, a wind energy fund, a coal fund, and so on.

Buying specific funds is one of the easiest ways to get exposure to the market. It's also a way to make sophisticated investments on your own. You can buy a short fund, for example, or a leveraged fund. You can buy a fund that tracks the daily return of crude oil or one that returns twice the daily return of crude oil.

An *exchange-traded fund* (ETF) is a security that tracks the return of an index, commodity, or basket of stocks and that trades like a stock on an exchange. These funds are bought and sold throughout the day, and the price fluctuates as a result. Because of this, an ETF doesn't have its net asset value calculated every day like a mutual fund.

Rather than track the return of an asset, a *mutual fund* pools together funds from many investors, and a professional money manager then invests those funds in stocks, bonds, money markets, or other investment vehicles. Because they're professionally managed and diversified, mutual funds give small investors access to strategies that would be difficult to deploy with little amounts of capital.

Instead of buying shares at the current market price like with ETFs, mutual funds are bought and sold at their *net asset value* (NAV) per unit, which is calculated once per day based on the closing market prices of the securities in the fund's portfolio. The per-unit price of the fund is calculated by dividing the total value of the securities it holds, minus any liabilities, by the number of outstanding fund units. Each unit holder profits proportionally to the gain or loss of the fund's NAV based on the number of units owned.

You should use ETFs if you know what sectors or indexes you want to invest in and have the confidence to buy and sell them on your own. Use mutual funds if you want to select general investment themes but want to leave the buying, selling, and diversification to a professional. Just know that you pay for this management with fees that eat into your returns.

Preparing for Your First Energy Investment

After you open and fund the necessary brokerage accounts, do some research, and decide what type of investment vehicle you want to buy, it's time to make your first energy investment. Assuming you don't have a managed account where a broker executes the trade, here are some things you need to know:

✔ What's a quote, and how do I read it?

✔ What's a ticker symbol?

✔ What kind of order types are there?

Getting familiar with important terms

A *stock quote* is made up of the name of the company or fund, the *ticker symbol, open price, bid* and *ask prices, current price,* and *volume.* Table 4-6 shows all this information for ExxonMobil at a random moment in time.

Table 4-6	ExxonMobil Quote Components					
Name	*Ticker*	*Open Price*	*Bid Price*	*Ask Price*	*Current Price*	*Volume*
ExxonMobil	XOM	$88.50	$88.31	$88.32	$88.31	2,414,003

In this example, ExxonMobil (NYSE: XOM) started trading at $88.50 for the day. At the moment in time you look at that quote, buyers are willing to pay $88.31 per share (the bid), sellers are willing to accept $88.32 (the ask), the stock is currently priced at $88.31, and over 2.4 million shares have already traded hands.

You then decide how many shares you want to purchase. Make sure you have enough money in the account to cover the total purchase price plus any fees. In this example, if you have $1,000 to invest, you can buy 11 shares of Exxon for a total of $971.52 (11 × $88.32 = $971.52), plus any per-trade commission the broker charges you.

Market and limit orders

After you determine how many shares you want to buy, you need to decide what type of order to place. When making a purchase, your options include a market order and a limit order.

A *market order* guarantees your trade will be executed but doesn't guarantee a price. It executes the trade at whatever the current ask price is. If you set a market order in the Exxon example, your shares would be purchased at $88.32. If the ask fluctuates while you're placing an order, your trade could be executed at a higher or lower price than you see in the quote.

A *limit order* guarantees a certain price but doesn't guarantee that your order will be completed. If you set a buy limit order for Exxon at $88.25, it won't be executed until the ask reaches that level. This is a much safer way to place trades because the trade isn't executed until the security reaches the exact price you're willing to pay. If the security doesn't reach the specified price, the trade isn't completed.

With a limit order, you may also be able to select options like *all or none* (AON), *good until canceled,* or *good until date.* All or none means you only want the trade to execute if you can get all the shares you've requested at that price. If you want 11 shares at $88.25, and only 5 become available at that price, the trade won't execute if you've selected all or none. Good until canceled means the order remains open until you cancel it, and good until date means the order remains open until the date you specify.

Figure 4-1 shows screen shots of buy market and limit orders for Exxon, as described in this example.

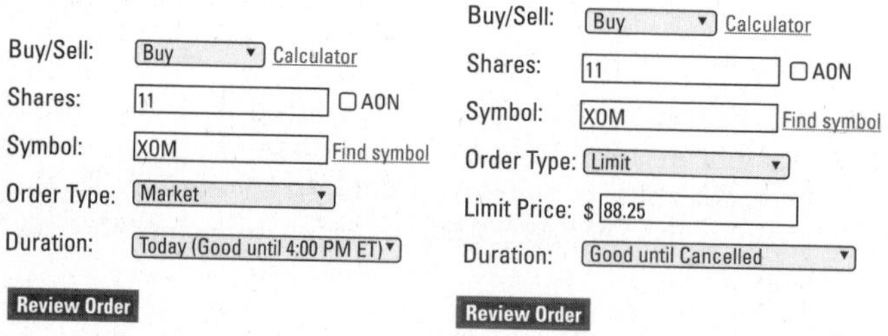

Figure 4-1:
Screen shot
of Exxon buy
orders.

Buy/Sell:	Buy ▼ Calculator	
Shares:	11	☐ AON
Symbol:	XOM	Find symbol
Order Type:	Market ▼	
Duration:	Today (Good until 4:00 PM ET) ▼	
Review Order		

Buy/Sell:	Buy ▼ Calculator	
Shares:	11	☐ AON
Symbol:	XOM	Find symbol
Order Type:	Limit ▼	
Limit Price:	$ 88.25	
Duration:	Good until Cancelled ▼	
Review Order		

Illustration by Wiley, Composition Services Graphics

Sell orders work in much the same way as buy orders. A market sell order executes at the current bid price. A limit sell order doesn't execute until the stock hits the price you specify. The strategy is simply reversed. You generally want to get the lowest price when buying and the highest price when selling.

Stop orders

There are a few more advanced options beyond market and limit orders. Able to be executed on both the buy and sell side, these include

- ✔ Stop-loss order, also known as stop order or stop-market order
- ✔ Stop-limit order
- ✔ Trailing-stop

A *stop-loss* is an order to buy or sell a security when the price rises above or falls below a specified stop price. After that price is reached, the stop order becomes a market order. A *stop-limit* order is the same thing, except that after the stop price is reached, the order becomes a limit order.

You use stop orders primarily to limit downside risk without having to constantly monitor your portfolio. They're a free insurance policy. For example, if you buy Exxon at $88.50 and want to limit downside risk to 5 percent, you'd set a stop-loss order for $84.07 (88.50 × .05 = 4.43; 88.50 − 4.43 = 84.07), and your position would be sold at market if the stock reaches that price. For even more security, you'd set a stop-limit order with a limit price you determine, so that if the stock is falling extremely fast, your shares aren't sold at market well below the stop price.

This concept can be hard to visualize, so Figure 4-2 shows images of a stop-loss and stop-limit order placed for Exxon.

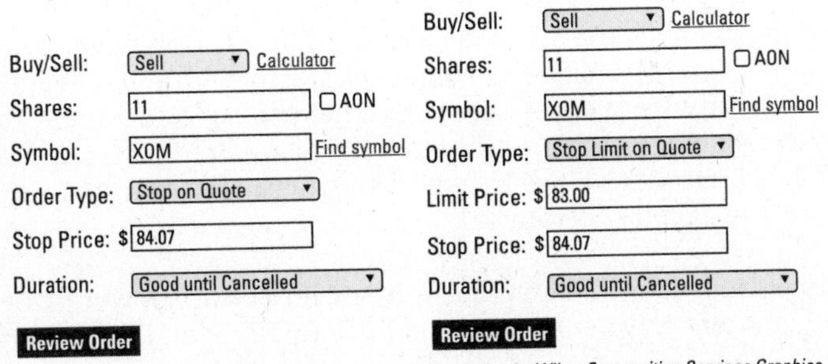

Figure 4-2:
Stop-loss and stop-limit sell orders for Exxon.

Buy/Sell:	Sell ▼	Calculator
Shares:	11	☐ AON
Symbol:	XOM	Find symbol
Order Type:	Stop on Quote ▼	
Stop Price:	$ 84.07	
Duration:	Good until Cancelled ▼	

Review Order

Buy/Sell:	Sell ▼	Calculator
Shares:	11	☐ AON
Symbol:	XOM	Find symbol
Order Type:	Stop Limit on Quote ▼	
Limit Price:	$ 83.00	
Stop Price:	$ 84.07	
Duration:	Good until Cancelled ▼	

Review Order

Illustration by Wiley, Composition Services Graphics

Conversely, you can use stop-loss and stop-limit buy orders to buy a stock only if it rises to a certain price. Though the objective is usually to buy as low as possible, some traders and technical analysts prefer to wait until a security is in a clear uptrend before buying. These types of orders help execute that strategy without staying glued to your computer.

A *trailing-stop* is a stop-loss order set at a percentage level or dollar amount below market price. It is "trailing" because the stop price is adjusted as the stock price fluctuates, allowing you to let profits run while minimizing losses. You can place a trailing-stop market order or a trailing-stop limit order.

For example, if you buy Exxon at $88.50 and want to lock in future profits if the stock ever falls 5 percent, you'd enter a trailing-stop sell order at $84.07. Then, if the price moves to $93.50, your trailing-stop would automatically rise to $90.82. If the price continues rising to $98.50, your trailing-stop would climb to $93.57. Then, if the price begins to fall, your trailing-stop stays at $93.57, and if the stock price reaches that level, the trailing-stop would trigger a sell, automatically protecting your profits. The trailing-stop only moves in the direction of the trade.

Don't set a trailing-stop that's too close to the market price because the market always fluctuates, and you don't want to sell prematurely.

Going long or short

When people talk about investing, they're almost always talking about *going long,* where the goal is to buy low and sell high. But you can also profit when the price of a security falls, known as *being short,* or *shorting.* The idea is still to buy low and sell high, only you do it in reverse, selling shares you borrow at a high price, and then buying when the price falls, profiting from the difference.

Short selling involves the selling of a stock that you don't own. When you short a stock, your broker lends you shares, either from its inventory or from shares it borrows from other clients that have margin accounts. You sell the borrowed shares short, and the proceeds are credited to your account. Eventually, you have to close the short by purchasing the same number of shares. This is called *covering.*

If the price drops as you expected, you buy it back at a lower price and profit from the difference. But if it rises, you have to buy it at a higher price, and you lose money.

You can usually hold a short position for as long as you want. Sometimes, however, you can be forced to cover if the lender wants the borrowed stock back. This is known as being *called away,* and you can lose out on potential profits if it happens. You must also pay the lender any dividends or rights declared while the short is open.

If you sold short 11 shares of Exxon at $88.50, and the stock falls to $80.50, you'd buy to cover at that lower price and earn a profit of $8 per share, or $88, minus any commissions or dividends issued while the position was open. If you cover higher than $88.50, you lose money. You can see these results in Table 4-7.

Table 4-7	Hypothetical Short Results		
Falling Price	*Amount*	*Rising Price*	*Amount*
Borrowed 11 shares of XOM at $88.50	$973.50	Borrowed 11 shares of XOM at $88.50	$973.50
Bought back (covered) at $80.50	−$885.50	Bought back (covered) at $96.50	−$1,061.50
Your profit	$88.00	Your profit	−$88.00

You can use market, limit, and stop orders for selling short and buying to cover. Just be aware that they work exactly in reverse because you want to sell high and buy low.

Safer ways to short

Playing price declines for profit doesn't have to involve the risky practice of short selling. Thanks to the advent of numerous exchange-traded products, you can buy an ETF designed to go up when the underlying investment vehicle goes down. There are short funds — called *inverse funds* — for both commodities and stock sectors. You can buy one that is short oil, for example, or short a group of stocks that operate in the oil and gas sector. You can also buy a *put option*, which gives you the right to sell a security at a certain price as its price falls. Both involve risk, of course, but neither involves borrowing shares.

Chapter 5

Risks and Rewards of Energy Investing

Any type of investment carries risk. Energy investing is no different. Laws change. Technology improvements foster creative destruction. Geopolitics shift in an instant. Speculators speculate. Identifying and properly managing the risks, however, can lead to above-average returns not delivered by many other sectors.

As I constantly illustrate in this book, energy is crucial for civilizations to thrive. The world doesn't need Big Macs, Coke Zero, or Macy's, but it needs energy. And if it wants fast food, soda, and department stores, all those things need energy, too. Indeed, between 1999 and 2012, the exchange-traded fund Energy Select Sector SPDR (NYSE: XLE) widely outperformed McDonald's (NYSE: MCD), Coca-Cola (NYSE: KO), and Macy's (NYSE: M) on the stock market, up 208 percent compared to 140 percent for McDonald's, 12 percent for Coke, and 72 percent for Macy's.

Performance isn't guaranteed, of course; you have to constantly work at it. In this chapter, I discuss the risks and rewards of energy investing to help you do just that.

Watch Your Step: Getting Familiar with the Risks

Lots of things affect the value of energy commodities and companies. Coal stocks that were up 500 percent or more from 2000 to 2008 have lost up to

80 percent of their value, as climate change policies have put restrictions on carbon emissions. Solar companies that bet on expensive technologies are now bankrupt, as old-fashioned silicon has proven to be cheaper and more efficient. Oil prices swing wildly anytime there's a hint of unrest in the Middle East or other oil-producing regions. Crude oil jumped 32 percent — from $85 to $112 per barrel — during the Libyan civil war and the Arab Spring of early 2011. All these circumstances and events drive speculation in both commodity and equity markets, compounding the volatility already inherent in the market.

These risks also yield large rewards. The following sections outline how to minimize these risks and manage them for profit.

Laws and policies

The laws of nations, states, and local entities have a great impact on the movement of energy markets. They address every aspect of the industry, including

- Energy consumption
- Energy distribution
- Energy production

And they do it through

- Conservation guidelines
- Incentives
- International treaties
- Legislation
- Subsidies
- Taxation

Every country, and even every U.S. state, has different policies. Covering them all would require a book of its own. Here I give a few examples of how global energy policy affects energy markets, including examples from major users, and I offer tools for you to explore these policies on your own.

Though the United States has no formal, overarching energy strategy, it has passed a series of energy acts that affect various markets, the most recent of which is the Energy Independence and Security Act of 2007. Its major provisions include

- Accelerated research of clean energy technologies
- Energy savings in building and industry

✔ Improved standards for appliances and lighting

✔ Improved vehicle fuel economy

✔ Increased production of biofuels

Hundreds of pages long, this act called for incentives for hybrid and electric vehicles, conversion from incandescent to high-efficiency light bulbs, a production minimum for biofuels, and much more. Established car companies, makers of conventional light bulbs, and fuel providers saw the act as a risk, but to the informed investor, it was a reward. High-efficiency lighting maker Veeco Instruments (NASDAQ: VECO) is up more than 75 percent since the act passed. Electric vehicle manufacturer Tesla Motors (NASDAQ: TSLA) has more than doubled since its initial public offering (IPO) in mid-2010.

To find out more about energy policy in the United States, including strategy and tax incentives, check out the following resources:

✔ http://energy.gov/mission

✔ http://energy.gov/savings

✔ www.epa.gov/lawsregs

International energy agendas

Global governments and organizations have a strong influence on the energy industry. You can see this influence in things like the United Nations' Kyoto Protocol, which sets binding targets for industrialized countries to reduce emissions of greenhouse gases. Nearly 200 countries have signed and ratified the Kyoto Protocol, and their efforts to curtail emissions dictate the types of energy they use and invest in. You can read about the ongoing implementation at the United Nations Framework Convention on Climate Change website: www.unfccc.int.

Despite global acknowledgement of the need to expand cleaner sources of energy, fossil fuel subsidies are still far greater than those given to renewable energy. In 2010, global renewable energy subsidies stood at $66 billion, while $775 billion was spent subsidizing oil, gas, and coal. And though world leaders pledged to phase out fossil fuel subsidies at the G-20 summit in 2009, the amount of fossil fuel subsidies continues to expand, signaling the need for government help to keep up with pressing demand. Figure 5-1 shows a breakdown of fossil fuel subsidies in 2012.

$775 Billion in Total International Fossil Fuel Subsidies in 2012

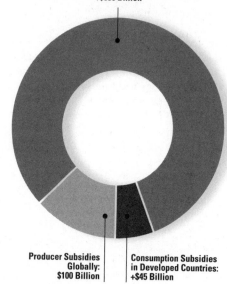

Consumption Subsidies in Developing Countries:
+$630 Billion

Figure 5-1:
Breakdown
of global
fossil fuel
subsidies,
2012.

Producer Subsidies
Globally:
$100 Billion

Consumption Subsidies
in Developed Countries:
+$45 Billion

Illustration by Wiley, Composition Services Graphics

You need to be aware of government involvement in energy markets because any fluctuation or outright deduction would have a clear effect on related energy investments. According to the International Energy Agency, the world would use more than 900 million fewer metric tons of oil equivalent from oil, gas, and coal if global subsidies were phased out, as seen in Figure 5-2. That would clearly be detrimental to the value of oil, gas, and coal commodities and countries and would be a boon for clean energy, so make sure you keep an eye on global energy policy. One of the best places to do so is at www.eia.gov/countries.

Technology

Keeping the pulse of constantly evolving energy technologies is vital because they can cause price swings in energy commodities or make once-dominant companies obsolete. New natural gas drilling technologies, for example, have allowed levels of recovery in the United States not seen for decades. As a result, natural gas prices fell to new lows in 2012, to $1.82 per MMBtu, as you can see in Figure 5-3. In 2008, prices were more than $13 per MMBtu, showing how much volatility technology can usher in.

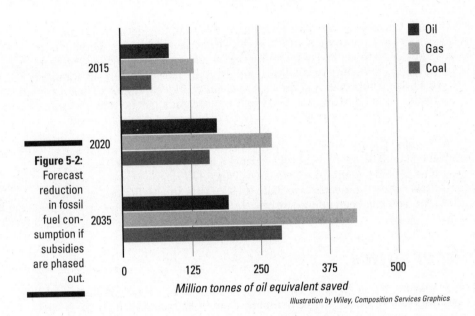

Figure 5-2:
Forecast
reduction
in fossil
fuel con-
sumption if
subsidies
are phased
out.

Million tonnes of oil equivalent saved

Illustration by Wiley, Composition Services Graphics

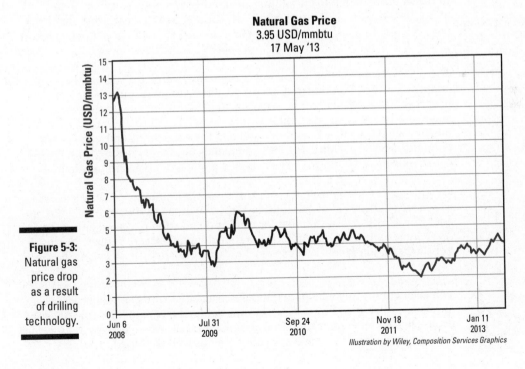

Figure 5-3:
Natural gas
price drop
as a result
of drilling
technology.

Illustration by Wiley, Composition Services Graphics

Changing technology can also put companies out of business. Just think of typewriters and computers, or horse-drawn carriages and cars. Though naysayers point to the failing of numerous clean energy companies as evidence the industry is doomed to fail, this is a part of the maturation of any industry. As technology improves and the cost of clean energy continues to fall, many companies won't make it. And you don't want to get stuck holding stock in a company whose technology is about to be defunct or cost-prohibitive.

One way to stay on top of new energy technology trends is to monitor the advancements being made at the Advanced Research Projects Agency-Energy (ARPA-E), modeled after the Defense Advanced Research Projects Agency (DARPA), whose innovations include the GPS, the stealth fighter jet, and the Internet. You can keep up-to-date at www.arpa-e.energy.gov.

Geopolitics

You may not be an expert on geopolitics and how they relate to energy and natural resources, but you've definitely seen them in action. If you've heard of Russia threatening to cut off European access to natural gas, or read about Venezuelan oil, or seen headlines about Iran's nuclear program or the Organization of the Petroleum Exporting Countries' (OPEC's) influence on oil prices, then you've witnessed how geopolitics influences energy.

The main reason for this is that energy resources aren't distributed evenly among countries. Nations that have abundant energy resources inevitably use them for political control or to improve their influence on the world stage. I've heard from companies who were permitted to operate in a country one day and then were kicked out and had their assets taken by the government the next day. This is the risk companies take when dealing with sovereign countries that control large deposits of oil, gas, coal, and uranium.

Consider Iran nationalizing the Anglo-Iranian Oil Company (now BP) in 1951, which led to the creation of OPEC in 1960, which led to the Arab oil embargo and the 1973 oil crisis. Or consider the nationalization of the oil industry in Venezuela in 1976, where all foreign companies were replaced with Venezuelan companies. You can see how that era affected oil prices in Figure 5-4.

You can't completely eliminate the risks associated with geopolitics. One way to manage them is to invest in larger international oil companies that have the experience and diversification to overcome geopolitical challenges rather than investing in smaller companies, which aren't as well equipped to do so.

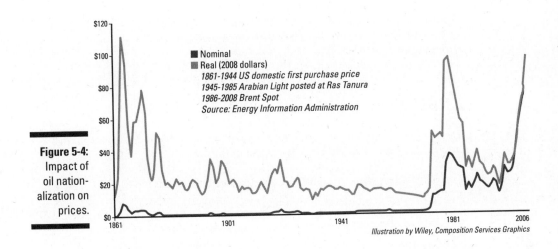

Figure 5-4:
Impact of oil nation-alization on prices.

Illustration by Wiley, Composition Services Graphics

Speculation

Speculation is a risk in any equity or commodity market because of the existence of traders interested only in making short-term profits by betting on whether a security's price will move up or down.

Unlike commercial investors who use price movements for hedging purposes, speculators have different motivations and tend to make the markets fluctuate in different ways. This can lead to wild price swings that cause the expansion and bursting of bubbles, like the dot-com bubble of the late 1990s, when the NASDAQ ran from 1,221 to 4,572 before collapsing to 1,172. Or the oil price bubble of 2007 and 2008, when crude prices went from $52 per barrel to more than $145 before plummeting below $40. Even though they're a small percentage of the market, speculators can cause you serious pain in a hurry.

Speculation can rapidly cause the value of securities to go well above or below the price the fundamentals indicate is fair. If you think prices are rising too far too fast, they probably are, and it's wise to take profits and get out of the market until normal trading patterns return.

Doing Due Diligence to Manage Risk

The best way to manage all investment risks is to make sure you do your *due diligence* — research all the angles of the investment you want to make before you make it. Don't simply take an investment position because you heard about it on a finance show on TV or because you think everyone else is doing it. Impulse buying almost always leads to more loss than gain.

Various energy investment vehicles require you to ask different questions and do diverse kinds of research. The next few sections cover how you should approach each type of energy investment.

Energy commodity futures

If you want to buy futures contracts for oil, natural gas, coal, uranium, or electricity, make sure you ask the following:

✔ Where (on what exchange) does the contract trade?

✔ Who else is involved in this market, and for what reason?

✔ What is the length of the contract you want to purchase?

✔ Are there margin requirements, and, if so, what are they?

Knowing the fundamentals of each commodity market may be the most important part of energy investing because the performance of all investment vehicles depends on the supply and demand of the resource and the numerous things that affect that delicate supply balance. Concerning each specific commodity, you want to know:

✔ Which countries control the largest reserves of it?

✔ What is the geopolitical situation of those countries?

✔ What are the production and consumption numbers for the commodity?

✔ What drives the usage of the commodity?

✔ Can the commodity be economically replaced with something else?

✔ Do seasonal patterns affect usage?

✔ What are the commodity's historic trading patterns?

Each energy commodity has a part in this book where I present the answers, or at least how to find out the answers.

Energy mutual funds

Before buying a managed mutual fund, you should find out:

✔ Who manages the fund? What is his or her track record?

✔ What is the manager's philosophy, and do you agree with it?

✔ What are the fees and how are they charged?

✔ What is the fund's goal, and does it align with your strategy?

✔ What is the fund's historic performance?

✔ What investment vehicles does the fund own?

If the fund owns energy companies, you also want to do some due diligence on them as if you were directly investing in the shares of those companies.

Energy companies

Ask the following questions before buying stock in any company:

✔ What is the firm's financial health, as determined by assets and liabilities?

✔ How does the company make money, and where is future growth going to come from?

✔ What is the company's organizational structure?

✔ Who manages the company, and what is the manager's history?

✔ Who are the company's competitors (peers), and how do they compare?

✔ Does the company have any regulatory or legal problems?

✔ How has the company performed cyclically?

You can find the answers to most of these questions in the annual (Form 10-K) and quarterly (Form 8-K) reports that companies have to file with the U.S. Securities and Exchange Commission. You can even participate in the conference calls most companies have to discuss these reports and ask questions directly to management.

Diversification

Beyond due diligence, one of the best ways to manage risks is to diversify. Not only should you diversify the types of investment vehicles you use — stocks, bonds, funds, commodities, and so on — but also the specific types of those vehicles you choose.

For example, owning oil stocks, oil funds, and crude oil futures isn't diversification. Mix it up among types of energy. You don't want to put all your eggs in one energy basket. Instead, you want exposure to asset classes that do well when others don't, so you can't get wiped out if one goes sour.

The Rewards of Energy Investing

If you acknowledge and mitigate the risks, energy investing can be very rewarding on multiple levels. Profits are typically the prime motivator, of course, but putting your dollars into energy markets can bring other rewards.

Reaping above-average returns

Because of the constantly rising demand for energy and the criticality of increasing supply, energy investments typically outperform the broader market.

For example, the Energy Select Sector SPDR fund, one of the most traded energy funds, had a ten-year annualized return of 15.3 percent as of the beginning of 2013. By contrast, both the Dow Jones Industrial Average and the S&P 500 had annualized returns of less than 9 percent during that period.

That fund largely holds oil companies. Other energy sectors haven't fared as well on a long-term basis, but the more you know about energy, and the more sophisticated techniques you employ, the easier it is to beat the market.

 You don't have to be long. The nuclear, coal, and renewable industries have all underperformed the market over the past few years. But if you're in tune with the energy markets, you can go short and still outperform. If you had shorted the nuclear industry the day of the Fukushima accident in March 2011, for example, you'd have outperformed the market twice over for the following year.

Similarly, knowing when to sell can also lead to higher returns than the broad market. Many clean tech companies were up hundreds to thousands of percentage points between 2006 and 2008. Investing in them and taking profits while the industry was hot would've left you significantly ahead of any broad index. As with most investments, higher risk means higher potential reward. And knowing when to sell is key.

Serving a purpose

Dabbling in energy can offer other benefits beyond investment returns.

Tracking and finding ways to reduce your personal energy, both at home and on the road, not only improves your overall bottom line but also offers contributions to society, like reducing energy demand. If you reduce the amount you spend on energy, you'll also have more free capital to inject in other aspects of the economy.

Investing in energy also allows you to participate in and contribute to what you believe in. Contributing personal funds to any sector or company is the ultimate way to put your money where your mouth is. And this doesn't have to be in the stock or commodities markets. You can become a member of an electricity co-op or fund a growing number of private energy projects whose objectives align with your beliefs.

A common saying is that the market knows everything. And when you have skin in the game, you become a piece of that market. Where you place your dollars plays a role in the direction of the all-knowing market.

Getting an education

Researching and investing in the energy market also gives you a hands-on education. You become aware of how the market operates because you're a part of it. You notice fluctuations in energy prices and also why they're fluctuating.

You start to understand the motivations behind how and why companies and governments do certain things. Because they affect the value of your investments, you'll become more concerned with policy and politics, allowing you to become a more informed citizen.

Most important, you'll eliminate surprises because you're ahead of the curve. You'll see a coming spike in oil or gas prices before it happens. You'll see a bubble bursting while it's forming. This foresight allows you to profit from world events and market swings that others are simply talking about in retrospect.

Part II

Oil and Gas Investments: Greasing the Global Economy

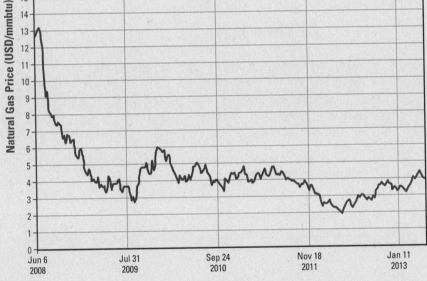

Natural Gas Price
3.95 USD/mmbtu
17 May '13

In this part . . .

- ✓ Grasp the fundamentals of the oil and gas market, including supply, demand, and reserves.

- ✓ Discover the various types of oil and production techniques used to recover it.

- ✓ See how oil and gas are traded as commodities.

- ✓ Identify the major players in the global oil and gas industry, from exploration to refining.

- ✓ Invest in oil and gas through index and exchange-traded funds (ETFs).

Chapter 6

The Crude Basics

Crude oil is the most important energy source in the world, responsible for one third of the total primary energy supply. In 2011, the world consumed 87.4 million barrels of it per day, enough to fill almost 6,000 Olympic-sized swimming pools. Oil is used for many things, from fuels to medicines to makeup. But it all starts with the black stuff that's extracted from beneath the earth's crust and brought to market.

I like to say that oil is responsible for greasing the global economy. But it's also the cause of much international strife. Oil is used to ship goods and provide cheap food for billions of people. But because of where some of the largest deposits of crude oil are located, dictators also use it to manipulate geopolitics and control populations.

Since it was first discovered, oil has been sought after for the great wealth it creates. The chase for it has created boomtowns, started wars, and led to technological breakthroughs. The money used to purchase oil even has its own name: *petrodollars*.

In this chapter, I break down oil market fundamentals. Making sure you understand how the key pieces of the oil market work in concert is crucial for putting together the oil investment puzzle. In the next few sections, I cover where the world's oil is located, what types of crude oil are available, and how much different regions produce and consume so you can build a solid base of oil knowledge before investing.

The Complex Landscape of the Oil Market

Oil supply and demand is constantly walking a tightrope. In fact, according to the U.S. Energy Information Administration (EIA), the world consumed more oil than it produced in 2011. Oil production totaled 87.1 million barrels per day, which was slightly less than consumption, which totaled 87.4 million barrels per day. The world lives on the margin, putting great faith that oil in stored reserves, in pipelines, and on ships and rail cars will arrive for just-in-time delivery. Understanding this margin and the factors that sway supply and demand is key to making successful oil investments.

It often amazes me how little people know about the energy source that drives their world. I've talked to people who think Saudi Arabia provides most of the world's oil. And I've talked to others who think presidents or prime ministers can simply increase production at will. Of course, neither of these things is true.

For all the talk of "oil from the Middle East," only 5 of the world's top 15 producers are located there (see Table 6-2, later in the chapter). It only seems like these countries produce so much because, until recently, they consumed much less than their European and North American counterparts. Only two countries from the Middle East rank on the list of top oil consumers (see Table 6-3, later in the chapter), so more of their oil is available for export.

How much a country consumes directly affects whether it's an importer or exporter. Norway, for example, is the world's 14th largest oil producer, but because it consumes so little of what it produces, it's the 7th largest exporter.

When just-in-time isn't in time

Because the line between consumption and production is razor thin, you often see real-life examples of oil shortages. When Hurricane Sandy struck the East Coast in October 2012, governments in New York and New Jersey resorted to rationing gas by license plate number to avoid shortages and chaos. Price gouging and illegal sales were rampant, underscoring not just how crucial crude oil is to people's lives but also just how fickle the supply-and-demand equation is.

When investing in oil, you need to keep an eye on a lot of moving parts. In the following sections, I break down the most vital ones (supply/demand, country reserves, and import/export figures) and how to use them to get a solid gauge of the global oil market. And because the industry is constantly changing, I point you where to go to find the most up-to-date information. Being armed with critical oil market data gives you an edge when it's time to invest.

Where the Oil Is: Reserves by Country

Before knowing where the world's oil reserves are, you must first understand different types of reserve estimates and realize that they change constantly. The main categories of reserves you commonly see used are:

- Proven (P90, 1P)
- Proven developed (PD)
- Proven undeveloped (PUD)
- Unproven
- Probable (P50, 2P)
- Possible (P10, 3P)

The Society of Petroleum Engineers (SPE) provides the most widely accepted definitions of these terms. You need to understand the definitions of these reserve types because they're an important factor in how to evaluate oil-producing countries and companies. In fact, the Securities and Exchange Commission (SEC) requires companies to disclose how much oil they have access to based on these definitions.

A demand shift

As of early 2013, six of the top ten oil-producing countries are also on the top ten list of oil-consuming countries. Their consumption rate is growing much faster than production growth, especially in Saudi Arabia and Brazil. When these countries had smaller populations and economies, they didn't need as much oil. Now that they're growing, they need more of their oil for themselves. And that means less oil available for the global market — and for importers like the United States and China. This is a long-term trend that will keep upward pressure on oil prices.

Proven reserves

Proven reserves are those thought to have at least 90 percent certainty of being developed given the current economic conditions and technology at the time of evaluation. Oil prices, cost of production, and type and depth of the deposit are all factored in to the level of certainty. Industry insiders refer to proven reserves as P90 or 1P. Proven reserves are further divided into two subcategories: proven developed (PD) and proven undeveloped (PUD). *Proven developed* reserves can be produced in and around existing oil fields and wells with little new investment. *Proven undeveloped* means additional capital investment is required to extract the oil.

The most recent data from the EIA estimates total world proven oil reserves at 1.3 trillion barrels. Table 6-1 shows the countries with the largest proven oil reserves as of 2010.

Table 6-1	Top Oil Reserves by Country
Country	*Proven Reserves (Billions of Barrels)*
Saudi Arabia	262.4
Venezuela	211.2
Canada	175.2
Iran	137
Iraq	115
Kuwait	104
United Arab Emirates	97.8
Russia	60
Libya	46.4
Nigeria	37.2

The countries in Table 6-1 account for around 90 percent of total world oil reserves. But simply having the most reserves doesn't automatically make a country a top producer. Venezuela, for example, has the second most oil reserves but isn't a top-ten producer. Lack of sustained investment, the perils of dictatorship, and the relationships that stem from geopolitics play a major role in a country's ability to effectively bring its reserves to market. This couldn't be more apparent than in the United States, which, even though it isn't a reserve powerhouse, is still the world's number three producer because of friendly investment and regulatory policies and its technological prowess.

Unproven reserves

Unproven reserves are evaluated using the same geologic and engineering techniques as proven reserves, but technological, economic, or political factors preclude them from having a 90 percent certainty of production. Unproven reserves are classified as either *probable* or *possible,* with probable reserves having about 50 percent certainty of recovery, and possible reserves having at least 10 percent certainty of production. In the industry, probable reserves are referred to as P50 or 2P, and possible reserves are referred to as P10 or 3P.

Getting accurate data

Evaluating these changing factors is a big part of making successful investment decisions. Various organizations and government entities evaluate them in different ways. And companies and countries have numerous reasons for misstating or being deliberately vague about their reserves, including company valuations and production quotas. Russia, for example, to be perceived as more of a powerhouse, has routinely reported reserves of more than 190 billion barrels, while credible reporting agencies peg its reserves closer to 60 billion.

To stay up to date on ever-changing global reserve numbers, make sure to check out the most recent reports at the following websites:

- ✔ U.S. Energy Information Administration (EIA): `www.eia.gov/countries`
- ✔ International Energy Agency (IEA): `www.iea.org/topics/oil`
- ✔ Organization of the Petroleum Exporting Countries (OPEC): `www.opec.org`
- ✔ American Petroleum Institute (API): `www.api.org`

Culture of crude

Many external factors help determine how much oil a country can bring to market. For example, four of the countries with the largest reserves fail to make the list of top producers: Iraq, Kuwait, Libya, and Venezuela. It takes more than having oil in the ground to get it to market. This is why, even though the United States doesn't make the top ten list of oil reserves, it's the world's third-largest producer of crude. America's position as a powerhouse of technology and commerce, coupled with a democratic regulatory framework, allows companies in the United States to access and recover oil at a much faster pace than countries lacking in these areas because of dictatorships and war.

Oil Production and Pricing: It's All about Supply and Demand

Everyone knows a bird in the hand is worth two in the bush. And that proverb applies to oil, too. Just because a country has oil doesn't mean it can or will viably produce it. Understanding which countries are the largest producers is part of the foundational knowledge you need to invest in oil. Table 6-2 lists them for you.

Table 6-2	Top World Oil Producers
Country	*Daily Production (Millions of Barrels per Day)*
Saudi Arabia	10.5
Russia	10.2
United States	9.7
China	4.3
Iran	4.3
Canada	3.4
Mexico	3.0
United Arab Emirates	2.8
Brazil	2.7
Nigeria	2.5

In total, the world produces about 87.1 million barrels of oil per day. The top ten production countries account for 60 percent of this output.

The supply of crude oil relative to demand is the basic factor that helps determine oil's price. Because demand often outpaces supply, the world relies heavily on new oil being produced and brought to market. So any disruption — or even perceived disruption — can send crude oil prices soaring. When Libya entered civil war in early 2011, crude oil prices surged from below $90 to more than $110 per barrel as its production plummeted from 1.8 million barrels per day to 500,000.

As you remember from freshman economics, price acts as a mechanism that helps balance supply and demand. When supply falls or demand rises, prices typically rise. So you must monitor these factors closely when investing in oil as commodity.

Because supply and demand have such a tenuous balance in the global oil market, you need to keep a close eye on production numbers. The EIA publishes up-to-date production numbers, short-term outlooks, and price forecasts at www.eia.gov/petroleum. Make sure to keep tabs on oil supply data whether you're directly trading benchmark crude contracts or investing in oil stocks.

Where crude oil is produced affects global energy flows and, therefore, investment flows. With North America ramping up production of shale reserves, the United States is expected to become a net oil exporter in the next two decades. This will shift as much as 90 percent of Middle Eastern oil exports to Asia. Iraq will also rapidly increase oil production as it recovers from a decade-long occupation. Iraq is expected to overtake Russia as the world's second-largest exporter, as its weapon of mass destruction becomes oil production.

The Consumption Junction: Global Oil Demand Numbers

Simply knowing where the oil is and which countries are producing it isn't enough information to successfully invest. You must also understand demand.

The United States is the world's largest oil consumer by far, requiring 18.8 million barrels per day, nearly twice what it produces, leaving it still 50 percent reliant on imports. The United States also consumes about twice as much oil as the next biggest consumer, China, although this gap will continue to close as China presses on with rapid industrialization. Table 6-3 shows you the world's top ten oil-consuming countries.

Table 6-3	Top World Oil Consumers
Country	*Daily Consumption (Millions of Barrels per Day)*
United States	18.8
China	9.8
Japan	4.5
India	3.3
Russia	3.2
Saudi Arabia	2.8
Brazil	2.6
Germany	2.4
Canada	2.3
South Korea	2.2

As you can see, many of the countries in Table 6-3 are still developing and will continue to consume more and more oil every year, keeping upward pressure on demand. In 2011, the world consumed just over 87 million barrels per day. The IEA forecasts global oil demand to hit 94 million barrels per day by 2020 and exceed 99 million barrels per day in 2035, which will drive prices to more than $120 per barrel. More than half of this growth will come from China, India, and the Middle East.

Growing demand in emerging markets

Saudi Arabia is the world's largest producer and exporter of crude oil and a vital player in the global oil market. But the country is also heavily reliant on crude oil to produce its own energy, and its needs are growing. It uses oil for more than 50 percent of its energy needs, and demand for it has tripled since 1990 with no signs of slowing down, as you can see in Figure 6-1. In the time Saudi Arabia's consumption has surged more than 200 percent, its production has grown only 27 percent. This increase in domestic consumption is leaving a growing gap in oil available for export, which means investment opportunities for new sources of production will abound.

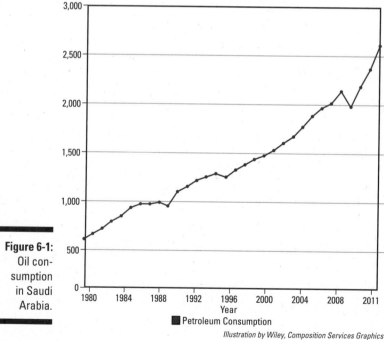

Figure 6-1: Oil consumption in Saudi Arabia.

Petroleum Consumption

Illustration by Wiley, Composition Services Graphics

In addition to demand growth in exporting nations, rapid increases in oil demand from developing nations will lead to numerous oil investment opportunities on the supply side. Demand in India has grown 60 percent since 2000 to more than 3.4 million barrels per day, yet it produces fewer than a million. China's demand has grown 82 percent in the same time. It now consumes about 9 million barrels of oil per day but produces only 4.3 million. The bulk of future demand is expected to come from developing countries like these, and identifying where the oil will be coming from to satiate demand is one of the surefire ways to successfully invest in oil.

Heading here and there: Imports and exports

It's not hard to see how production and consumption come together to form a global oil market. All you have to do is look at imports and exports. This data reveals how well a country is sating its own demand or, conversely, how much oil it has available for sale.

Less-industrialized countries are typically exporters, while industrialized nations are importers. Taking the pulse of global oil flows and monitoring how they change helps you make smart decisions when trading oil prices and investing in oil companies. I present investment strategies for how to capitalize on the flow of oil from these countries in Chapter 9.

Table 6-4 reveals the world's top oil exporters, according to the most recent data from the EIA.

Table 6-4	Top World Oil Exporters
Country	*Exports (Millions of Barrels per Day)*
Saudi Arabia	8.2
Russia	7.5
United Arab Emirates	2.6
Kuwait	2.3
Nigeria	2.2
Iran	2.2
Iraq	1.8
Norway	1.8
Angola	1.8
Venezuela	1.5

And you can see the largest importers in Table 6-5.

Table 6-5	Top World Oil Importers
Country	*Imports (Millions of Barrels per Day)*
United States	8.8
China	4.6
Japan	4.3
India	2.5
Germany	2.2
South Korea	2.2
France	1.7
Spain	1.4
Italy	1.3
Netherlands	1.0

One glance at Tables 6-4 and 6-5 and many macro energy and economic trends become readily apparent:

✔ The continued reliance of the United States on imports

✔ The energy supply vulnerability of Europe and why it's constantly dependent on Russia

✔ The OPEC nations' continued dominance of the export picture

✔ The world's largest economies by gross domestic product (United States, China, Japan, Germany, and France) are also the most reliant on oil imports

Getting familiar with the broader implications of oil import and export data is the foundational knowledge you need to make the energy investments outlined in later chapters. In a practical way, this data also has major impacts on every sector of the global economy.

If crude prices go up, industrialized nations suddenly face much higher costs, while exporting countries generate higher revenues. Driving, transporting goods, and manufacturing items for which oil is a feedstock costs more. And you can see a direct correlation to this in the stock market. The stocks of companies that have oil as a variable cost invariably fluctuate inversely with the price of crude.

Norway's oil model

Though you wouldn't guess it, Norway is one of the world's largest oil exporters. It also has what many call the best model for managing its oil reserves and the revenue those reserves generate. Instead of putting the revenue in sovereign funds, as Saudi Arabia does, Norway puts it in open funds. The revenue belongs to the entire population rather than to a small and select few. The country is transparent about where it invests the money. The country also effectively manages its reserves, deciding in the 1960s not to extract them all at once but instead to bid them out in blocks. Today, Norway has a near half-trillion-dollar fund from its oil revenues and exports more oil than Venezuela.

OPEC and Geopolitics

More than half a century ago, in 1960 to be exact, a few oil-exporting countries decided to band together and form an organization. Today, you know these countries as the Organization of the Petroleum Exporting Countries, or OPEC. When it was first founded, OPEC had five member nations:

- Iran
- Iraq
- Kuwait
- Saudi Arabia
- Venezuela

Over the past 40 years, countries have joined and vacated the organization. Currently, it has 12 members, including those in the preceding list plus the following:

- Qatar (joined 1961)
- Libya (joined 1962)
- United Arab Emirates (joined 1967)
- Algeria (joined 1969)
- Nigeria (joined 1971)
- Ecuador (joined 1973; vacated 1992–2007)
- Angola (joined 2007)

Together, these countries produced 29.8 million barrels of oil per day in 2011. That equates to just over 34 percent of total world oil production. Proven reserves of OPEC nations total 1.2 trillion barrels, or some 85 percent of the world's 1.3 trillion barrels. Because OPEC produces more than a third of the world's oil and possesses such a large portion of total reserves, knowing why it exists and how it operates should be compulsory knowledge for energy investors.

OPEC's mission is "to coordinate and unify the petroleum policies of its member countries and ensure the stabilization of oil markets in order to secure an efficient, economic, and regular supply of petroleum to consumers, a steady income to producers, and a fair return on capital for those investing in the petroleum industry."

To do this, the member nations meet twice a year at the OPEC Conference to discuss the global economic picture and determine production quotas that are in their best interest. They consider economic growth rates, oil supply-and-demand scenarios, and other factors when deciding how much oil the organization needs to produce to maintain stable prices and steady supplies to oil consumers.

OPEC doesn't control the oil market or oil prices. It produces 34 percent of the world's oil and 19 percent of its natural gas. But because its members consume less oil than developed nations, it's responsible for about 60 percent of the crude oil traded internationally. As such, it has a large, but not controlling, influence on the oil market.

From the early 1970s through the mid-1980s, OPEC did set oil prices. However, this is no longer the case. Today, the free market determines the price of oil, as indicated by the three major international exchanges on which it's traded. I examine these exchanges in Chapter 8.

You can find out more about OPEC, its member nations, production rates, and more at www.opec.org.

Conventional and Unconventional Oil

Until now, I've only discussed crude oil. But not all crude is created equal. The most basic division is between conventional and unconventional oil.

Conventional oil is oil produced using standard drilling techniques. These large pools of oil simply need to be drilled into so the oil can be extracted.

This is what typically comes to mind when you think about oil. Jed Clampett's "Texas tea" was conventional oil. It's the cheapest and most efficient oil to produce.

For years, the world has relied on the production of conventional oil. But after decades of intense extraction to meet growing demand, finding viable conventional oil reserves is getting harder and harder. In fact, the International Energy Agency has said global production of conventional oil peaked in 2006 at 70 million barrels of oil per day and will plateau around 69 million barrels per day through 2015.

Unconventional oil, by contrast, is any oil produced with nontraditional techniques. Unconventional crude includes the following sources:

- Oil shales
- Oil sands
- Coal-based liquids
- Biomass-based liquids
- Natural gas–based liquids

The inclusion of these resources is why you see different numbers when looking at reserves, supply, and demand. Make sure to check whether the numbers you come across are for just crude oil or total oil. These additional resources lumped into the unconventional group are why the world can produce less oil than it consumes. Some of the margin is made up by these other liquids.

As you invest in oil companies, you want to know what kind of oil they produce and what the related costs are. Conventional oil costs much less to produce than unconventional, so companies producing conventional oil have a much higher profit margin.

Saudi Arabia, for example, with its vast reserves of conventional oil, is estimated to have total production costs between $4 and $6 per barrel. Oil shale is estimated to cost between $52 and $113 per barrel to produce. If the current price of oil is lower than a company's cost of production, there's no money to be made, and it's likely not a good investment. You should be looking for companies that have the highest margin between the price of oil and their production costs.

Table 6-6 shows various types of oil fields and recovery techniques and their estimated production costs.

Table 6-6	Oil Production Costs
Oil Field/Source	*Estimated Production Costs, in Dollars*
Mideast/North Africa	$6–$28
Other conventional oil fields	$6–$28
CO2 enhanced recovery	$30–$80
Deepwater	$32–$65
Arctic	$32–$100
Heavy oil/bitumen	$32–$68
Oil shale	$52–$113
Gas to liquids	$38–$113
Coal to liquids	$60–$113

Because the production of conventional oil has peaked, the world must increasingly rely on more expensive unconventional oil. By 2035, some 30 percent of the world's supply will be from unconventional sources. This growing dependence on unconventional oil is one of the main drivers behind rising oil prices. Getting oil from hard-to-reach places like oil sands and miles beneath the ocean floor simply costs more.

Sweet and sour, heavy and light

The terms *conventional* and *unconventional* simply relate to how the oil is produced. Whether conventional or unconventional, it's all still crude oil. Variations in the oil's makeup are what determine how it's classified and sold.

Crude quality is measured in terms of density (light or heavy) and sulfur content (sweet or sour).

The first property of the oil that matters is the density, or viscosity, which equates to how gooey the oil is. This is measured by its gravity on the American Petroleum Institute (API) scale. Light crude has an API gravity higher than 31.1 degrees, medium crude between 22.3 degrees and 31.1 degrees, and heavy oil lower than 22.3 degrees. The higher the number, the lighter the crude. Oil that's too viscous to flow on its own, like that produced from Canada's oil sands, is called *bitumen* and has an API gravity lower than 10 degrees.

The second difference is sulfur content. To turn crude oil into the products people use every day, the sulfur must first be removed. To be considered *sweet,* the crude must contain less than 0.5 percent sulfur. If it contains any more than this, the oil is considered to be *sour.*

The lighter and sweeter the crude, the easier and cheaper it is to refine it into the products people use, like gasoline. Because production of conventional oil has peaked, the remaining oil will get progressively heavier and sourer. If you've filled up your tank in the past five years, you've seen firsthand how this is playing out at the pump.

When traded as a commodity, light, sweet crude fetches a higher price than heavier, sourer crude because it's cheaper to process, and more value-added products can be made from it.

Major oil fields

The importance of major oil fields can't be overstated. Half of all oil produced comes from just 0.03 percent of all oil fields. But many of them are aging and starting to produce less and less oil each year. Each oil field has a finite amount of oil, and when that oil is extracted, it's gone forever. As this trend continues, the world is scrambling to find resources to replace these fields. This is one reason so much attention and capital has been spent developing unconventional resources over the past few years.

Because they're so large, giant oil fields were the first to be discovered. The Ghawar field in Saudi Arabia, for example, was discovered in 1948 and hit peak production in 2005. Mexico's Cantarell field was discovered in 1976 and now produces just 400,000 barrels per day after peaking at 2.1 million barrels per day in 2004. Big fields like these may continue to be discovered, but the oil won't be as easy or cheap to produce because of the type of oil or its location.

Figure 6-2 illustrates the number and size of the world's oil fields and what percentage of the world's oil they produce.

The decline in production from major oil fields means crude oil prices will rise as harder-to-get resources are exploited at higher costs. This is a great scenario for investors who profit from investing in crude prices or for those who invest in oil companies with lower production costs. It also means you'll have many opportunities outside of the traditional oil powerhouse countries.

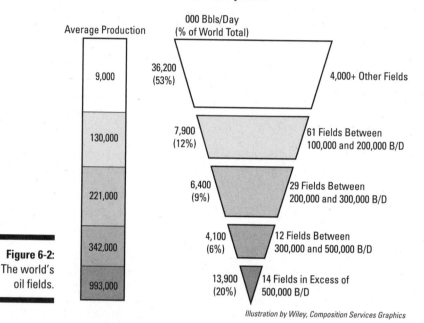

Figure 6-2:
The world's
oil fields.

Illustration by Wiley, Composition Services Graphics

Offshore oil

Some of the biggest discoveries of late have been offshore oil fields. Drilling for oil under the ocean isn't new. The first submerged wells were drilled off piers in California in 1896. The technology has come a long way since then, and companies can now drill up to 2 miles beneath the ocean floor many miles off the coast. Of course, that comes at a price. Royal Dutch Shell (NYSE: RDS) has spent $3 billion building its Perdido hub in the Gulf of Mexico.

Today, nearly 700 offshore oil rigs operate around the world. Table 6-7 shows the areas where most of these rigs are located.

Table 6-7	Offshore Oil Rigs
Region	*Number of Rigs*
Europe (North Sea)	165
North America (Gulf of Mexico)	95
Middle East (Persian Gulf)	93

Region	Number of Rigs
South America (Brazil)	92
Asia (Southeast)	89
Africa (West)	63

It's possible to invest in the companies that own these fields, as well as companies that provide the necessary technology and rigs to produce the oil. I discuss these opportunities in Chapter 9.

Hydraulic fracturing

One of the ways to access unconventional oil is with *hydraulic fracturing,* or *fracking.* Developed in the United States, this is the process of using water pressure to create fractures in rock formations that allow once-trapped oil and gas to escape and flow out of a well. Using this technology, hundreds of billions of barrels of oil once thought inaccessible may be developed.

Already, the technology is being credited with igniting an oil renaissance in the United States, where oil production peaked in the 1970s. It's already increased production by 700 percent in North Dakota, where production went from 100,000 barrels per day to more than 700,000 barrels per day between 2008 and 2012. Using this technology, U.S. oil production has rebounded to levels not seen since the early 1990s, as shown in Figure 6-3. Because of this technology, the IEA forecasts that the United States will exceed 11 million barrels per day of production, potentially surpassing Saudi Arabia.

Brazil's offshore oil fields

One of the largest offshore oil basins in the world was discovered off the coast of Brazil in 2006 and is currently being developed. Known as the Santos Basin, it has already spawned three big oil fields. The first field, called Tupi, may hold 7.5 billion barrels. The second, found in 2007 and called Sugar Loaf, may hold 25 billion barrels. And the most recent, Jupiter, found in 2008, may hold 17 billion barrels. They're being developed by Petrobras (NYSE: PBR) in conjunction with BG Group.

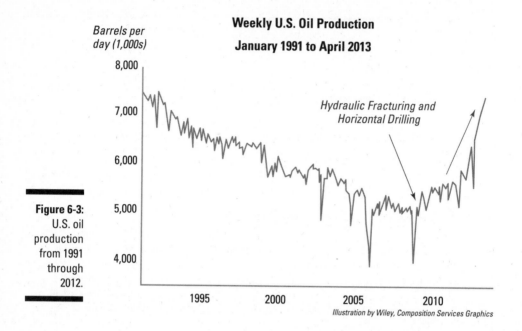

Figure 6-3:
U.S. oil
production
from 1991
through
2012.

With those kinds of results, the rest of the world is hungry for fracking technology. China has made numerous multibillion-dollar acquisitions of U.S.
drillers to gain expertise in the area, many of which have led to substantial
returns for investors. You can find a full discussion of investing in drilling
companies in Chapter 9.

Chapter 7

Grasping Gas

*L*ike crude oil and coal, natural gas is a nonrenewable fossil fuel resource and major source of energy across the globe. Cleaner burning and more cost-effective than its coal counterpart, natural gas is playing an increasingly larger role in energy consumption.

Historically speaking, humans have been using natural gas for a long time. Ancient Greeks built temples around naturally occurring gas seeps ignited by lightning. More than 2,500 years ago, the Chinese used natural gas to evaporate water they collected from the sea to produce salt. Fast forward to the early 19th century, and the first gas company was founded in London to provide fuel for lighting. I'd be remiss if I didn't mention that the first use of gas lamps in the United States took place in Baltimore, just a few blocks down the street from my office. A few years after Baltimore's gas lamps were put into place, the first natural gas well in the United States was put into production.

A reader once asked me why I had become so bullish on natural gas over the last five years. On the surface, prices declined dramatically in North America in 2011 and 2012 thanks to a newfound abundance of supply. Is this low-price natural gas environment really a good place to find a strong energy investment?

In this chapter, I show you. This chapter is designed to give you a basic understanding of natural gas markets on both a regional and global scale; to show you who's lucky enough to have cheap, abundant supplies of natural gas available; and to illustrate the major players that'll shape the future of the gas industry.

Considering the Gas Basics

Natural gas is a composition of hydrocarbons formed from millions of years of pressure and heat in thick layers of silt, sand, and mud. It is odorless and tasteless, has no discernible color, and more important, is combustible. Its combustibility is the characteristic that makes it so valuable. Burning natural gas provides you with the vital energy you use in everyday life. You can cook your food with it, heat your home, and use it to generate electricity.

Because of its odorless nature, distributors and utilities add a harmless chemical called *mercaptan* to natural gas. This chemical gives natural gas its distinctive smell, usually described as rotten cabbage or eggs. The mercaptan is primarily added for safety purposes (imagine the increased danger of gas leaks without it!).

The everyday natural gas you come across is nearly all methane because it has been refined. But when it first comes out of the ground, it has a completely different makeup. Like crude oil (see Chapter 6 for details), natural gas must be refined into usable fuels. The makeup of the raw gas is between 70 and 90 percent methane and up to 20 percent ethane. Raw gas also contains smaller quantities of several other gases, including carbon dioxide, oxygen, nitrogen, hydrogen sulfide, propane, and butane.

Typically, there are two types of natural gas production. Oil and gas companies often target specific gas fields depending on the price environment. The two main categories of natural gas are

- ✔ **Dry natural gas:** Production that's composed of nearly all methane. In the United States, natural gas is considered *dry* when it has less than 0.1 gallon of heavier hydrocarbons (like propane and butane) for every 1,000 cubic feet. Dry gas is what's delivered to consumers after the impurities have been removed.

- ✔ **Wet natural gas:** Whenever you hear a company talk about *wet* gas, it means the gas has a greater presence of heavier hydrocarbons. These hydrocarbons are generally separated from the gas in the form of a liquid during natural gas processing. These natural gas liquids (NGLs) hold value for oil and gas companies because they can be sold on the market.

Companies typically report their oil and gas production in terms of barrels of oil equivalent (BOEs). Essentially, one BOE is the amount of energy generated by burning one barrel of crude oil. One BOE is roughly equal to 5,800 cubic feet of natural gas. However, the U.S. Geological Survey (USGS) calculates that approximately 6,000 cubic feet of natural gas is one barrel of oil equivalent.

Natural gas can be measured in several ways. The two you see the most are

- Cubic feet for volume, which is used in standard natural gas futures contracts
- British thermal unit (Btu) for energy content, which is the amount of energy necessary to heat 1 pound of water by 1 degree Fahrenheit

When converting between the two, note that 1 cubic foot is equal to approximately 1,027 Btus. Table 7-1 shows you the most common natural gas volume and energy equivalent terms with abbreviations for each.

Table 7-1	Gas Abbreviations Made Easy
Natural Gas Volumes/Equivalents	*Abbreviations*
One cubic foot	1 cf
One thousand cubic feet	1 Mcf
One million cubic feet	1 Mmcf
One billion cubic feet	1 Bcf
One trillion cubic feet	1 Tcf
One cubic foot of natural gas equivalent	cfe
One thousand cubic feet of natural gas equivalent	Mcfe
One million cubic feet of natural gas equivalent	Mmcfe
One billion cubic feet of natural gas equivalent	Bcfe
One trillion cubic feet of natural gas equivalent	Tcfe

For perspective, the United States consumed in excess of 25.5 trillion cubic feet (Tcf) of natural gas in 2012, and the world consumed around 119 Tcf.

Moving from the wellhead to your doorstep

Five basic steps take natural gas from deep underground to your stovetop:

- **Exploration:** When geologists locate a possible natural gas reservoir, they conduct extensive tests by using seismic technology to determine the best site for drilling. Typically, companies drill exploratory wells to evaluate the economic potential of the area. If successful, a company can go forward with a drilling program. An exploratory well that yields no significant quantities of oil or gas is called a *dry well.*

✔ **Production:** After a site gets the green light, companies begin drilling new wells and placing them into production. I cover natural gas production investments in Chapter 9.

✔ **Transportation:** Although crude oil producers have several options available to get their barrels to customers, natural gas is limited to using pipelines. More than 2.5 million miles of oil and gas pipelines snake through the United States. That's enough to circle the earth more than 100 times! This vast array of pipelines includes gathering pipeline systems for receiving natural gas from the wellhead, transmission pipeline systems to transport the gas from processing or storage facilities to distribution centers, and distribution pipeline systems that send it directly to the consumer. I give you more details on pipeline investments in Chapter 9. (Flip ahead to Figure 7-1 to see the highly complex series of natural gas pipelines built within the United States.)

✔ **Storage:** Natural gas is traditionally considered a seasonal fuel because demand is highest during the winter months, so it's typically injected into underground storage facilities. (Note that the seasonal fuel concept is changing because of its increased consumption in other sectors.) Underground storage fields can include depleted oil and gas reservoirs, salt caverns, and aquifers. As of 2011, more than 400 underground storage fields were in the United States. Keeping tabs on the amount of natural gas in storage is critical when investing in natural gas futures (covered in Chapter 8), and you do that with the U.S. Energy Information Administration's (EIA's) *Weekly Natural Gas Storage Report* at http://ir.eia.gov/ngs/ngs.html.

✔ **Distribution:** After natural gas is produced from a wellhead, processed at a facility to remove impurities, and ready for consumption, it's transported directly to either large-volume customers or distribution points such as a local gas utility and delivered to customers through smaller pipelines.

Knowing major gas drivers

As an investor, knowing what factors affect the short- and long-term success of the U.S. gas industry is a critical part of making successful decisions. I discuss the specifics of natural gas consumption later in this chapter. First, here's a discussion of what drives natural gas demand.

Natural gas demand is generally perceived to be cyclical because of its relationship to heating. Weather, as it turns out, is top on the list of short-term catalysts for natural gas. For the most part, a colder-than-average winter can portend stronger residential and commercial demand, while a hot summer can directly lead to higher demand in power plants. It makes perfect sense, doesn't it? People usually turn up their heat during the coldest months of the year. Conversely, they inevitably use less during the warm months of summer.

The temperature outside isn't the only piece of this puzzle. Weather-related events are a major wild card because of their unpredictability. A particularly strong storm can be potentially devastating to a major production area, which everyone learned all too well during the 2005 hurricane season.

Prior to the devastating impact of Hurricane Katrina in late 2005, the United States was having a difficult enough time as natural gas demand outstripped supply. When the hurricane struck the Gulf of Mexico, it took out about 18 percent of annual U.S. production. At the time, the Gulf Coast accounted for 40 percent of U.S. natural gas production. Prices skyrocketed from $8 to almost $16 per MMBtu in the three months after the hurricane made landfall.

Both Hurricane Katrina and Hurricane Rita caused gas supplies to remain much tighter throughout the winter heating season and showed how vulnerable the gas industry was to weather.

Along with weather, the economy can also play a significant role in driving demand. Strong economic growth gives demand a boost, including for industrial, residential, and electricity applications. A weaker economy inevitably erodes demand.

Taking into account natural gas supply and demand

I find that long-term trends in the natural gas industry are primarily dependent on demand projections. Barring the short-term fluctuations, these projections tell you what to expect decades down the road. One of the best places to look for these growth trends are from regular reports of the EIA and International Energy Agency (IEA).

The EIA's *Annual Energy Outlook* provides long-term supply and demand projections for the United States. According to the early release of its 2013 report, U.S. natural gas consumption is expected to increase 17 percent from current levels to 28.7 Tcf in 2035. The IEA's *World Energy Outlook* shows that, globally, natural gas demand will rise even more — some 47 percent, from 120 Tcf to 176 Tcf — in the same time.

Despite projecting long-term supply and demand trends, these organizations don't always get it right. In 2007, the EIA held an overly bullish outlook for coal consumption. At the time, natural gas prices were rising, averaging $7.51 per Mcf, and the now-famous shale plays hadn't yet made it into the spotlight. In that report, imports of U.S. natural gas imports rose significantly to 2030, while coal demand grew steadily. Now it's six years later, and the EIA has changed its outlook. In fact, the 2013 projections show that natural gas will be the only one of the fossil fuels to increase its share of the overall U.S. energy mix.

The following resources can be quite helpful for finding global growth trends for natural gas. Look for their annual reports:

- ✔ http://www.eia.gov
- ✔ http://www.iea.org
- ✔ http://www.ingaa.org

Table 7-2 shows the top natural gas–consuming countries, using the most recent data available

Table 7-2	Top Natural Gas Consumers
Country	*Annual Consumption (Billion Cubic Meters)*
United States	690.1 Bcm
Russia	424.6 Bcm
Iran	153.3 Bcm
China	130.7 Bcm
Japan	105.5 Bcm
Canada	104.8 Bcm
Saudi Arabia	99.2 Bcm
United Kingdom	80.2 Bcm
Germany	72.5 Bcm
Italy	71.3 Bcm

And Table 7-3 shows the top-producing natural gas countries.

Table 7-3	Top Natural Gas Producers
Country	*Annual Production (Billion Cubic Meters)*
United States	651 Bcm
Russia	607 Bcm
Canada	160 Bcm
Iran	152 Bcm
Qatar	147 Bcm
China	103 Bcm

Country	Annual Production (Billion Cubic Meters)
Norway	101 Bcm
Saudi Arabia	99 Bcm
Algeria	78 Bcm
Indonesia	76 Bcm

Eyeing the importance of imports and exports

Before liquefied natural gas (LNG) could be viably shipped, the natural gas industry was tied down to regional markets. It all boils down to how the resource is transported. Unlike crude oil, which can be shipped via freight, tanker, pipeline, and even trucks, the overwhelming amount of natural gas is supplied by pipeline.

In other words, the price for 1,000 feet of natural gas in China can drastically differ from the price for the same amount you can buy in Louisiana — and it certainly does! Today, natural gas prices in Europe and Asia are double, even triple, the prices in North America because of the supply glut currently seen in the United States. If America begins to export natural gas, the gap could be closed.

Before the rapid development of shale gas plays began in 2006, the United States was growing increasingly dependent on foreign gas supplies. To show you how crucial pipelines are for natural gas exports, look no further than the United States. Almost 95 percent of all U.S. natural gas imports are received by pipeline from Canada. North America is flooded with natural gas because of two main factors:

- ✔ U.S. domestic gas production increased 26 percent to about 29.7 Tcf in 2012, which was more than the country consumed.

- ✔ The first exports of North American LNG aren't expected to begin until 2015.

If you're interested in exactly how the shale gas boom has changed the picture, consider the following: U.S. imports of liquefied natural gas rose almost nine-fold between 1997 and 2007. Today, they've fallen to levels not seen in more than a decade, as gross withdrawals from shale gas wells increased by more than 300 percent.

The advent of LNG exports, however, will finally allow the natural gas industry to do something it has never done before — trade on a global scale.

The process of liquefied natural gas involves chilling natural gas to approximately –260 degrees Fahrenheit. At that temperature, it turns to a liquid that takes up only 1/600th the volume of typical natural gas and can be transported by special tankers.

Nearly 20 countries exported LNG to more than two dozen others during 2012. Although the amount of LNG being exported worldwide makes up a trivial quantity compared to pipeline exports, the LNG trade is quickly gaining steam. Table 7-4 shows the top ten natural gas–exporting countries in 2011, including pipeline gas and LNG.

Table 7-4	Top Natural Gas Exporters
Country	*Annual Net Exports (Billion Cubic Meters)*
Russia	196 Bcm
Qatar	119 Bcm
Norway	99 Bcm
Canada	63 Bcm
Algeria	49 Bcm
Indonesia	46 Bcm
Netherlands	33 Bcm
Turkmenistan	29 Bcm
Nigeria	26 Bcm
Malaysia	22 Bcm

I see a mad dash by companies in both Canada and the United States racing to become the first LNG exporters in North America. At the beginning of 2013, the only project approved that was scheduled to begin exporting LNG as early as 2015 was Cheniere's (NYSE: LNG) LNG terminal, located on the Sabine River between Texas and Louisiana.

Before a company can begin production on a new LNG facility, it must receive approval from both the Department of Energy (DOE) *and* the Federal Energy Regulatory Commission (FERC). As of April 2012, eight projects were approved by the DOE, with one under review and one approval pending. FERC had approved only the Sabine Pass project. For a complete list of the proposed and approved projects in the United States, check out FERC's website at http://ferc.gov/industries/gas/indus-act/lng.asp.

Oh Henry: The heart of the U.S. gas trade

Located in Erath, Louisiana, the Henry Hub has been the distribution hub for U.S. natural gas for the past 23 years. It's owned by Sabine Pass LLC, a subsidiary of Chevron (NYSE: CVX). Every day, natural gas futures contracts exchange hands on the New York Mercantile Exchange (NYMEX) for the gas that arrives there. Henry Hub is the heart of the natural gas industry and the lifeblood of future U.S. power plants, and it sets the benchmark for natural gas prices across Canada and the United States.

When looking for the right natural gas investment, remember that North American LNG exports will take between three and five years to get started — and that's assuming there are no major delays along the way. As of today, the United States is still a natural gas importer. You can see the top natural–gas importing countries in Table 7-5.

Table 7-5	Top Natural Gas Importers
Country	*Annual Net Imports (Billion Cubic Meters)*
Japan	116 Bcm
Italy	70 Bcm
Germany	68 Bcm
United States	55 Bcm
South Korea	47 Bcm
Ukraine	44 Bcm
Turkey	43 Bcm
France	41 Bcm
United Kingdom	37 Bcm
Spain	34 Bcm

Knowing Where the Gas Is

Five years after the first gas lamps started popping up on the streets of Baltimore, the first natural gas well was drilled by William Hart in western New York. The well was 27 feet deep and dug by using shovels. Hollowed-out logs sealed with tar were used as a pipeline to transport production. The

Fredonia gas well was located just 80 miles north of the famous Drake well in Pennsylvania that kick-started the U.S. oil industry, and the search has been on for oil and gas ever since.

Who's got gas?

A close friend of mine once remarked that he was hesitant to invest in the oil and gas industry because it was dominated by *national oil companies* (NOCs). An NOC is a company that's owned — either wholly or through a majority stake — by a national government. A few of the most recognizable names include Saudi Aramco, Gazprom, China National Petroleum Corporation (CNPC), Petróleos de Venezuela (PDVSA), Petróleos Mexicanos (Pemex), Oil and Natural Gas Corporation Limited (ONGC), Statoil, and Petróleo Brasileiro (Petrobras).

Were his fears of investing in oil and gas abroad unfounded? Even some of the largest public oil and gas companies in the world get the short end of the stick from NOCs sometimes. Exxon was ousted from Venezuela after then-President Hugo Chavez nationalized the country's oil industry and took possession of foreign oil assets still in the country.

The world's top oil-producing countries are a veritable who's who of countries with powerful NOCs (see Chapter 6 for a list of these countries). More than half of the global production and nearly 90 percent of the world's proven oil reserves are in the hands of these companies.

The same can be said about natural gas. NOCs control about the same percentage of global gas production but less than 70 percent of the world's gas reserves. Table 7-6 shows you the top ten countries by natural gas reserves.

Table 7-6	Top Ten Countries by Proven Gas Reserves
Country	*Proven Gas Reserves (Trillion Cubic Meters)*
Russia	55 Tcm
Iran	33.5 Tcm
Turkmenistan	26.2 Tcm
Qatar	25.4 Tcm
United States	9 Tcm
Saudi Arabia	8.2 Tcm
Azerbaijan	6 Tcm

Country	Proven Gas Reserves (Trillion Cubic Meters)
Venezuela	5.5 Tcm
Nigeria	5.2 Tcm
Algeria	3.8 Tcm

Fracking: It's shale, dummy!

One reason why natural gas investment prospects are better in North America than the rest of the world is because a real bona fide natural gas boom is happening right now. Figure 7-1 illustrates my point perfectly, showing how the majority of U.S. natural gas production comes from shale and tight gas.

These are reserves of natural gas trapped deep in shale and sedimentary rock that are too hard to drill through. Hydraulic fracturing, or fracking, solves this problem by combining water, sand, and chemicals and injecting this mixture at high pressures to fracture the rock and release the gas. U.S. companies have perfected the technique, allowing the United States to pass Russia as the world's top natural gas producer. Fracking is now being pursued in many other countries around the world.

U.S. Dry Natural Gas Production by Source, 1990-2040

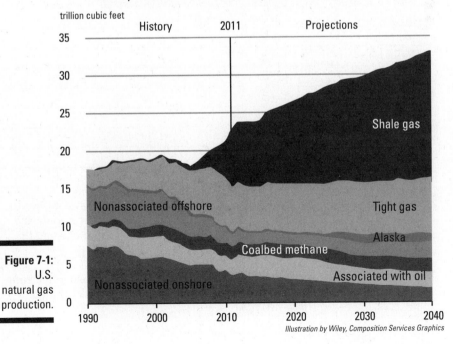

Figure 7-1: U.S. natural gas production.

Illustration by Wiley, Composition Services Graphics

Although every other source of U.S. dry natural gas output is set to drop between now and 2040, production from shale and tight gas is projected to increase. Interestingly, many natural gas investors I encounter aren't able to separate the two from each other.

It may seem subtle, but the differences exist:

- **Tight gas:** This source of natural gas is pretty much what it sounds like — deposits of natural gas trapped in a tight rock formation, typically sandstone or limestone, with little to no porosity.

- **Shale gas:** Shale gas is found in layers of sedimentary rock such as shale. Because the rock lacks the porosity to let the gas flow freely from the formation, companies combine horizontal drilling with hydraulic fracturing to make these plays commercially viable.

These two sources account for nearly all growth in natural gas production to 2040. Shale gas made up nearly one-third of total production in 2011. It's expected to make up half of U.S. total domestic gas output by 2035. In Table 7-7, I list some of my favorite shale gas plays that are worth checking out further.

Table 7-7	Top Shale Gas Formations
Shale Formation	**Undeveloped Technically Recoverable Shale Gas (Trillion Cubic Feet)**
Marcellus	141 Tcf
Haynesville	75 Tcf
Barnett	43 Tcf
Fayetteville	32 Tcf
Woodford	22 Tcf
Eagle Ford	21 Tcf
Antrim	20 Tcf

Despite the added benefits and hype surrounding U.S. shale plays, it pays to keep a level head. Two major hurdles for shale companies to overcome are steep decline rates during the early life of wells in these formations and the exorbitant price tag that comes with each one.

When you're doing your due diligence when researching a prospective company focusing on shale gas production, always check to see how the company is dealing with these two major hurdles.

Encana Corporation (NYSE: ECA), one of the leading natural gas producers in North America, shocked investors in February 2013 by announcing that it would actively drill the Haynesville shale in Louisiana. Encana was able to lower drilling costs by employing a new drilling method called *multi-well pad drilling*. I believe it's only a matter of months or years before multi-well pad drilling becomes the norm for shale plays throughout the United States.

This technique increases efficiency and lowers costs in many ways, as it allows multiple wells to be drilled from a single location, called a *pad*. Reducing the number of pads but increasing the number of wells:

✔ Reduces land and surface disturbance

✔ Gives landowners more control over where and how many pads are placed

✔ Eases the permitting process because most cities require a permit for each pad

✔ Increases efficiency by getting more gas out of a reservoir faster

✔ Reduces equipment costs by consolidating operations

Companies using this technology, including Devon Energy (NYSE: DVN), are fast gaining an edge over the competition.

Forecasting the future

You don't need your crystal ball to see the fundamental shift taking place in the North American natural gas industry. In a relatively short period of time, North America has increasingly relied on unconventional sources to meet demand.

To judge how significant a role unconventional natural gas sources are playing, look no further than the EIA's breakdown of the growth in withdrawals and production between 2007 and 2011, which I include in Table 7-8.

Table 7-8	Annual Natural Gas Gross Withdrawals by Source (Trillion Cubic Feet)				
Source	*2007*	*2008*	*2009*	*2010*	*2011*
Gas wells	15	15.1	14.4	13.3	12.3
Oil wells	5.7	5.6	5.7	5.8	5.9
Shale gas wells	2	2.9	4	5.8	8.5
Coal-bed wells	2	2	2	1.9	1.8

The fracking conundrum

Since the 1940s, the single most important technology to affect the U.S. oil and gas industry has been hydraulic fracturing. Even the politicians on Capitol Hill understand how important it is to U.S. domestic energy production. The process involves blasting the targeted formation with millions of gallons of water, proppant (typically sand), and chemicals to create fissures in the rock to allow the oil and gas resources to flow more freely.

Industry insiders have suggested that as many as nine out of every ten new wells will need to receive some form of fracture stimulation. For ways to invest in fracturing technology today, check out Chapter 9.

When deciding between North American gas stocks and playing the international field, always weigh a specific country's history with developing its unconventional resources. In Europe, and particularly in France, an anti-fracking sentiment only hinders production. In the case of France, the government imposed a moratorium on hydraulic fracturing back in 2011. Barring a miracle, it won't be lifted anytime soon.

Nearly the same fight happened when New York imposed a similar ban on hydraulic fracturing after a media blitz stoked fears over contaminated water. In March 2013, the New York Assembly passed a second, two-year ban on the practice.

Having a lot of gas doesn't necessarily mean that a country will successfully develop it soon. According to an EIA report in 2011, China holds the largest amount of recoverable shale gas in the world, yet the country may be decades away from producing shale gas because it lacks the advanced technology available in the United States.

Burn It if You Got It: Examining How Gas Is Used

One of the most attractive features of natural gas is that it's the cleanest burning fossil fuel. When you burn natural gas, it creates less carbon dioxide (CO_2) emissions than both oil and coal. Table 7-9 highlights the cleaner-burning benefits associated with natural gas.

Table 7-9	Fossil Fuel Emissions (Pounds per Billion Btu of Energy)		
Pollutant	*Natural Gas*	*Oil*	*Coal*
Carbon dioxide	117,000	164,000	208,000
Carbon monoxide	40	33	208
Nitrogen oxides	92	448	457
Sulfur dioxide	1	1,122	2,591
Particulates	7	84	2,744
Mercury	0	0.007	0.016

Natural gas is clearly cleaner than other fossil fuels, but that doesn't mean oil and coal will suddenly fizzle out of your life. The EIA projects all three fossil fuels will have a role in the world's future energy consumption. I show their projections in Figure 7-2, where fossil fuels compose more than three-quarters of total energy demand in 2040.

U.S. Primary Energy Consumption by Fuel, 1980-2040

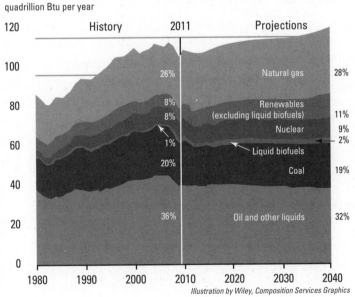

Figure 7-2: U.S. primary energy consumption.

Illustration by Wiley, Composition Services Graphics

Although the majority of natural gas is burned to produce electricity, it also has a wide variety of other uses, including water and air heating, fertilizer and other petrochemical production, and transportation. Table 7-10 shows the end uses of natural gas in the United States as of 2011. And the upcoming sections discuss its rising use in electricity generation and as a transportation fuel.

Table 7-10	Natural Gas End Uses	
Use	*Amount (Trillion Cubic Feet)*	*Percent of Total*
Electric power generation	7.57 Tcf	31%
Industrial	6.9 Tcf	28%
Residential	4.71 Tcf	19%
Commercial	3.15 Tcf	13%
Lease and plant fuel	1.32 Tcf	5%
Pipeline and distribution	0.68 Tcf	3%
Vehicle fuel	0.03 Tcf	<1%

Electricity generation

Another compelling piece of evidence that natural gas is slowly taking its place as the most important source of energy is through its growing role in power generation.

Between now and 2035, approximately 80 percent of total additions to electrical generation will come from gas-fired generators. The overwhelming number of electrical generators being produced run on natural gas. Notice in Figure 7-3 that consumers are quickly phasing coal out of the big picture.

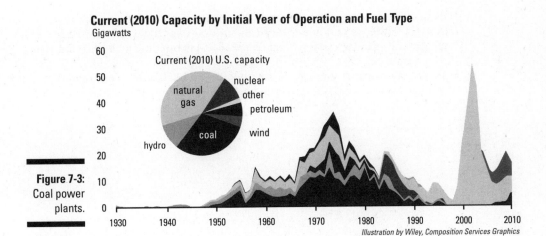

Current (2010) Capacity by Initial Year of Operation and Fuel Type
Gigawatts

Current (2010) U.S. capacity

natural gas · nuclear · other · petroleum · hydro · coal · wind

Figure 7-3:
Coal power
plants.

Illustration by Wiley, Composition Services Graphics

Transportation

At less than one percent of end uses (refer to Table 7-10), transportation is the natural gas wild card. Truthfully, I don't often come across investors who give it much thought. But they should, because the investment rewards will be huge as it plays out.

Without question, the single most dominated sector in U.S. energy is transportation. Americans love gas guzzlers, and even $4 a gallon at the pump hasn't scared the SUVs off the road. Petroleum accounted for a whopping 93 percent of the transportation sector in 2011.

But many fleets (think the postal service, trash trucks, and taxis) are beginning to operate their vehicles on natural gas. It's cheaper and much cleaner than gasoline or diesel. Natural gas prices between $2 and $4 translate into 25 to 50 cents per gallon of gasoline equivalent (GGE). Even with $1.75 refining cost, that still translates to $2 to $2.25 for a gallon. I've been paying more than that for more than five years.

Across the United States, companies are racing to create the infrastructure necessary to start relying more heavily on natural gas for many needs: rigs, gas-to-liquid plants, pumping stations, pipelines, engines, and more.

This boom is creating a ring of wealth from coast to coast. Clean Energy Fuels (NASDAQ: CLNE) is building "America's Natural Gas Highway" — 150 LNG fueling stations in two years. Shell (NYSE: RDS) is building an additional 100.

Keep in mind the fortunes that were built on the back of oil. The transition won't necessarily take place overnight, but it's an inevitable move to make as gasoline prices climb ever higher.

Chapter 8

Buying the Barrel, Trading the Therm

*O*il and natural gas present many different ways to invest beyond just the Exxons and BPs of the world. Trading energy futures is one such opportunity. Few retail investors take the time to trade futures contracts, and they rarely understand them enough to do so successfully.

Energy futures is a world of speculation and is often considered more volatile and risk-laden than your average stock trade. Many times, people lose their entire initial investment and are even required to pay more because they trade on margin. So you can see why few people dip into this realm of energy investing. Those who have the capital and risk appetite to do it, however, can enjoy returns that exceed the stock market.

In this chapter, I familiarize you with how standard futures contracts work, where to begin when looking for a futures broker, and what steps you can take to avoid potential pitfalls. I also dive into the supply-and-demand drivers behind oil and natural gas prices.

The Basics of Oil and Gas Futures

Futures trading isn't a new phenomenon. Agricultural futures contracts have been trading on the Chicago Board of Trade for nearly 150 years, and over time the futures market has grown to include a wide number of commodities. Investors trying to capitalize on short- and long-term price trends in the energy sector have turned to trading oil and natural gas futures.

So what exactly does futures trading entail? This is one of those cases where it sounds exactly like it is: *Futures* are simply an investment instrument whereby someone agrees to buy or sell a specific amount of units for a specific price with a set delivery date in the future. The only variable in place is the price of the contract.

Traders and hedgers

There are two main types of futures traders:

- **Speculators:** Although the mere phrase *oil speculator* conjures harsh images of greedy billionaires hiking oil prices and causing the average Joe considerably more pain at the pump, there's a little more to it. Speculators are driven to take a long or short position in a commodity to make a profit. They're taking a gamble, and they aren't as evil as you may first think. In fact, speculators play a critical role in the futures market. Remember, these investors don't manipulate the market as if it were a puppet on strings but instead identify a specific trend and then successfully profit from it. Speculators take on the risk that other people want no part of, and in the process, they make the market more fluid.

- **Hedgers:** An individual or group hoping to minimize their price risk will establish a short or long hedge in a commodity. Their goal is to effectively manage the risk of future price volatility. Oil and natural gas companies routinely lock in a price for future production. For example, Encana Corporation has approximately 1.5 billion cubic feet per day (Bcf/d) of its 2013 natural gas production hedged using fixed price contracts at an average of $4.39 per million cubic feet (Mcf) on the New York Mercantile Exchange (NYMEX), well above the average spot price projected for the year.

Hedgers employ two different techniques:

- **A short hedge** is a strategy producers can use to secure a price of the commodity for future delivery. The hedger essentially establishes a short futures position while still owning the commodity. If the price of the commodity falls, the value of the short position offsets some of the revenue lost upon delivery.

- **A long hedge** involves taking a long futures position to protect against future price increases.

In addition to these specific categories, the style you adopt for trading futures contracts also directly affects how you trade contract futures. Futures traders typically fall under one of two classes:

✔ **Day trading:** Day traders conduct several trades throughout the day. They're focused on getting in and getting out in a relatively short period of time. I've always found that your average individual investor simply doesn't have the time or discipline to properly day trade. Day trading is difficult for beginner investors to learn, and you can also quickly rack up commissions and fees that can reduce your overall return.

✔ **Position trading:** This style of trading is your typical buy-and-hold strategy. It's much easier than day trading to learn and doesn't require being in front of a computer all day.

Inside the futures contract

Think of trading futures as the transfer of risk from the producers (the ones doing the hedging) to the speculators. It's the most effective way to mitigate price volatility because the standardized contracts are only bought and sold on regulated exchanges.

The New York Mercantile Exchange, or NYMEX, is home to the energy complex, and it's where you find listed futures contracts for crude oil, gasoline, heating oil, and natural gas. In 2008, CME Group purchased the NYMEX in a cash and stock deal. By September 2009, the NYMEX was fully integrated into CME Group.

Along with Commodity Exchange, Inc. (COMEX), on which you can trade precious metals futures, CME Group is also composed of the Chicago Board of Trade and the Chicago Mercantile Exchange. It's officially your one-stop shop for trading futures and options. The Intercontinental Exchange, also called ICE, is a bit different from CME group insomuch that futures contracts are bought and sold over the counter, meaning that all the transactions are conducted over the Internet.

You can find more information regarding these two exchanges on their respective websites:

✔ www.cmegroup.com

✔ www.theice.com

In Table 8-1, I provide a list of contracts for oil, natural gas, and refined products that gives you a starting point for your futures investments.

Table 8-1	Structure of Oil and Gas Futures Contracts		
Exchange and Product	Symbol	Contract Size	Settlement Type
NYMEX Light Sweet Crude Oil (WTI)	CL	1,000 barrels	Physical
Henry Hub Natural Gas Futures	NG	10,000 million British thermal units	Physical
RBOB Gasoline Futures	RB	42,000 gallons	Physical
New York Harbor No. 2 Heating Oil	HO	42,000 gallons	Physical
E-mini Crude Oil Futures	QM	500 barrels	Financial
E-mini Natural Gas (Henry Hub)	QG	2,500 million British thermal units	Financial
ICE Brent Crude Futures	B	1,000 barrels	Financial
ICE WTI	T	1,000 barrels	Financial
ICE RBOB Gasoline 1st Line Future	RBS	1,000 barrels	Financial
ICE Henry Hub Natural Gas	HEN	2,500 million British thermal units	Financial

Futures Broker: Best Friend or Worst Enemy

Choosing the right broker is a long and arduous process, and rarely will you find one early on in your search. You have a set of expectations, and the wrong choice can be costly to your portfolio.

All brokerage firms must be registered with the U.S. Commodity Futures Trading Commission (CFTC) as a Futures Commission Merchant (FCM) or an Introducing Broker (IB), and they have to be a member of the National Futures Association (NFA).

A Futures Commission Merchant can be either an individual or an organization that solicits or accepts orders to buy or sell futures contracts or options on futures and that accepts money from its clients for these orders.

An Introducing Broker can solicit and/or accept orders to buy or sell futures contracts, but with one major difference compared to an FCM: Introducing Brokers don't accept any money or margin deposits. Basically, they solicit accounts for an FCM and bring in new clients.

If you're new to trading futures contracts, skip the discount brokerages where you're responsible for making all the decisions. You don't receive as much support and may even have to do your own research. I find that starting with a full-service brokerage is best. The higher fees can feel burdensome at times, but you won't regret the decision when you consider all that's involved in doing everything on your own.

Choosing an individual broker

After making your selection, you may also have to pick an individual broker. The first three questions you should ask are:

- **What services do you offer, and what are your commission fees?** Remember, higher fees aren't necessarily a deal-breaker (some brokers need to make a living from their commissions).

- **How knowledgeable are you when it comes to the markets?** Nothing is worse than paying someone who knows less than you do about the energy sector. Does the broker have personal contacts within the market that offer a good analysis into market news?

- **What is your track record?** Although you can't take past performance as a guarantee of future profits, knowing the broker's track record helps sort out potential disasters. Also along this line of questioning, find out about the broker's investing strategies and trading ideas to see whether they match your own.

Keep in mind that not everyone is looking out for your best interests. I've come across several hustlers in the past and found that having a few red flags can save you a lot of time, frustration, and most important, money. Here are some of the warning signs I look out for:

- Whenever something seems too good to be true, it probably is. Be wary of promises of guaranteed profits or can't-lose claims.

- The broker insists that you can make gains from news or data that is already public.

- The broker suggests that you borrow money or take out a loan to make an investment.

- The broker dismisses the value of the disclosure statement, which can help you evaluate the risks involved.

- The broker pressures you to make a lot of trades so he can pile up the commission fees.

Opening an account

After you nail down a broker, your next step is to open a futures trading account. Each broker may have a different process to do this, but the process nearly always involves you filling out an application, either online or through the mail. The broker will want to know a little bit about you before you start trading futures — things like how much income you earn and how much trading experience you have.

Understanding orders

After you open an account, it's important to know the difference among the various order types and when it's appropriate to use each.

Don't get overwhelmed if you're suddenly confronted with an order type you've never encountered before. Individual investors usually stick to limit orders with a trailing stop-loss to protect gains, but here I run through all the order types so you can cover your bases:

- A **market order** indicates that you want to execute a trade immediately at the best available price. This order is a double-edged sword because, though the order is filled right away, you may regret the entry price you get. The biggest red flag for when to avoid using market orders is with low-volume trades.

- **Limit orders** have always been my go-to trade order because it means I'm buying at my price. These orders take a little extra attention on your part because they may not be immediately filled.

- A **stop order** is just a market order that's executed when a specified price is reached. When you use a *stop limit*, you give two prices — a stop price and a limit price. When the price surpasses the stop price, the order then becomes a limit order. Investors use this order to protect gains or limit losses on a long or short position.

- You can also use **conditional orders** along with individual orders to strengthen your entry and exit strategy. *One cancels another*, or OCA orders, for example, allow you to set up a protective exit price (via a stop order) and a target exit price (using a limit order). If one gets filled, the other is canceled.

Watching the margin

A *margin* is the minimal amount of money needed to trade a futures contract through your broker. Basically, the margin is in place to guarantee that you have the money to settle potential losses from a trade.

Unlike stocks, where you can sometimes trade on large margins (with a 50 percent margin, you can trade $10,000 worth of stock with only $5,000), futures contracts have a much lower margin, usually between 5 and 15 percent of the contract, that is enforced by the exchange. Different types of margins include

- ✔ **Initial margin:** The amount of capital necessary to initiate a futures position. The exchange sets the initial margin.

- ✔ **Clearing margin:** A safeguard that ensures that both clearing brokers and corporations conduct the open contracts of their customers.

- ✔ **Customer margin:** This ensures that both buyers and sellers of futures contracts fulfill their contract obligations.

- ✔ **Maintenance margin:** The minimum margin per outstanding futures contract that you must have to keep your margin account.

The final type of margin, the *day-trade margin,* is set by your brokerage firm, rather than the exchange on which the commodity trades. Contact your individual broker for more details. As an example, TD Ameritrade's day-trading margin requirement is $25,000. So to conduct futures trades, you must have minimum capital of $25,000 in your account at the start of the day.

Doing some homework before you trade

If you decide to leap into oil and natural gas futures, have identified the associated risks, meet all the qualifications, located the perfect broker to suit your needs, and are ready to start trading after doing all your due diligence, then there are just a few more questions to ask yourself before you begin.

The following is an easy and helpful checklist the U.S. Commodity Futures Trading Commission put together to review before conducting any trades. I highly recommend taking this one last step.

- ✔ Have you clearly identified your financial goal, including the amount of risk and loss you can sustain?

- ✔ Have you determined how much assistance you want from a trading advisor in making trading decisions?

- ✔ Did you double-check the registration status and history of the advisor or pool you chose with the National Futures Association, or NFA? (You can view the NFA's website here: www.nfa.futures.org.)

- ✔ Did you receive and review the disclosure document before opening your account? The disclosure document gives you the statement of fees, potential for loss, your right to withdraw funds, and a break-even analysis.

- ✔ Do you recognize that you're trading a contract for only a small portion of the entire value, which opens the door for a flood of gains, as well as substantial losses? Make sure your account doesn't fall below the minimum margin or else you'll have to deposit more cash or be forced to exit your position.

Factors Affecting Futures

To successfully trade oil and gas futures, understanding the basic drivers behind oil and gas prices is imperative. In a perfect world, a market's fundamentals would revolve entirely around demand. That is, you have a buyer with a specific amount in mind, willing to pay a certain price.

Rarely, however, is that the case. You've seen firsthand that oil and natural gas prices aren't set in stone. One day you fill up your gas tank for $4 per gallon, and the next day you regret the decision because prices are suddenly 20 cents cheaper.

Three basic factors are at work here: a mishmash of supply, demand, and market opinion (from both a geopolitical and technical perspective) that come together to shape prices over the short and long term.

Over the barrel

My old economics professor would tell you that everything comes down to supply and demand and that price is simply a reflection of the relationship between the two. In a nutshell, higher supply leads to lower prices and vice versa.

By now, you should know that oil markets don't play by the usual rules. How high the price at the pump climbs doesn't matter because, chances are, your car (and more than 90 percent of the transportation sector) won't run on a different fuel at the drop of a hat. If your house runs on heating oil, that leaves you relatively few options during the winter months — buy more heating oil or pay to switch fuels. You can lower the thermostat, but you're still going to heat your home.

Supply

It takes different crudes to move the world, and not all crudes were created equal. You may only be familiar with the top grades of crude: West Texas Intermediate (WTI) and Brent Blend from the North Sea.

The quality of crude oil is based on its American Petroleum Institute (API) gravity, which measures the weight of the liquid compared to water. Typically, having an API gravity higher than 10 indicates that the crude is lighter than water. Anything less than 10 is heavier and sinks. WTI has an API gravity of approximately 39.6. Extra-heavy oil from Venezuela's Orinoco belt comes in with an API gravity of 8.

The sulfur content of crude oil is also measured. When it has a sulfur level of more than 0.5 percent, it's considered *sour.* Anything less than 0.42 percent sulfur is considered *sweet.* Overall, light, sweet grades of crude are more desirable for refineries because they're cheaper and easier to refine.

In total, there are more than 100 different grades and types of crude oil. Table 8-2 is a list of some of the more familiar ones found within the United States.

Table 8-2	Types of U.S. Crude Oil	
Type	*API Gravity*	*Sulfur Content*
Alaska North Slope	31.9	0.93%
Bakken Blend	42.0	0.17%
Bayou Choctaw Sour	32.2	1.43%
Bayou Choctaw Sweet	36.0	0.36%
Bonito Sour	35.5	0.99%
Heavy Louisiana Sweet	32.9	0.35%
LA Mississippi Sweet	40.7	0.34%
Light Louisiana Sweet	35.6	0.37%
Mars Blend	30.3	1.91%
Port Hudson	45.0	1.97%
South Louisiana Sweet	35.9	0.33%
West Texas Intermediate	39.6	0.24%
West Texas Sour	31.7	1.28%
Williams Sugarland Blend	40.9	0.20%

For a long time, West Texas Intermediate was considered the global benchmark for crude oil. Its top quality makes it ideal for refiners to produce gasoline. Location is an added bonus — WTI is produced close to the Midwest refiners, as well as those found along the Gulf Coast area.

Every Wednesday, the U.S. Energy Information Administration (EIA) releases its weekly petroleum report after 10:30 a.m. The report offers you analysis and market data for crude oil and petroleum products. Along with crude oil futures and contract prices, you can also check out changes to stock levels (supply), production and imports, and refinery inputs for crude oil, gasoline, distillates, and propane. The report is published on the EIA's website: www.eia.gov.

Another helpful report comes from the API: www.api.org/statistics. Called the *Monthly Summary Report,* it offers data about oil and gas production, imports, and costs. The report is published on the third Thursday of every month.

Members of the Organization of Petroleum Exporting Countries (OPEC) control about 80 percent of the world's oil reserves. The OPEC reference basket is also used as an important benchmark for oil prices. It's the average of prices for its members' crude blends, which you can find in Table 8-3. OPEC publishes its basket price daily at www.opec.org.

Table 8-3	OPEC Oil Basket
Crude Blend	*Country*
Saharan Blend	Algeria
Girassol	Angola
Oriente	Ecuador
Iran Heavy	Iran
Basra Light	Iraq
Kuwait Export	Kuwait
Es Sider	Libya
Bonny Light	Nigeria
Qatar Marine	Qatar
Arab Light	Saudi Arabia
Murban	United Arab Emirates
Merey	Venezuela

Within the last few years, Brent Blend crude oil successfully replaced WTI as the global benchmark for crude pricing. The two have historically traded relatively close, but the price gap began to widen in 2010, and Brent now trades at a considerable $15 per barrel premium to WTI. Figure 8-1 shows the price divergence since 2007.

Although it usually comes down to who you ask, it seems that more analysts and government reporting agencies are starting to accept that Brent crude is a better reflection of a global price benchmark. In fact, the EIA adopted Brent crude for its price forecasts for the first time in its *Annual Energy Outlook 2013.*

Brent Blend is made up of production from about 15 different fields in the North Sea. The API gravity of Brent crude is 38.3, with a 0.37 percent sulfur content. In other words, it's not exactly as light as WTI.

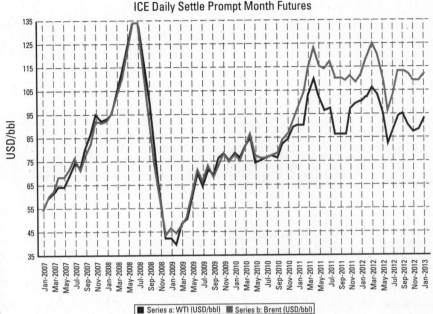

Illustration by Wiley, Composition Services Graphics

Figure 8-1:
WTI and
Brent
crude price
divergence.

Demand

Contrary to popular belief, future demand growth for crude oil won't come from the United States. America may account for one-quarter of global demand today, but that dynamic is going to change dramatically over the course of a few decades.

The largest growth will come from countries outside the Organisation for Economic Co-operation and Development (OECD), specifically from China, India, and countries in the Middle East. This demand growth is illustrated in Figure 8-2, which I've taken directly from BP's *Energy Outlook 2030* report.

There's a good reason why demand slows or declines in these developed countries. Oil and liquids demand is centered on the transportation sector. Countries with high consumption rates (like the United States) experience a decline in demand for various reasons, such as better vehicle efficiency or the substitution of other fuels in place of oil.

In non-OECD countries like China, for example, total liquids demand is projected to reach 17 million barrels per day (mb/d) in 2030, nearly double its current consumption rate.

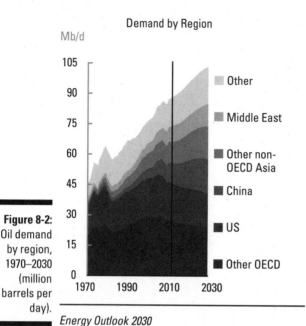

Demand by Region

Figure 8-2: Oil demand by region, 1970–2030 (million barrels per day).

Energy Outlook 2030

Illustration by Wiley, Composition Services Graphics

Geopolitical mess

If you want to find one wild card in the oil industry that can swing crude prices, geopolitical volatility is by far the most unnerving, unpredictable force out there. Some reports have suggested that conflict in the Middle East adds a $20 to $30 premium to crude oil prices.

To understand why, remember that disruptions in areas like the Strait of Hormuz can have a major impact on the petroleum trade. The strait is a natural choke point between the major oil-producing members of OPEC (Saudi Arabia, Iraq, and Kuwait) and open water. In 2009, about one-third of the world's oil-borne sea trade was shipped through the strait. Overall, that accounts for almost one-fifth of the world's oil supply.

When supply disruptions do occur, you must take other factors into consideration. When Libya's oil production was curtailed in 2011 during its six-month civil war, countries like Saudi Arabia decided to make up the shortfall. An immediate problem that surfaced was the quality of Saudi Arabia's spare capacity. Unlike Libya's light, sweet crude, the Saudis' spare capacity was of poorer quality. The European refineries that it went to, however, weren't set up to process the heavy, sour grade of crude.

My point here is that OPEC's inability to add high-quality oil indicates a potential problem during future supply disruptions. Failure to deal with these events can lead to short-term price shocks.

Gambling on gas

Years ago, you could almost always depend on the seasonality of the natural gas market. I had a colleague once that swore by one rule: Buy low in the summer and sell high in the winter. He used a seasonal approach to trading natural gas.

Usually, the weakest time of year for natural gas demand was during the hot summer months. Conversely, heating during the cold winter months historically marked the peak times for demand. Keeping a ten-day weather forecast can help you prepare for temperature changes that can cause a short-term price swing.

The rise of unconventional production from shale formations and natural gas locked in impermeable rock, called *tight gas,* across North America has caused a supply glut, while pushing prices to decade lows.

The EIA publishes a weekly report on natural gas storage levels. This report can keep you updated on weekly draws on working gas storage. Other important data points to digest are long-term trends you can determine by comparing current natural gas storage levels to the five-year average. This report is released on Thursday mornings on the EIA website: www.eia.gov.

Trading natural gas futures in today's market requires an extraordinary amount of attention. Stepping away from a trade for a few hours can have a devastating effect on your position. For this reason, most retail investors stick with other investment options, such as exchange-traded funds that track a commodity's price, which I cover in Chapter 10.

Chapter 9

Drilling Down, Extracting Profits: Investing in Oil and Gas Companies

. . . .

. . . .

After you're armed with the basics of the oil and gas sector, it's time to put that knowledge to use (check out Chapters 6, 7, and 8 if you're not yet armed with those basics). The next logical step is to find out what investments are out there. You don't have to be on the inside, have intimate knowledge of future drilling tests, or even sit on a board of directors to identify an appropriate investment.

Trading oil and gas stocks for the first time can be a daunting venture. Where do you begin? Who are the major and minor players in this piece of the energy puzzle? As you narrow down the field to find a suitable company, how do you evaluate each company along the way? Do you place more value on a company's production or the amount of oil the company has in the ground? Does the stock jumping out at you from your computer screen fit your portfolio? In other words, how can you properly evaluate these oil and gas players?

This chapter gives you an in-depth look into oil and gas investments, helps you sort out the major and minor players from the sector, and provides you with a little clarity on how to approach a new trade.

Evaluating Oil and Gas Stocks

Properly evaluating a future oil and gas investment is perhaps the most important skill you can learn as an investor. It can mean the difference between securing that nest egg for the future and losing your shirt because of a bad craps throw.

Instead of diving into the oil and natural gas industry and picking names out of a hat, properly assess a company's current position to determine its future value.

Size matters

Before diving right into the deep end, I humbly offer one piece of advice that will help you deal with the immensity of these industries: *Nobody has it all figured out.*

That encompasses more than individual investors like you and me. It goes for both amateur and seasoned investors, fund managers, analysts, day traders, and insiders as well.

When you're kick-starting the search for a new oil and gas investment, look first at size and sector. Here's how the size of companies is broken down:

- **Nano cap:** Companies with market caps below $50 million are considered nano caps and carry the greatest risk.

- **Micro cap:** These companies have a market cap between $50 and $300 million. These stocks typically cost pennies on the dollar and can be extremely volatile.

- **Small cap:** With a market cap between $300 million and $2 billion, still in the speculative range, small cap stocks also carry plenty of growth opportunity.

- **Mid cap:** These stocks have a market cap above $2 billion but below $10 billion, and like small caps, offer potential growth for investors.

- **Large cap:** Market caps for large caps are between $10 billion and $200 billion or higher. As you may guess, these caps are at the other end of the risk spectrum. These stocks come with lower risk and are much more stable than smaller companies.

Although it typically goes without saying that you expect a small growth stock to deliver higher returns than a stock with a larger capitalization, that isn't always the case. In fact, some of the strongest returns delivered to investors last year came from large cap stocks in the refining sector.

Figure 9-1 illustrates the performance of two such investments during 2012: Marathon Petroleum (NYSE: MPC) and Valero Energy (NYSE: VLO), which have market caps of $29 billion and $24 billion, respectively.

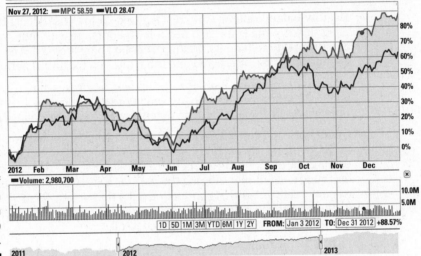

Figure 9-1: 2012 stock performance of Marathon Petroleum and Valero Energy.

Illustration by Wiley, Composition Services Graphics

Putting it all together

Every time I'm about to make a new trade, I ask myself several questions — a kind of inner checklist that assures I'm on the right track or warns me of a potential blockbuster mistake headed my way.

This simple checklist of things to consider can save you quite a bit of time down the road and help you do your due diligence:

- ✔ **Location:** Depending on the specific sector, where the company is operating is sometimes as important as (if not more important than) who's doing the drilling. It could mean the difference between drilling in the Bakken formation, which has fueled North Dakota's oil boom for the past five years, and drilling one dry hole after another.

- ✔ **Assets:** Whether a company is a fully integrated oil company with assets upstream, midstream, and downstream, or a small E&P company holding on to an exploration license, always take note of a company's assets. For upstream activity, this could mean leases or reserves (refer to Chapter 6 for a detailed overview of different reserves). Midstream assets include storage and transportation facilities, trucks, pipelines, or even tankers to ship millions of barrels of crude oil. Downstream assets can include oil refineries, pipelines, trucks, or other means of transporting refined oil and gas products.

✔ **Growth trends:** Has the company managed to increase revenue in the previous year? And does it expect to meet future revenue and earnings during the next four quarters?

✔ **Healthy balance sheet:** Is there a major debt load burdening the company? If not, what is its cash position? A company with little to no debt and the ability to fund its drilling program going forward is more than enough to get me interested and is a good sign for future performance.

✔ **Attractive valuation:** What is the company's price/earnings ratio? Is it under 10? Moreover, a company with a price/earnings to growth (PEG) ratio less than 1 could indicate that it's currently undervalued.

✔ **Quality of reserves:** This category doesn't usually get much attention from investors. Personally, I blame the growing number of reports coming out that report production and reserves in terms of barrels of oil equivalent without offering the details. To use the Bakken play as an example, remember that production from that area is 98 to 99 percent light sweet crude, as opposed to an area that has more natural gas, which is sold at a discount compared to oil.

✔ **Cash flow problems:** What are the company's present and future funding needs, and will raising money dilute the stock?

✔ **Yield:** Many oil and gas companies offer a secure annual dividend paid out to shareholders on a regular basis. When searching for a safe dividend, determine whether the company has increased, maintained, or even lowered its dividend during the past five years. Furthermore, find out the payout ratio, which is the amount of earnings paid out in the dividend. A company with a high payout ratio may not provide a secure dividend to shareholders.

National Oil Companies (NOCs): Puppet Masters Pulling Supply Strings

A national oil company is an oil company owned by a national government. Although a few of them are traded publicly, the majority stake is owned by the government, and you can bet they're the ones calling the shots.

A few years ago, I asked readers of *Energy & Capital* to write in and tell me their thoughts regarding the world's largest oil companies. The answers I received were staggering. I got e-mails ranging from concern that ExxonMobil was the culprit behind the high price for gasoline to accusations toward BP and its lack of environmental awareness. It wasn't the individual opinions that perplexed me but rather that people believed these were the largest oil and gas companies in the world.

Name recognition aside, the truth is that those two major oil companies don't even crack the top 5 list of who controls the world's oil and gas reserves. Table 9-1 shows you a list of the 20 largest oil and gas companies by reserves.

Table 9-1	Largest Oil and Gas Companies by Reserves	
Company	**Country**	**Total Reserves in Barrels of Oil Equivalent (boe)**
Petróleos de Venezuela	Venezuela	327 billion
National Iranian Oil Company	Iran	315 billion
Saudi Aramco	Saudi Arabia	260 billion
Qatar General Petroleum Corporation	Qatar	178 billion
Iraq National Oil Company	Iraq	135 billion
Abu Dhabi National Oil Company	United Arab Emirates	128 billion
Kuwait Petroleum Corporation	Kuwait	112 billion
Nigerian National Petroleum Corp.	Nigeria	69 billion
National Oil Company	Libya	55 billion
Sonatrach	Algeria	39 billion
Gazprom	Russia	29 billion
Rosneft	Russia	22.8 billion
PetroChina	China	22.4 billion
BP Corporation	United Kingdom	17.8 billion
Egyptian General Petroleum Corp.	Egypt	17.5 billion
ExxonMobil Corporation	United States	17.4 billion
Petróleos Mexicanos (Pemex)	Mexico	13.3 billion
Lukoil	Russia	13 billion
Royal Dutch Shell	Netherlands	12.5 billion
Petróleo Brasileiro	Brazil	12.5 billion

In total, the companies in Table 9-1 own approximately 88 percent of the world's oil reserves and more than 40 percent of daily production. The figures get slightly better for the natural gas industry, where the top national oil companies (NOCs) account for 54 percent of reserves and 37 percent of daily production. Furthermore, about 60 percent of the oil traded around the world comes from the national oil companies of the Organization of the Petroleum Exporting Countries (OPEC).

Just because a country is rich in reserves doesn't necessarily mean it will close the door to outsiders. Contracts can still be made with foreign oil companies to develop assets. You're most likely to come across one of these four types of contracts:

- ✔ **Concession agreements** can be struck with a government to give a company the right to operate in a specific area. They typically spell out the rules under which the foreign company will develop the country's oil and/or gas resource in question during a specific time frame.

- ✔ **Production sharing agreements** (commonly referred to as PSAs) are contracts that offer each party a certain percentage of production. These contracts usually last between 25 and 40 years, or sometimes even longer. The oil company will invest its capital in return for control of the field and a portion of its revenue.

- ✔ **Joint ventures**, or JVs, are made between two parties to combine resources for a specific project. They can sometimes be beneficial for a country without the specific technology to develop a play. An example is the deal between Rosneft and ExxonMobil to develop tight oil projects in western Siberia. Russia's goal is to utilize drilling and completion technology that ExxonMobil uses through its North American shale activity.

- ✔ **Technical service agreements** (TSAs) outline specific services done by a company for a national oil company. The foreign company typically doesn't receive any revenue from production but instead is given a fixed fee per barrel.

A fifth type of contract used by governments is called a *unit agreement*. It occurs when the government offers a contract among several companies that hold contiguous leases over a specific reservoir. It typically assigns one company to be the operator over all activities and usually commits the parties to aggressive exploration and development of the area.

Always use extreme caution when dealing with investments in foreign governments. Many of these oil- and gas-rich countries don't take kindly to outside oil companies making a profit from their resources, and things can turn ugly in the blink of an eye. In 2007, then-President Hugo Chavez nationalized Venezuela's oil and natural gas assets. This included every ship, rig, and piece of equipment still in the country after May 1. In addition to forcing all foreign oil companies out of the country, Chavez offered monetary compensation for the seized assets at a much lower price than they were worth.

This change led to long, drawn-out court battles between Venezuela and companies not willing to take the offers. ExxonMobil, for example, was seeking more than $10 billion from the Venezuelan government and was awarded a mere $900 million in a court decision in early 2013. Venezuela agreed to pay just $255 million of the amount.

Discussing OPEC: Inside an oil cartel

It's impossible to have a discussion about national oil companies without shining a light on OPEC. By the end of 2011, more than 80 percent of the world's proven oil reserves rested in the hands of the 12-member oil cartel.

OPEC was created in the 1960s by five founding members: Iran, Iraq, Kuwait, Saudi Arabia, and Venezuela. At the time, international oil companies ruled the world's oil supply.

Take a quick glance back at Table 9-1 and you may notice that the ten largest NOCs are in OPEC. Only one of them, however, holds all the cards: Saudi Arabia. Figure 9-2 breaks down OPEC reserves by individual members.

OPEC Share of World Crude Oil Reserves 2011

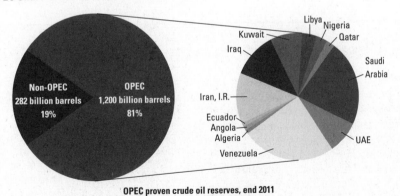

Figure 9-2: OPEC reserves by country.

OPEC proven crude oil reserves, end 2011
(billion barrels, OPEC Share)

Venezuela	297.6	24.8%	Iraq	141.4	11.8%	Libya	48.0	4.9%	Algeria	12.2	1.0%
Saudi Arabia	265.4	22.1%	Kuwait	101.5	8.5%	Nigeria	37.2	3.1%	Angola	10.5	0.9%
Iran, I.R.	154.6	12.9%	United Arab Emirates	97.8	8.2%	Qatar	25.4	2.1%	Ecuador	8.2	0.7%

Illustration by Wiley, Composition Services Graphics

Saudi Arabia's Ghawar oil field is the largest of its kind. Considered a super-giant oil field, Ghawar pumps out a monstrous 5 million barrels per day and has been in production for more than 60 years.

As shown in Chapter 6, four of the top ten oil-producing countries in the world are OPEC members — Saudi Arabia with 10.5 MMbbls/d, Iran with 4.2 MMbbls/d, United Arab Emirates with 2.8 MMbbls/d, and Nigeria with 2.4 MMbbls/d. Because OPEC members raise and lower their production targets and quotas based on the current supply and demand, the amount of spare capacity has become a major issue. *Spare capacity* refers to the ability of a country to produce more oil. Basically, will OPEC be able to increase production in the event of a supply constraint?

This is a more serious problem for OPEC than you may first think because the only member with significant spare capacity is Saudi Arabia. In the event of a supply constraint, the entire world is relying solely on Saudi Arabia to turn on the taps and pick up the slack. Failure to do so would result in a spike in oil prices.

Although you can't directly trade state-owned oil companies in OPEC like Saudi Aramco, the 12-member cartel can provide vital information and greatly influence global oil markets. Periodic meetings can swing oil prices in both directions depending on any changes in production.

Don't confuse government-owned national oil companies with *multi-national corporations,* which are simply companies that operate in more than one country.

Seven stepsisters who lost the glass slipper

Before OPEC rose to prominence during the 1970s and became the most dominant force in the global oil industry, just seven international oil companies controlled approximately 85 percent of global petroleum reserves. Later dubbed the *Seven Sisters* by Eni's CEO Enrico Mattei, this group formed after the breakup of Standard Oil. It consisted of Standard Oil of New Jersey (Esso), Royal Dutch Shell (Anglo-Dutch), Anglo Persian (APOC), Standard Oil of New York (Socony), Standard Oil of California (Socal), Gulf Oil, and Texaco. Four of those members survive today after a series of consolidations. Of course, you know them as BP, Chevron, Royal Dutch Shell, and ExxonMobil.

I call them *stepsisters* because they weren't meant to be together. The Seven Sisters were formed in an effort to bring Iranian oil back online after Iran nationalized its oil industry in 1951. The Seven Sisters remained dominant until the formation of OPEC. This is important and interesting at the same time because it reminds you that no one entity permanently owns anything.

Buying your way into state-owned profits

The following is a list of oil and gas companies that are partially government-owned but that you can still trade on certain stock exchanges:

- **Petróleo Brasileiro:** Petrobras, in which the Brazilian government owns a 64 percent stake, has approximately 11.4 billion barrels of oil equivalent in reserves and produces slightly more than 2.5 million barrels of oil equivalent per day. In 2008, Petrobras discovered what's considered the world's third-largest oil field. Located off the coast of Rio de Janeiro, the Tupi field holds an estimated 8 billion barrels of oil equivalent. Petrobras trades on the New York Stock Exchange under the symbol PBR.

- **China National Offshore Oil Corporation:** CNOOC (NYSE: CEO) is the third-largest national oil company in China and the largest offshore drilling company in China. Among the perks of being majority-owned by the Chinese government, CNOOC receives a 51 percent stake in every offshore oil and gas project in which a foreign company is involved.

- **PetroChina Ltd.:** PetroChina (NYSE: PTR) is the traded segment of state-owned China National Petroleum Corporation. This integrated oil and gas company is involved with oil and gas exploration, production, refining, marketing, and transportation of oil, natural gas, refined products, and petrochemicals.

- **Statoil ASA:** With 67 percent of all shares, the government of Norway is the largest owner of Statoil (NYSE: STO). The company is the largest offshore operator in the world.

- **Gazprom:** If you like natural gas, Gazprom (NYSE: OGZPY) is worth a closer look. It's the largest natural gas company out there, with 29.8 trillion cubic meters of natural gas reserves. The Russian government owns a hair more than 50 percent of the company, just enough to keep control.

National oil companies can also cause dramatic moves in smaller exploration and production stocks from buyout announcements and joint venture agreements. In October of 2011, Statoil spent $4.4 billion acquiring Brigham Exploration for a 20 percent premium.

Non-NOC Oil and Gas Companies: Fighting over Scraps

After thumbing through the NOCs, you may feel as if nothing is left in the pot. Fortunately, that isn't the case. More and more, NOCs are migrating out of their domestic comfort zones into up-and-coming oil and gas hot spots.

Thanks to the development of unconventional oil and gas resources in North America, state-backed companies are making an appearance. Often they have an ulterior motive pushing them into the U.S. and Canadian oil patch. China, for example, has the largest amount of shale gas resources in the world. The Energy Information Administration reported in 2011 that China holds 1.3 *quadrillion* cubic feet of recoverable shale gas. All of it, unfortunately, is locked underground until Chinese companies develop the technology to extract it. And they're buying U.S. companies to get that expertise.

I'm not the only one with a bullish outlook on non-OPEC supply. Actually, OPEC shares the same sentiment. In OPEC's *World Oil Outlook 2012*, non-OPEC liquids supply is projected to outpace OPEC's own supply growth. Table 9-2 shows you the long-term growth in OECD supply to 2035.

Table 9-2	World Liquids Supply (mb/d)					
Source	*2010*	*2015*	*2020*	*2025*	*2030*	*2035*
OECD	20.0	21.8	22.6	23.3	24.1	24.9
Developing countries, excluding OPEC	16.9	17.8	19.2	19.3	19.1	19.3
Eurasia	13.4	13.9	14.3	14.7	15.1	15.5
Processing gains	2.1	2.4	2.6	2.7	2.9	3.0
Total non-OPEC supply	52.4	55.7	58.7	60.0	61.2	62.7
OPEC natural gas liquids (NGLs)	4.9	6.2	7.2	8.0	8.9	9.4
OPEC crude	29.3	29.6	30.9	32.5	33.8	34.9
Total OPEC supply	34.2	35.8	38.1	40.5	42.7	44.3

From a trading perspective, you may strongly consider looking at a different playing field of oil and gas companies — the ones that don't answer to the government.

Integrated oil companies

When an oil and gas company is involved in the entire process from exploration to distribution, it's considered an *integrated oil company*. You're likely to recognize these companies right from the get-go, and for good reason.

Why? Well, it's because they're the most visible face of the oil industry. At least, they are to the end user. You drive by their drilling rigs, pump your gas at their gas stations, and consistently hear them tout their environmental awareness and alternative energy ambitions on television. They operate upstream (exploration and production), downstream (refining and distribution), and everywhere in between.

You may know some of these key players by another name: Big Oil. A select few of them go by another name: *supermajors*. The supermajors represent the best in show, the biggest kids on the block, or the most potent polluters, depending on how you view the industry. Table 9-3 lists the six supermajors and shows you what makes them so big.

Table 9-3		How the Supermajors Stack Up		
Company	*Symbol*	*Market Capitalization*	*Revenue, in Millions (FY 2012)*	*Daily Production (boe)*
ExxonMobil	XOM	$400 billion	$482,295	5.3 million
BP	BP	$128 billion	$388,285	4.1 million
Royal Dutch Shell plc	RDS	$200 billion	$467,153	3.9 million
Chevron	CVX	$230 billion	$241,909	3.5 million
Total S.A.	TOT	$115 billion	$224,252	2.7 million

ConocoPhillips (NYSE: COP) would've made the list until 2012, when it split into two companies. The spinoff, Phillips 66, comprises the downstream refining segment, while ConocoPhillips maintains the production operations. Because upstream and downstream operations were separated, it's no longer technically an integrated oil company.

Integrated oil companies often fall into a specific portfolio group called *widow-and-orphan* stocks. Don't run for cover — the name sounds a lot worse than it is. Widow-and-orphan stocks typically provide a low-risk investment and have a stable, long-term dividend attached to them. For example, each one of the supermajors offers an annual yield between 2 and 5 percent.

If you're looking for fast-paced growth and lured by the excitement of huge returns over a relatively short period of time, this class of investments may not be your cup of tea. But they can also provide you with a little safety if you're heavily invested in smaller, more volatile stocks.

A balanced portfolio spread across several sectors should always include a group of stable, healthy-yielding income investments. These stocks are the ones you can buy and forget about. These are the energy income stocks I prefer, because you have to revisit them only a few times each year.

Playing the independent field

Okay, so maybe you want more bang for your buck. Who doesn't? Then perhaps you'll make time to mull over the independents. It's the group of stocks I'm asked about the most, and nearly all my major trading successes were found here.

So what are they? Put simply, independent oil and gas stocks companies have no downstream activity. The downstream sector of the petroleum industry involves the refining and processing operations, along with marketing and, finally, distribution. I tend to include midstream operations, too, which involve the transportation and storage of oil and gas production.

Essentially, that leaves my personal favorites: the exploration and production companies, ranging from the smallest wildcatters to some of the largest oil and gas producers in the United States and Canada.

I once met a reader of mine who wanted to know why anyone would like an oil company that wasn't considered part of Big Oil. Bigger was better, or at least it was in his eyes. When I look at the U.S. oil and gas boom that's taken place since 2008, Big Oil seems like it's always late to the party. ExxonMobil's biggest deal in over a decade was to acquire XTO Energy in 2009 for $35 billion. At the time, XTO Energy was an independent company heavily invested in shale gas plays across the country.

A useful place to whittle the field and find new opportunities is the Industry Center of Yahoo! Finance. You can find a complete index of independent oil and gas companies at `http://biz.yahoo.com/ic/121.html`. Your broker is also an excellent place to find and filter potential investments. Use Table 9-4 as a stepping block to begin your search of independents.

Table 9-4	Top Independent E&P Companies	
Company Name	*Exchange: Ticker*	*Market Capitalization*
Anadarko	NYSE: APC	$41.5 billion
Canadian Natural Resources	NYSE: CNQ	$34.2 billion
Apache	NYSE: APA	$29.6 billion
Noble	NYSE: NBL	$20.1 billion
Continental Resources	NYSE: CLR	$16.7 billion
Encana Corp.	NYSE: ECA	$14.2 billion
Chesapeake Energy	NYSE: CHK	$13.7 billion
Cabot Oil & Gas Corp.	NYSE: COG	$13.5 billion
Tullow Oil	NYSE: TLW.L	$11.3 billion
Denbury Resources	NYSE: DNR	$6.8 billion

Small independent companies are among the most susceptible to the wild price swings of oil and natural gas. Always keep a stop-loss in place to prepare for the worst.

Chapter 10

Investing in Oil and
Indexes and Fund

....

In This Chapter

▶ Determining whether oil and gas funds are right for you

▶ Getting started with oil and gas funds

▶ Playing oil and gas price swings with funds

....

Speculation can be a portfolio killer. Don't get me wrong — I believe there's a time and place for it, especially when it comes to up-and-coming growth stocks that litter the oil and gas investment landscape. Sometimes, the results pay off handsomely, and watching your stock's share price soar to new heights is a great feeling.

That potential treasure trove, however, always comes with a great degree of risk. A string of bad news can have devastating consequences that shake your nerves and make you hesitant in future speculative stock trades. And then, of course, you have the financial sting of a hefty loss.

So how do you offset the added risk factor? A smart investor always expects the best performance from speculative plays but prepares for the worst at the same time.

Get ready to discover how to add a bit of diversity to your portfolio. Throughout this chapter, I cover the ins and outs of various oil and gas funds, including how to properly trade these investment vehicles, where to begin your search, what to look for when adding one to your portfolio, and how to use commodity funds to both invest in stronger long-term outlooks and/or effectively hedge your position to offset unforeseen setbacks.

A Fund for Any Occasion

Investment funds offer you an opportunity for diversification. A *fund* is essentially an amount of money collected from a large group of investors and managed by a fund manager. Sounds pretty simple, right? Essentially, an investment fund lets you toss your hat into the ring with thousands of other investors.

Because these investments are a valuable way to put some diversity into your portfolio, I start with some basics. In the grand scheme of things, there are two main types of investment funds (I give you details about both of these types throughout this chapter):

- **Mutual funds:** According to the U.S. Securities and Exchange Commission, a *mutual fund* is defined as a company that brings together money from many people and invests it in stocks, bonds, or other assets. These holdings make up the fund's portfolio.

- **Exchange-traded funds:** Commonly referred to as ETFs, *exchange-traded funds* are investment companies legally classified as open-end companies or unit investment trusts. The goal of most ETFs is to track the performance of a specific market index, much like an index fund.

Mutual feelings, mutual profits

Investment management companies want to make money, and so do you. To achieve this goal, they create funds with certain objectives. Like-minded investors who have the same goal as the fund pool their money together, giving control to a fund manager who's responsible for building a collective portfolio filled with investments that fall within the specific criteria, and voilà.

Three basic types of mutual funds are available to investors, and each comes with its own strategy to suit your needs:

- Fixed-income funds (bonds)
- Money market funds
- Equity funds (stocks)

For the purpose of focusing your investments within the oil and natural gas industries, I narrow down the playing field to stock funds, often referred to as equity funds.

Stock funds can be broken down into several categories:

- **Growth funds** focus on returning large capital gains for investors rather than steady dividends.

- **Income funds** are exactly what they sound like. These funds concentrate on stocks that offer regular dividends.

- **Index funds** try to mirror the return of a specific market index by investing in stocks found within that index. For example, a fund attempting to replicate the performance of the Dow Jones Industrial Average builds a portfolio consisting of either all or at least a sample of stocks on the Dow.

✔ **Sector funds** target a particular industry or sector of stocks.

Energy funds broaden their investments beyond simple exploration and production stocks. They also include service stocks or those that offer transportation and equipment.

Although sector funds offer you the chance to diversify your portfolio, these funds also have a greater systemic risk compared to a fund that uses a broader investment strategy. For example, a fund's portfolio built entirely around oil assets can rise and fall alongside crude oil prices because of higher or lower profits generated from companies within that sector.

Today, energy mutual funds represent a huge amount of investment capital. Table 10-1 shows you five of the top-ranked energy mutual funds available for long-term investors according to combined ratings from Morningstar, Lipper, Zacks, TheStreet.com, and Standard & Poor's.

Table 10-1	Top-Ranked Energy Mutual Funds		
Name	*Ticker Symbol*	*Net Assets*	*Top Five Holdings*
Icon Energy Fund	ICENX	$622 million	ExxonMobil Corporation, Chevron, Valero Energy Corp., Schlumberger, Tesoro Corporation
Integrity Williston Basin/ Mid–North America Stock Fund	ICPAX	$548 million	National Oilwell Varco, Kodiak Oil & Gas Corp., Halliburton, Oasis Petroleum, Whiting Petroleum
Fidelity Select Energy Portfolio	FSENX	$2.1 billion	ExxonMobil Corporation, Chevron, Occidental Petroleum, National Oilwell Varco, Hess Corp.
Fidelity Select Natural Resources Portfolio	FNARX	$1.1 billion	Occidental Petroleum, Hess Corp., Halliburton, Suncor Energy, National Oilwell Varco
Vanguard Energy Fund	VGENX	$11.8 billion	ExxonMobil Corporation, Chevron, Royal Dutch Shell, BP PLC, Occidental Petroleum

Table 10-1 may bring to mind the old cliché "Birds of a feather flock together." As you sort through the multitude of investment funds out there, you'll notice that many of them often hold the same assets. Beginner investors can use this fact to their advantage when looking for new opportunities. I once had a reader of mine explain that he liked to pick his individual stock trades from a long list of top mutual fund holdings.

Bigger doesn't always mean better. If a fund is too big and/or limited to investing in energy entities with large market caps, the return may not be as you hoped.

And because funds come in all different shapes and sizes, each with its own specific investment goals and objectives, you must consider several factors when choosing an energy mutual fund. Identifying the right fund for you can be just as difficult as evaluating individual oil and gas stocks. So what do you look for, and more important, how do you find your answers? Consider the following:

- **Performance:** Contrary to popular belief, a mutual fund's performance in the past isn't as critical as you may think. Smaller funds new to the market may appear extremely attractive because they've invested in just a few stocks. As funds increase in size, their portfolio size also grows, making it less likely that the fund will repeat its short-term success. A mutual fund's performance, however, gives you some insight into its volatility during a specific time frame — more volatility leads to higher risk.

- **Risk:** Every investment you ever make in the market comes with a certain degree of risk. If that weren't the case, everybody would invest, and everybody would cash in on the market. Unfortunately, that simply isn't the case. To mitigate risk, read a fund's prospectus from top to bottom to learn its investment strategy, and determine whether it's best suited to meet your level of risk.

- **Fees:** Along with risk, always factor cost into your decision to buy a fund. You can expect to see typical things like shareholder transaction fees charged to you every time you buy and sell a fund's shares. Among these fees are sales charges on purchases, purchase fees, deferred sales charges, redemption fees, exchange fees, and account fees.

- **Expenses:** Another important piece of due diligence is determining the operating expenses levied against you on a yearly basis. These expenses can include management fees paid right out of a fund's assets and distribution fees (or *12b-1 fees*) that cover the expenses associated with marketing and selling the fund's shares. The total annual fund operating expenses can be found on the fee table, and prudent investors use the expense ratio as a comparison among several potential funds.

Not everyone was born with a gift in mathematics, myself included. If the thought of calculating these numbers has you rethinking this whole venture into mutual funds, I have some good news for you. You can find mutual fund cost calculators online, and they'll help you analyze a mutual fund's expenses. I prefer to use one from the Financial Industry Regulatory Authority (or FINRA, for short), which you can find at `http://apps.finra.org/fundanalyzer/1/fa.aspx`.

At your disposal are several sources of information that you can use to evaluate a prospective new fund. The following documents should be available either on the fund's website, by contacting a broker that sells the fund, or by directly contacting the fund itself:

- ✔ **Profile:** A fund's profile gives you a brief description of the fund, sums up the prospectus, and is a good starting point when narrowing down your list of potential funds.

- ✔ **Prospectus:** Even though a fund is required by law to provide you with a prospectus, it's always prudent to get your hands on a copy before you decide on the investment. The prospectus contains a wealth of information, including the fund's primary strategies, objectives, and core risks. It tells you who's in charge of the fund and how to buy and redeem shares.

- ✔ **Statement of Additional Information:** Known as *Part B* of the registration, this document goes deeper into a fund's operations than the prospectus. It gives you details on the fund's history; includes fund policies on borrowing and concentration; identifies its officers, directors, and other information regarding tax matters; and offers performance and average total return information. To get this statement, consult the back cover of the prospectus.

- ✔ **Shareholder Reports:** These regular reports give you up-to-date financial information and current holdings.

The dawn of ETFs

When exchange-traded funds (ETFs) stepped onto the investment scene in the 1990s, nobody was happier than individual investors. This type of investment offers you the opportunity to diversify your portfolios like traditional mutual funds without some of the hassles.

An *exchange-traded fund* is an investment fund that can be traded on an exchange. Like mutual funds, ETFs hold assets like stocks, bonds, or commodities, but with much more flexibility. There's quite a difference between trading the two — look at ETFs like a mutual fund that you can trade like a stock. With mutual funds, the price isn't set until the end of the day, which is when the *net asset value* (NAV) is calculated.

To calculate NAV, first take the total value of the fund's assets minus the liabilities and then divide that number by the total outstanding shares. The formula looks like this:

NAV = (assets − liabilities)/shares outstanding

An ETF, on the other hand, can trade higher or lower than its net asset value per share depending on market demand throughout the trading day.

The differences don't end there. ETFs have the following key advantages over mutual funds:

- **Tax efficiency:** Capital gains taxes are incurred only when the ETF is sold. With mutual funds, capital gains taxes are charged as shares are traded within the fund throughout its existence.

- **Cost and expenses:** Mutual funds are actively managed by a fund manager, so it's easy to watch their fees and related expenses stack up. Those expenses are limited with ETFs because only one transaction is involved, and lower expense ratios add to your savings.

- **Flexibility and transparency:** The ability to trade an ETF like a stock gives you more control over when to buy and sell. Also, ETFs must report their holdings at market close, which means you know exactly what they own. Sometimes it can take up to two months before a fund reveals that information.

- **Shorting:** It's entirely possible for investors with bearish outlooks to short ETFs. Shorting may not sit well with a long-term investing strategy, but it can offer you the chance to hedge through a short position. You can find a discussion of conventional shorting in Chapter 4.

Picking the proper ETF

When pitting one potential ETF against another, it's important to compare a few key metrics to help you sort them out. Follow these simple guidelines when deciding whether a certain ETF is right for you:

- **Strategy, strategy, strategy:** Because you know exactly what cards each ETF is holding, take the time to see how the ETF is positioned. In other words, do the ETF's holdings offer you the diversification you're looking for? Is one of the ETFs more top-heavy than the other? If you wanted more risk, you could have just gone after an individual stock.

- **Expense ratios:** Effectively keeping expenses under control means all the difference with investment funds. Despite their advantage over mutual funds in this category, remember that there's a wide range of expense ratios among ETFs. However, you also need to look beyond the management fees. Some ETFs are commission-free, which can pay off over time.

✔ **Discounts:** Look for an ETF that's trading at a discount to its net asset value. With enough due diligence, you'll quickly discover that deals can be found under any market conditions if you just look hard enough.

✔ **Dividends:** A strong yield by a prospective investment fund can be the deciding factor when evaluating its volatility. What's more, dividends can differ greatly as you dig around potential ETFs.

✔ **Liquidity:** You can tell that ETFs are more liquid than traditional mutual funds, but liquidity is an important factor because you can conduct these trades during market hours. The ability to quickly buy or sell a position is paramount when determining a proper entry and exit price (especially if it means buying at a strong discount!).

✔ **Volatility:** No matter where you look in the market, some investments simply carry more volatility than others. Having a lower volatility generally attracts more investors. I typically use the 200-day volatility metric to gauge how a specific ETF has performed in the past.

Never forget to thoroughly review an ETF's prospectus before the purchase. The prospectus tells you everything you need to know about the ETF. Some ETFs send you a summary ETF instead of the entire document. The whole prospectus is nearly always available on the Internet, although you're perfectly within your rights to request a paper copy from the company at no charge.

You can find shortcuts for sorting through the investment funds available all over the Internet. I've had a lot of success by using the following websites:

✔ http://etf.stock-encyclopedia.com/category/

✔ http://etfdb.com/

Differentiating between ETFs and ETNs

Know your note! Exchange-traded notes, commonly referred to as ETNs, are like an ETF's twin — they appear to be identical, can easily confuse newcomers, and rarely do I come across a small investor who can tell me the difference between the two. An ETN is a note that's a liability of the issuing company. Basically, it's a debt note that's linked to the performance of a specific market benchmark or strategy. While an ETF is a basket of assets that track an index and parts of a sector, an ETN focuses on a particular niche of a sector. Think of it like a bond, where it guarantees investors the return on the index with a specific maturity date — and there are no tracking errors when it comes to ETNs.

Mutual funds for the oil and gas sector

Although thousands of mutual funds are floating out there, the following are among the top-ranked energy equity funds available, again using a combination of ratings from multiple agencies.

Those ratings take into account risk-adjusted historical returns, the fundamentals of the underlying holdings of a fund, tax efficiency, and other factors. The information I include about each fund gives you a sense of its longevity, costs, and size. Optimally, you're looking for a fund that has the longest history of success, with the lowest costs and largest assets. Everything in life is a trade-off, though, so you want to look for funds that have the best blend of these features.

Name: Integrity Williston Basin/Mid–North America Stock Fund Class A
Ticker: ICPAX
Fund start date: April 5, 1999
Category: Equity Energy
Total assets: $548 million
Expense ratio: 1.44%
Dividend/annual yield: N/A
Top five holdings: National Oilwell Varco, Kodiak Oil & Gas, Halliburton, Oasis Petroleum, Whiting Petroleum

Description: According to the Integrity Funds prospectus, this investment seeks long-term capital appreciation. The fund normally invests at least 80 percent of its net assets in stock of domestic and foreign issuers that are participating or benefiting from the development of the resources in the Williston Basin and/or Mid–North America area. It may not invest in companies that have recently commenced operations and don't have significant revenues.

Name: Putnam Global Energy Fund
Ticker: PGEAX
Fund start date: December 18, 2008
Category: Equity Energy
Total assets: $19 million
Expense ratio: 1.69%
Dividend/annual yield: 0.71%
Top five holdings: ExxonMobil Corporation, Royal Dutch Shell, Eni SpA, Suncor Energy, Chevron Corp.

Description: According to the Putnam Investments prospectus, the investment seeks capital appreciation. It invests mainly in common stocks (growth stocks, value stocks, or both) of large and mid-sized companies worldwide that the advisor believes have favorable investment potential. Potential investments include companies engaged in the exploration, production, development, and refinement of conventional and alternative sources of energy. It may also use derivatives — such as futures, options, certain foreign currency transactions, warrants, and swap contracts — for both hedging and non-hedging purposes, and may engage in short sales of securities.

Name: Fidelity Advisor Energy Fund
Ticker: FANAX
Fund start date: September 3, 1996
Category: Equity Energy
Total assets: $658 million
Expense ratio: 1.17%
Dividend/annual yield: 0.41%
Top five holdings: ExxonMobil Corporation, Chevron Corp., Occidental Petroleum, National Oilwell Varco, Hell Corp.

Description: According to Fidelity's fund overview, the investment seeks capital appreciation. The fund invests primarily in common stocks. It normally invests at least 80 percent of assets in securities of companies principally engaged in the energy field, including the conventional areas of oil, gas, electricity and coal; and newer sources of energy, such as nuclear, geothermal, oil shale, and solar power. The fund invests in domestic and foreign issuers. It uses fundamental analyses of factors such as each issuer's financial condition and industry position, as well as market and economic conditions, to select investments.

Name: BlackRock Energy & Resources Portfolio
Ticker: SSGRX
Fund start date: March 2, 1992
Category: Equity Energy
Total assets: $776 million
Expense ratio: 1.34%
Dividend/annual yield: 0.12%
Top five holdings: Plains Exploration & Production Company, EQT Corp., Consol Energy Inc., Range Resources, Energy XXI (Bermuda) Ltd.

Description: According to the BlackRock Funds prospectus, the investment seeks long-term growth of capital. The fund invests at least 80 percent of its total assets in equity securities of global energy and natural resources companies and companies associated in businesses, as well as utilities (such as gas, water, cable, electrical, and telecommunications utilities). It intends to emphasize small companies but may from time to time emphasize companies of other sizes. The fund may invest without limit in companies located anywhere in the world and will generally invest in at least three countries and in companies tied economically to a number of countries.

Name: Cushing MLP Premier Fund Class A
Ticker: CSHAX
Fund start date: October 19, 2010
Category: Equity Energy
Total assets: $796 million

Expense ratio: 3.30%
Dividend/annual yield: 6.61%
Top five holdings: Kinder Morgan Management LLC, Plains All American Pipeline LP, Enterprise Products Partners LP, NGL Energy Partners LP, Energy Transfer Equity LP

Description: The investment seeks to produce current income and capital appreciation. The fund normally invests at least 80 percent of net assets in MLP investments. MLP investments include investments that offer economic exposure to MLPs in the form of common units, subordinated units, or debt securities that are derivatives of interests in MLPs, including I-Shares, and derivative instruments in which the fund may invest that have economic characteristics of MLP securities.

Name: Fidelity Natural Gas Portfolio
Ticker: FSNGX
Fund start date: April 21, 1993
Category: Equity Energy
Total assets: $651 million
Expense ratio: 0.86%
Dividend/annual yield: 0.81%
Top five holdings: Halliburton, Anadarko Petroleum, Apache Corp., National Oilwell Varco, Canadian National Resources Ltd.

Description: This investment seeks capital appreciation. The fund normally invests at least 80 percent of assets in securities of companies principally engaged in the production, transmission, and distribution of natural gas and involved in the exploration of potential natural gas sources, as well as those companies that provide services and equipment to natural gas producers, refineries, co-generation facilities, converters, and distributors. It invests primarily in common stocks. The fund invests in domestic and foreign issuers.

Dipping into oil and gas ETFs

Right away, you'll notice the lower expense ratios associated with ETFs included in the list of oil and gas sector ETFs.

Name: Energy Select Sector SPDR Fund
Ticker: XLE
Fund start date: December 16, 1999
Category: Equity Energy
Total assets: $8 billion
Expense ratio: 0.18%
Dividend/annual yield: $1.30/1.65%

Top five holdings: ExxonMobil Corporation, Chevron Corp., Schlumberger, Occidental Petroleum, ConocoPhillips

Description: This investment seeks to provide investment results that, before expenses, correspond generally to the price and yield performance of publicly traded equity securities of companies in the Energy Select Sector Index. In seeking to track the performance of the index, the fund employs a replication strategy. It generally invests substantially all, but at least 95 percent, of its assets in the securities comprising the index. The index includes companies from the following industries: oil, gas and consumable fuels, and energy equipment and services.

Name: Vanguard Energy Index Fund
Ticker: VDE
Fund start date: September 23, 2004
Category: Equity Energy
Total assets: $3 billion
Expense ratio: 0.14%
Dividend/annual yield: $1.99/1.78%
Top five holdings: ExxonMobil Corporation, Chevron, Schlumberger, ConocoPhillips, Occidental Petroleum

Description: This investment seeks to track the performance of a benchmark index. The fund employs an indexing investment approach designed to track the performance of the MSCI U.S. Investable Market Index (MI)/Energy 25/50, an index made up of stocks of large, mid-size, and small U.S. companies within the energy sector, as classified under the Global Industry Classification Standard (GICS). It attempts to replicate the target index by investing all, or substantially all, of its assets in the stocks that make up the index, holding each stock in approximately the same proportion as its weighting in the index.

Name: Market Vectors Oil Services ETF
Ticker: OIH
Fund start date: December 20, 2011
Category: Energy Equity
Total assets: $2 billion
Expense ratio: 0.46%
Dividend/annual yield: $0.40/0.94%
Top five holdings: Schlumberger, Halliburton, National Oilwell Varco, Transocean Ltd., Baker Hughes Inc.

Description: The investment seeks to replicate as closely as possible, before fees and expenses, the price and yield performance of the Market Vectors U.S. Listed Oil Services 25 Index. The fund normally invests at least 80 percent of its total assets in securities that make up the fund's benchmark index. Its benchmark index is composed of common stocks and depositary receipts of U.S. exchange-listed companies in the oil services sector.

Name: iShares Dow Jones U.S. Energy Sector Index Fund
Ticker: IYE
Fund start date: June 12, 2000
Category: Equity Energy
Total assets: $1 billion
Expense ratio: 0.47%
Dividend/annual yield: $0.68/1.52%
Top five holdings: ExxonMobil Corporation, Chevron Corp., Schlumberger, ConocoPhillips, Occidental Petroleum

Description: The investment seeks investment results that correspond generally to the price and yield performance, before fees and expenses, of the Dow Jones U.S. Oil & Gas Index. The fund generally invests at least 90 percent of its assets in securities of the underlying index and in depositary receipts representing securities of the underlying index. The underlying index measures the performance of the oil and gas sector of the U.S. equity market. The underlying index includes companies in the following industry groups: oil and gas producers and oil equipment, services, and distribution.

Name: iShares S&P Global Energy Sector Index Fund
Ticker: IXC
Fund start date: November 12, 2001
Category: Equity Energy
Total assets: $1 billion
Expense ratio: 0.48%
Dividend/annual yield: $0.97/2.41%
Top five holdings: ExxonMobil Corporation, Chevron Corp., BP PLC, Royal Dutch Shell, Total SA

Description: This investment seeks investment results that correspond generally to the price and yield performance, before fees and expenses, of the S&P Global 1200 Energy Sector IndexTM. The fund generally invests at least 90 percent of its assets in the securities of the underlying index and in depositary receipts representing securities of the underlying index. The underlying index measures the performance of companies that Standard & Poor's Financial Services LLC, a subsidiary of the McGraw-Hill Companies, deems to be part of the energy sector of the economy and the S&P believes are important to global markets.

Name: SPDR S&P Oil & Gas Exploration & Production ETF
Ticker: XOP
Fund start date: June 19, 2006
Category: Energy Equity
Total assets: $912 million

Expense ratio: 0.35%

Dividend/annual yield: $0.65/1.05%

Top five holdings: PDC Energy Inc., Delek U.S. Holdings Inc., Berry Petroleum, Valero Energy Corporation, Cabot Oil and Gas Corporation

Description: The investment seeks to provide investment results that, before fees and expenses, correspond generally to the total return performance of an index derived from the oil and gas exploration and production segment of a U.S. total market composite index. The fund employs a replication strategy in seeking to track the performance of the S&P Oil & Gas Exploration & Production Select Industry Index. It generally invests substantially all, but at least 80 percent, of total assets in the securities comprising the index. The fund may invest in equity securities that aren't included in the index, cash and cash equivalents, or money market instruments.

Oil and Gas Price-Tracking Funds

Let's face it: Energy outlooks vary greatly. You can utilize commodity ETFs and take advantage of broad trends in commodity prices. A *commodity ETF* is an exchange-traded fund whose goal is to mirror the performance of a physical commodity like crude oil. Some commodity ETFs are also designed to leverage investors against price declines.

The strategy involves an intimate knowledge of how the particular market typically trades. If you miss the trend, it can end up painful. Use these steps to trade the price of a commodity without buying an actual futures contract for it:

1. **Identify the market weakness or strength.**

2. **Look at a price chart for the commodity and identify two higher highs or two lower lows that signal an uptrend or downtrend.**

3. **Choose an appropriate commodity ETF whose objectives coincide with that uptrend or downtrend.**

4. **Establish your long or short position.**

Table 10-2 is a list of ETFs tracking oil and natural gas prices in which investors can play broad market trends through short and long positions.

Table 10-2	Commodity-Tracked ETFs			
Fund Name	Ticker	Commodity Tracked	Position	Objective/Tracking
United States Oil Fund	USO	Crude oil	Long	WTI spot performance
PowerShares DB Oil Fund	DBO	Crude oil	Long	Price and yield of Deutsche Bank Liquid Commodity Index
Teucrium WTI Crude Oil Fund	CRUD	Crude oil	Long 2X	Daily change in closing settlement prices for futures delivered to Cushing
United States Short Oil Fund	DNO	Crude oil	Short	Inverse percentage changes of spot price of oil delivered to Cushing
ProShares UltraShort DJ-AIG Crude Oil ETF	SCO	Crude oil	Short 2X	Twice the daily inverse of the Dow Jones UBS Crude Oil Sub-Index
PowerShares DB Crude Oil Double Short	DTO	Crude oil	Short 2X	Twice the daily performance of Deutsche Bank Liquid Commodity Index Optimum Yield Oil Excess Return
United States Natural Gas Fund, LP	UNG	Natural gas	Long	Seeks to replicate the performance of natural gas prices traded on the NYMEX that is near month and set to expire
United States 12 Month Natural Gas Fund	UNL	Natural gas	Long	Seeks to reflect the changes of the spot price of natural gas delivered at the Henry Hub

Fund Name	Ticker	Commodity Tracked	Position	Objective/Tracking
Horizons BetaPro NYMEX Natural Gas Inverse	TSX: HIN.TO	Natural gas	Short	Seeks to replicate the inverse daily performance of the NYMEX natural gas futures contract for the next delivery month
Horizons BetaPro NYMEX Natural Gas Bear Plus	TSX: HND.TO	Natural gas	Short 2X	Seeks to replicate two times the inverse of the daily performance of the NYMEX natural gas futures contract for the next delivery month

Part III

Investing in Coal

U.S. Primary Energy Consumption by Fuel, 1980-2040

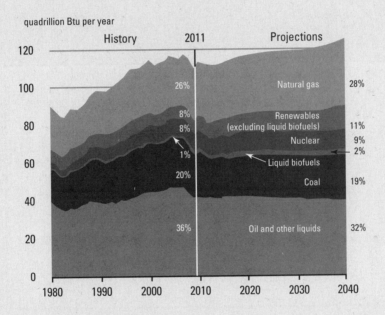

quadrillion Btu per year

History | 2011 | Projections

- Natural gas 26% / 28%
- Renewables (excluding liquid biofuels) 8% / 11%
- Nuclear 8% / 9%
- Liquid biofuels 1% / 2%
- Coal 20% / 19%
- Oil and other liquids 36% / 32%

So much of the energy we use comes from coal, so you'd think that investing in this commodity would be simple. Don't be so sure. Visit www.dummies.com/extras/energyinvesting for information on Asian coal demand.

In this part . . .

- Grasp the fundamentals of the coal market, including major drivers, supply, demand, reserves, and types.

- Understand the debate surrounding coal and pollution.

- Get a look at the future of coal, how it's being used in cleaner ways, and which countries will use the most of it going forward.

- Identify the major miners in the world's best coal-producing regions.

- Invest in coal companies, funds, and futures.

Chapter 11

Coal: Still the King

*W*hen people think of energy investing, they usually first think of oil and the big dogs in the industry like ExxonMobil (NYSE: XOM) or BP Inc. (NYSE: BP). But what you may not know is that coal, though it may not be sexy, is one of the best energy investment vehicles in the world.

Over the past 10 to 15 years, you could have made a fortune on lowly coal investments. For example, the blue-chip coal stock Peabody Energy Corporation (NYSE: BTU) went from $5 a share in 2002 to $80 a share in 2008 — a 1,500 percent return (Exxon returned 160 percent by comparison).

And that's not all. If you bought Peabody in 2009 at $20 a share, you would have tripled your money again as it hit $80 in 2011. And today, due to the slowdown in China, you get another chance. In early 2013, Peabody is back down below $25 per share.

Coal is cyclical, as evidenced by those wide Peabody price swings. The buy low/sell high mantra works time and time again. Furthermore, coal is a basic commodity. Not only is it simple to understand, but you can drop it on your foot. In this way, it can't be devalued through printing money.

Coal is the main fuel used in electricity production around the world. Over the past 30 years, the amount of electricity produced from coal globally has more than tripled. Coal is the second most heavily used hydrocarbon overall, after oil, but it's gaining fast. The International Energy Agency (IEA) predicts that coal will surpass oil as the world's most used fuel source within ten years.

Coal has a long and vibrant history. It was sought out by Romans as early as the second century and was used to heat baths and villas, as well as for smelting iron. Coal stocks have been found stored by the Romans at Hadrian's Wall.

Written records show that coal was traded in the United Kingdom during the Middle Ages. As early as 1228, sea coal from the northeast was being taken to London. In 1575, Sir George Bruce of Culross, Scotland opened the first coal mine from a moat pit on the Firth of Forth.

Most people know that coal stoked the fires of the industrial revolution. Its availability as a cheap energy source was as important as the technological advances in steam engines. What most people don't know is that coal is just as important today.

In this chapter, I tell you where coal comes from, where it goes, and what to look for to turn a profit. But first, I go back to the beginning by breaking down coal market fundamentals, including where the coal is buried, how it's produced. Finally, I discuss the political and environmental opportunities in clean coal.

Discovering the Coal Basics

Many investors in North America and Europe think that coal is the energy of the past. It's dirty and a major contributor to greenhouse gas emissions. Therefore, in the "developed" countries, *coal* is a bad word. People point to the coal ash and other byproducts as dangerous pollutants, and rightly so. They look at the dangers of mining in places like West Virginia and the cave-ins in China, and place heavy regulations on the industry. But as every good investor knows, every problem has a profitable solution.

Despite what you may have heard in the press, coal is growing both in production and in use. Coal provides 30.3 percent of global primary energy needs and generates 42 percent of the world's electricity. It's the fastest growing source of energy in the world. As such, it can't be ignored by any energy investor. In fact, because it is so despised, coal is a great contrarian investment.

Considering major coal drivers

Coal, oil, and every other commodity run in business cycles. When times are booming, companies expand and use more energy. Feedstock assets like coal, iron, and silver go up as demand increases. When there is a cyclical bust and times are bad, companies cut back. They shutter factories and fire people. During these times, the cost of commodities like coal drops. When coal goes down in price, mines close, and supply shrinks.

This in turn leads to booms. When commodities are cheap, business margins increase, companies get confident, and they start to expand. Expansion creates demand, which creates higher prices. Higher prices mean that coal mines that were unprofitable during the bust are reopened. More supply feeds the boom until eventually there's a bust and it starts all over again.

This is your basic business cycle. Cheap coal begets expensive coal, which begets cheap coal.

In 1998, there was a massive currency and debt crisis in emerging markets called the *Asian Contagion.* This bust created a drop in commodity demand. Two years later, the dotcom bust hit the rest of the world. The effects of those events compounded to create a cyclical bottom in commodities, including coal. I remember at the time you could buy coal companies for less than the cash they had in the bank. No one wanted them. I was literally laughed at for buying coal. That's when you know you're right.

From 2000 to 2008, the world witnessed what has since been termed the *Commodity Supercycle.* China was growing at a 10 to 12 percent annual rate, and it was buying every commodity, including coal, to feed its raw material needs. Coal, uranium, oil, and every other commodity hit all-time highs.

In 2008 and 2009, a banking crisis led to the "Great Recession." A lot of money was invested by hedge fund managers on margin in coal. These fund managers were chasing the supercycle dream on heavy margin and got caught in the banking crisis. They got hit with margin calls and had to sell. And sell they did — fast and hard. Some 6,000 hedge funds went out of business. With no buyers, coal prices fell and fell and fell.

Four years later, the economy is limping along. Coal mines have shut down. The price of coal in places like the Northern Appalachian Basin has fallen from $150 a ton to $65 a ton. Coal production has fallen 7 percent in the United States. In South Africa, the price of high-quality thermal coal has fallen to $84 a ton. If it falls below $80, many more mines will become unprofitable and will close. In Australia, coal is selling for $94 a ton because it's closer to the prime Asian markets, but it's still well off the highs.

The answer to what drives coal prices is the business cycle coupled with specific global demand. In early 2013, coal is cheap because the global economy is on the downside of the business cycle. Geography also is a factor. Coal costs more the closer you get to Beijing, and less the closer you get to Coal City, West Virginia.

Digging up the coal

Companies mine coal out of the earth's crust by using three techniques:

- Traditional underground mining
- Surface mining
- Mountaintop mining

Underground mining is what most people think of when they think of coal mines. Miners with lights on their hard hats dig tunnels down into the earth to find coal seams. A *seam* is layer of coal that can be hundreds of feet deep. Using heavy automated equipment, miners then start digging caverns or rooms into the seam. They leave behind large columns of coal to support the roof. This technique is called room and pillar mining. As the miners dig, a conveyor system carries the coal to the surface.

More than half the coal mined around the world comes from underground mining. It's dangerous and expensive work. It's much better if the coal is located close to the surface. Surface open pit mines are faster, cheaper, and safer. This technique is also called strip mining. Strip mining uses excavators, front-loaders, conveyor belts, and the biggest dump-trucks in the world to mine the coal.

When investing in a coal mining company, you should know that open pit mining is better than shaft mining.

A newer and more controversial method of coal mining is called mountaintop mining. It's common in West Virginia. In this method, miners literally blast the top off a mountain and carry away the coal underneath. Hundreds of mountains have disappeared due to this practice.

Coal company stocks can be crushed due to new regulations, lawsuits, and mine disasters. They can also move up rapidly when these problems are rectified or abated.

Grouping types of coal

When investing in coal, you need to know what type of coal you're dealing with. Just like crude oil or cars, with coal, quality is everything.

Coal was formed some 300 million years ago as sediments and earth-quakes buried peat-bogs under the earth. How it was buried and under what kind of pressure determine whether you get cheap brown coal or expensive anthracite.

Drier, harder coal is worth more than wetter, less dense coal. The type of coal is determined by:

- What kind of vegetation it's sourced from
- How deep it's buried
- The temperature and pressure at that depth
- How long it was buried

Coal is then ranked based on its physical and chemical properties. Ranking goes from the least expensive to the most expensive, with higher carbon content fetching the highest prices.

The ranks of coals, from those with the least carbon to those with the most carbon, are:

- Lignite
- Sub-bituminous
- Bituminous
- Anthracite

Lignite is also known as *brown coal*. It is common in China and is the primary cause of that country's heavy air pollution because it burns dirtier than coal that has purer carbon content.

Anthracite is the most valuable type of coal and is turned into coking coal for use in the production of steel. Like diamonds, the longer coal has been hardened and purified by the heat and pressure of the earth's crust, the more pure and valuable it is.

When investing in coal, the quality of the coal is more important than the quantity.

Coal is divided into two basic types:

- **Thermal coal:** Used for electricity
- **Metallurgical or coking coal:** Used for making steel

Studying coal's uses

The main use for coal is generating electricity. Nearly three quarters of the world's coal is used for this purpose, and it generates about 40 percent of global electricity. Table 11-1 shows the countries that produce the most electricity by burning coal.

Table 11-1	Countries Producing the Most Coal-Fired Electricity
Country	*Coal-Fired Electricity Produced (Terawatt-Hours)*
China	3,373
United States	1,994
India	653
Japan	304
Germany	274
South Africa	242
South Korea	219
Australia	181
Russia	166
Poland	138

Coal is cheap and plentiful. Coal plants are also low-cost and easy to build. Therefore, consumption growth is driven by the low cost of building and running coal-fired power plants, and the strong demand from emerging markets in countries like China and India for electricity. Their growing infrastructures and populations demand electricity. Currently 1.3 billion people are without electric power in the world, and they want refrigerators and TVs just like everyone else. Coal is the cheapest way for them to get it.

Approximately 15 percent of total hard coal production is currently used by the steel industry, and more than 60 percent of total global steel production is dependent on coal. Through 2035, more than 80 percent of the increase in global coal demand will come from electricity generation.

Looking at supply and demand

Total world coal production reached a record level of 7,678 million tonnes (Mt) in 2011, increasing by 6.6 percent over 2010. Since 1990, coal production has grown 64 percent from 4,677 Mt.

As you can see in Table 11-2, China is the number-one producer of coal in the world by a large margin. China produces more than three times its nearest competitor, the United States.

Table 11-2	Top Coal-Producing Countries	
Country	*Annual Production (Million Tonnes)*	*Percent of World Total*
China	3,576	45.9
United States	1,004	12.9
India	586	7.5
Australia	414	5.3
Indonesia	376	4.8
Russia	334	4.3
South Africa	253	3.3
Germany	189	2.4
Poland	139	1.8
Kazakhstan	117	1.5

China is also the world's largest consumer of coal. You can see the top ten coal-consuming countries in Table 11-3.

Table 11-3	Top Coal-Consuming Countries
Country	*Consumption (Million Tonnes)*
China	3,753
United States	909
India	654.4
Russia	232.8
Germany	232.7
South Africa	182.7
Japan	174.9
Poland	152.9
South Korea	126.2
Australia	118.9

At current consumption rates, coal consumption is expected to rise about 50 percent through 2035 to more than 11,700 million tonnes. A true growth trend is happening in coal right now; it's one of the most undervalued commodities in the world. But it won't be that way for long. You could make a very solid case that coal will be one of the best-performing assets over the next ten years.

Knowing the Location of the World's Coal

The two internationally recognized methods for assessing world coal reserves are as follows:

- The first is produced by the German Federal Institute for Geo-sciences and Natural Resources (BGR) and is used by the IEA as the main source of information about coal reserves.
- The second is produced by the World Energy Council (WEC) and is used by the BP Statistical Review of World Energy.

According to BGR, 1,004 billion tonnes of coal reserves are left. That's equivalent to 130 years of global coal output in 2011. Coal reserves reported by WEC are much lower — 861 billion tonnes, equivalent to 112 years of coal output.

Since 1983, China has been the world's top producer of coal. But that doesn't mean it has the most, just that it has the highest demand. Production has less to do with reserves than it does with demand. As Table 11-4 shows, the United States has by far the world's largest reserves of coal. Some estimate that the United States has enough coal to last 500 years.

Table 11-4	Top Ten Countries by Coal Reserves
Country	*Coal Reserves (Billion Tonnes)*
United States	237.3
Russia	157
China	114.5
Australia	76.4
India	60.6
Germany	40.7
Ukraine	33.9
Kazakhstan	33.6
South Africa	30.2
Colombia	6.7

When weighing coal-investment options, you need to look at not only value metrics like price to equity ratios, cash flows, and debt levels, but also the proximity to high-demand markets.

For example, Indonesia, Australia, and the United States export to Asia. South Africa and Kazakhstan export to India, and Russia exports to Germany, China, and Japan. Because coal production is low-cost and low-tech, any country with a rail line, a port, and an abundance of coal can be a major exporter. Digging coal out of a pit mine is nothing like drilling two miles under the North Sea for oil. If coal spills, you pick it up. There are no blowout wells.

Table 11-5 lists the largest exporters of coal. Note that Indonesia leads the list in exports but doesn't even make the top ten in reserves. Indonesia had 5.5 billion tonnes of coal reserves in 2011, and exports 82 percent of its annual production. It's estimated that 90 percent of the 3.5 billion tonne coal demand growth in Asia will come from Indonesia in the next 20 years (at which point it will run out).

Table 11-5	Top Net Exporters of Coal
Country	*Coal Exports (Million Tonnes)*
Indonesia	309
Australia	285
Russia	99
United States	85
Colombia	76
South Africa	70
Kazakhstan	34
Canada	24
Vietnam	23
Mongolia	22

As opposed to other energy sources, there is an almost endless supply of coal. No one talks of "peak coal." Therefore, coal isn't affected by new finds, dwindling supply, or politics in the Middle East. In this way, it's the most honest of energy commodities. You buy at the bottom of the business cycle and sell at the top. (That's not to say the price of coal isn't affected by politics; for details, see the next section.)

Table 11-6 reveals the top importers of coal. China, Japan, and South Korea import the most coal. But future demand growth will come from China and India.

Table 11-6	Top Net Importers of Coal
Country	*Coal Imports (Million Tonnes)*
China	177
Japan	175
North Korea	129
India	101
Taiwan	66
Germany	41
United Kingdom	32
Turkey	24
Italy	23
Malaysia	21

Being Aware of the War on Coal

"If someone wants to build a coal-powered plant, they can. It's just that it will bankrupt them."

—President Barack Obama, 2008

A highly charged debate about coal has been raging since Al Gore won an Oscar.

President Obama and his administration have pushed hard and generally succeeded in fulfilling his 2008 election promise to end the expansion of the coal industry in America. This campaign has been helped along by the low cost of natural gas. Most new power plants in the United States are gas-fired.

The decline of the U.S. coal industry

According to data from the U.S. Energy Information Administration, U.S. coal production in the first half of 2012 was down 11 percent compared with the first half of 2007. And that's just the start. The federal government's anti-coal stance is focused on more than just production. It's also against burning coal, as evidenced by these new regulations:

> ✔ **New source performance standards for greenhouse gas emissions from new coal-fired power plants.** These rules will ban new coal-fired power plants that don't capture carbon dioxide emissions. As you see in Chapter 12, the technology is prohibitively expensive. Grandfathered

plants don't have to meet these rules, but they will get hit by the next set of regulations, called MATS.

✔ **Mercury and air toxics standards (MATS).** This regulation aims to reduce emissions of mercury and other foul substances from power plants. According to the EPA, the cost of this regulation is $10 billion per year. The combination of these two rules could end coal-fired power plants in the United States within the next ten years. It will certainly push utility companies to go for natural gas or nuclear power instead.

As an investor, you should know that the Obama administration is being true to its word and waging a war on coal-fired power plants. That doesn't mean there aren't investment opportunities. The United States has the highest quality and highest quantity of low-cost coal in the world. There are plenty of ways to invest. Even if no coal is burned in America, it will be exported and burned in China. This is why Warren Buffet has been buying up railroads that run from major resource centers to ports on the West Coast.

Coal's destructive effects on the environment

In this section I reveal the dark side of burning coal in terms of pollution and climate change. The basic problem is that coal is much cheaper than other fossil fuels ($1 to $2 per MMBTU, compared to $6 or $12 for oil). It's also a heavier pollutant than its peers. The good news, which I tell you about in Chapter 12, is that the low cost of coal means that high-cost solutions to pollution and climate change can be adopted, and king coal will remain competitive as a global energy source.

Coal mining takes a tremendous toll on the environment by destroying mountain ranges and polluting waterways. Black lung is a killer for miners. Underground seams of coal have been known to catch fire and burn for years. Thousands of underground seam fires are currently burning around the world. The most publicized is perhaps the one that started in 1962 and is still burning underneath the now empty town of Centralia, Pennsylvania. One in India has been burning since 1916.

But the real problem is the waste products that are produced after coal is burned in power plants.

Coal plants produce the largest amount of carbon dioxide (CO_2) emissions in the world. Scientists believe that CO_2 is the primary cause of global warming, or climate change. The combustion of coal, whether for electricity, heat, or cooking, is the leading cause of toxic air pollution that causes smog and acid rain. China has an epic problem with air pollution. Recent air pollution was so bad that it was reported as "beyond index" according to the U.S. Embassy's American Air Quality Index. Air quality is a very real problem. These emissions can be fixed with scrubbers and other technologies, but they're expensive and inefficient.

The goal of investing is to make money. In modern litigious times, it's important to know what negative effects an investment can have on the environment and what drag that can have on your bottom line. No one wants to see years of gains wiped out by an EPA lawsuit or some other black-swan event. On the flip side, some companies make money by cleaning up hazardous situations and/or producing the systems that make coal burning cleaner.

One of the biggest problems with coal burning is that it produces acid rain. Acid rain is a serious problem in the eastern United States and Canada. It kills fish and trees and causes harm to animals that must deal with a loss of habitat. It even has been known to destroy the paint on cars. Acid rain is caused by a mixture of sulfur dioxide ($SO2$) and nitrogen oxides (Nox) mixing with water in the atmosphere and falling as rain.

The good news is that the effects of acid rain in the United States have been greatly reduced. The 1975 Clean Air Act and its 1990 amendments forced coal utilities to add scrubbers to their plants. EPA data shows a steady decline in the sulfate content in the air and rain, as well as the acid in lakes in the northeastern United States.

The second largest environmental problem from coal plants is fly ash. This is particulate matter or soot that causes lung problems like bronchitis and asthma. Fly ash can be abated by using bag houses, which are like giant fabric air filters for coal-fired power plants.

The last major environmental and health concern regarding coal burning is that it produces mercury. In fact, half of mercury pollution created by humans is put out by coal-burning power plants. Mercury is a toxic heavy metal that is extremely poisonous. A small amount — less than a thimble full dumped in a small lake — can make fish inedible.

Despite the benefits of abundance and low cost, burning coal can be a nasty business. Besides the aforementioned three problems, coal-fired power plants also emit lead, cadmium, carbon monoxide, hydrocarbons, and arsenic.

But as an investor, every problem presents an opportunity. Companies that are searching for clean-coal technologies include Duke Energy (NYSE: DUK), ConocoPhillips (NYSE: COP), Hitachi (OTC: HTHIY), and Siemens (NYSE: SI).

Chapter 12

The Future of Coal

Back in the early 2000s, I used to flip houses for fun and profit. It was still early enough in the game that you could buy a distressed house at a distressed price. My goal was to find the ugliest house out there and offer the seller 20 percent less than the asking price. My favorite find was a 1950s-style box that had mold problems. The insurance company would gut the place, kill all the mold, and sell it at a discount as compared to non-gutted houses because consumers think a gutted house needs too much fixing up, and they aren't willing to pay actual market value. What other home buyers didn't know at the time was that when you were buying a house to fix up, it was cheaper to buy the gutted one. It saved you from having to gut it yourself.

Coal is the ugly, mold-infested house of energy. Let's face it: You don't impress your golf buddies by telling them you bought a bunch of Arch Coal (NYSE: ACI) at five-year lows. Heck, they'll probably laugh you out of the 19th hole. But if you do a little research and know what you're doing, you can make a fortune. I'm not saying it's for the faint of heart. You have to have a little courage to zig when the market zags. But being a contrarian and having patience is a time-tested market strategy for success. Like the 1950s house, coal is currently undervalued because of its perception as a dirty fuel.

Yes, coal is ugly, polluting, and abundant. It's also a highly leveraged force that's cyclical in nature and easy to understand and profit from. That said, be aware of some basic trends in coal and the obstacles to overcome. All investments climb a wall of worry, and all investments have a price. The question you should ask yourself is: How much of the negative is priced relative to the positives? In other words, which of the following scenarios is more likely to happen?

> ✔ They discover more harmful environmental problems for coal
>
> ✔ Or they create a solution

And does the price reflect either one of these scenarios?

Taking control of your investments means that you have to answer these questions yourself. This chapter gives you the basic points of contention of which you need to be aware. I talk about two major geographic trends in coal, plus the technology that's attempting to change the environmental impact of burning coal — so-called *clean coal*. I also outline where the import/export picture is heading, and how World War II–era German technology is still being used today to turn anthracite into jet fuel.

Coal and the Climate

Both mining and burning coal create a whole gamut of health problems (see Chapter 11 for details). These problems range from coal dust to a toxic slurry of chemicals and heavy metals that get into the environment. Perhaps the largest problem with coal is that burning it emits the largest amount of greenhouse gas in the world: CO_2.

Developed and developing

Coal has two markets — the developed market represented by the United States and the developing market represented by India and China.

Burning coal in the United States is responsible for 37 percent of the country's total carbon dioxide emissions. The use of coal is being gradually reduced both due to the low cost of natural gas — now abundant due to fracking — and measures taken by the EPA in response to President Obama's efforts to clean the environment.

Due to the regulatory cost of clean coal, the last coal-fired power plant in the United States has probably been built. Natural gas in America has undercut coal's natural advantages. That is, natural gas is now abundant and cheap, and it has the added benefit of burning much cleaner than coal. As you can see in Table 12-1, the projected cost of advanced coal with clean coal technology, or *carbon capture and sequestration* (CCS), will soon eclipse the cost of using natural gas.

Utilities use the levelized cost of electricity generation, or the price they must charge to break even after all costs and depreciation are accounted for, to determine which types of energy assets to acquire. This number is reported in dollars per megawatt-hour, which can also be broken down into cents per kilowatt-hour. Utilities look for the source with the lowest levelized cost that meets all their emissions and generation requirements. Coal is competitive on its own but becomes prohibitively expensive when you start adding clean-coal technology.

Table 12-1	Estimated Cost of New Generation Resources, 2017
Plant Type	*Total System Levelized Cost ($/MWh)*
Natural gas advanced combined cycle	65.5
Natural gas conventional combined cycle	68.6
Hydro	89.9
Natural gas advanced CC with CCS	92.8
Wind	96.8
Conventional coal	99.6
Geothermal	99.6
Natural gas advanced combustion turbine	105.3
Advanced coal	112.2
Advanced nuclear	112.7
Biomass	120.2
Natural gas conventional combustion turbine	132.0
Advanced coal with CCS	140.7
Solar PV	156.9
Solar thermal	251.0
Wind — offshore	330.6

Despite the consumption drop in the United States, coal consumption globally is going up. Coal has significant advantages for the developing world, which is why it's the most-used fuel for electricity production. Over the last three decades, the amount of electricity produced from coal has grown more than 200 percent worldwide. China alone is adding an average of two coal-fired power plants per week. These additions put staggering stress on the environment.

During the 2008 Beijing Olympics, you may have seen air so bad that some runners refused to compete. China now burns 3.8 billion tons of coal each year, almost as much as the rest of the world combined. China's CO_2 emissions rose by 9.3 percent in 2011 to 720 million tons. Pollution and dust generated in China are causing smog in Japan and have been found as far away as California. In January 2013, the index for fine particle pollution rose to 1,000 micrograms per cubic meter — or 40 times what the World Health Organization says is safe. It was literately off the chart. An estimated 750,000 people die in China each year as a result of air pollution. Table 12-2 shows global CO_2 emissions by country.

China's reason for not signing the Kyoto Protocol, which is the United Nations treaty to reduce global emissions, was that its emissions were much lower per capita than developed nations. That's true, but it's also a red herring. Though the United States has more than twice the per-capita carbon emissions as China, total U.S. emissions are about half of China's. Both per capita and total emissions figures are important, but you must also consider geographic and demographic factors. China's coal plants are closer to more densely populated cities, so their problems are exacerbated.

Table 12-2	CO2 Emissions by Country	
Country	*CO2 Emissions (Thousand Tonnes)*	*Emissions per Capita (Tonnes)*
China	9,700,000	7.2
United States	5,420,000	17
India	1,970,000	1.6
Russia	1,830,000	12.8
Japan	1,240,000	9.8
Germany	810,000	9.9
South Korea	610,000	12.6
Canada	560,000	16.2

No one wants to live with horrific air pollution, and the recent conditions have forced Chinese leadership to talk up plans to cut pollution. They already have strict targets in their five-year plan to cut air pollution in major cities by 40 to 50 percent by 2016. It seems unlikely that China will meet these goals because 70 percent of its electricity still comes from coal. Something has to give. It's a good bet that China will embrace the use of clean coal technology.

Considering the possibility of cleaner coal

When people talk of *clean coal,* they mean coal that's processed to remove pollutants created when it is burned. This trend is being driven by a global technological drive to reduce carbon dioxide emissions. Coal burning is the leading cause of carbon dioxide being released into the atmosphere. Carbon dioxide is a greenhouse gas, in that it floats into the higher atmosphere and acts like the glass in a greenhouse, trapping heat from the sun. Scientists believe this trapping of heat, known as the *greenhouse effect,* causes climate change, melting of the polar icecaps, rising ocean waters, increased storms, and the desertification of farmlands.

Thus, environmentalists are making a concerted effort to cut down or eliminate coal-burning power plants. Their opposition believes that coal has a future in the United States. These people look to new technology that will sequester, scrub, or otherwise limit CO2 discharge and the other toxins released from burning coal.

Former president George W. Bush pushed heavily for clean coal, beginning in his first term in office. He believed that such technology could limit U.S. dependence on foreign oil. In his second term, Bush funneled $3.4 billion in Troubled Asset Relief Program (TARP) money to clean coal efforts that advanced the field of study.

Environmental groups such as Greenpeace want to eliminate coal burning altogether. They claim that burning coal emits 29 percent more CO2 than other hydrocarbons like oil or natural gas. And as I discuss in Chapter 11, coal emits a toxic mix of mercury and other waste products that get into the food chain. It should be noted that no fiscally feasible methods are currently available to remove this mercury with clean coal technology.

The other side claims that if coal isn't burned in the United States, it will be burned with no scrubbing technology in Asia. Furthermore, the United States won't suddenly shut down 50 percent of its electricity production. Nor is it likely that the United States will let 500 years of coal reserves go to waste.

The environmentalists say the answer lies in renewable energy. President Barack Obama has called for 10 percent of U.S. electricity to come from renewable sources by 2012 and 25 percent by 2025, and he has spent more than $32 billion to bring about this change. You can find the investment opportunities associated with renewable energy in Part V of this book.

In the end, as an investor you should know that coal-burning power plants are on the wane in the United States. New legislation means that older plants will close, and some of the more modern ones will be further enhanced to reduce emissions. The trend is clear in the developed world. And it's anti-coal.

Coal will never be completely clean. Vaclav Smil, an environmental professor at the University of Manitoba, says that there's no economically feasible way to eliminate the carbon dioxide emissions from coal-fired power plants. If one were to bury just 10 percent of CO_2 put out annually by the global coal-burning industry, it would equal the volume of oil produced every year. The money required would be in the trillions of dollars. There's no easy answer to so-called greenhouse gas emissions. As a coal industry investor, you should know that environmentalists will never be on your side.

The next trend in coal for the United States is to export it to Asia. Coal miners, railroad companies, port companies, and unions are applying tremendous pressure on governmental agencies to build export facilities in British Columbia, Washington, and Oregon. Warren Buffett has bought the railroads that run east/west and has been seen touring the coal mines in Wyoming. This movement is being fought by local municipalities and environmental movements like Voters Taking Action on Climate Change and the Wilderness Committee, among others, which point to the threat of coal dust from transport as well as fears that the United States would just be exporting its greenhouse gas emissions to China.

Gas and Liquid: Coal Gets a Makeover

In addition to burying or scrubbing coal emissions after the fuel is burned, there are other ways to make coal cleaner. By converting coal in a gaseous or liquid fuel, it can be used for much more than just boiling water to make steam.

Several publicly traded companies break apart and recombine coal molecules into their varying components. This process, called *gasification,* separates and removes the various chemicals. It's the most environmentally friendly use of coal for energy needs because it removes up to 99 percent of all pollutants. It also improves power plant efficiency from 40 to 70 percent.

Gasification has been around for hundreds of years. Jan Baptista van Helmont, a Flemish scientist, discovered a vapor that escaped from wood and coal when heated. In 1609, he coined the term *gas.* Helmont's discovery was commercialized in Germany in 1825 when the town of Hannover made gas by blowing oxygen and steam through coal while applying heat.

After coal is turned into gas, it can be further synthesized by using the Fischer–Tropsch technique. It's a complex process that's important for investors because it refines the gas from coal into synthetic oil products. Unlike with other clean coal processes, this one offers pure play investment opportunities.

The Fischer–Tropsch process was used by Nazis to provide fuel for their war machine because oil was hard to come by. It was further improved during the apartheid period in South Africa. Over time, the process of turning coal into liquids was advanced. Today, the market leader in coal-to-liquid technology is Sasol (NYSE: SSL) of South Africa.

Due to the economic embargo that resulted from apartheid, historically South Africa lacked access to oil imports and was forced to turn to coal-to-liquid technology. The fuel is used in automobiles and as jet fuel. In fact, about 30 percent of South Africa's gas and diesel requirements come from coal.

Coal-to-liquid works in countries that have a large supply of coal but have to import expensive oil. The upside is that liquid fuels from coal work just like regular gasoline. They're distributed from your standard gas pump and fuel your standard gas burning car or truck.

Sasol (NYSE:SSL) is the leader in this field and, like many South African blue chips, it has gone global. The company is currently building the first major refinery in the United States, near Lake Charles in Louisiana. It will be situated to take advantage of the end of the natural gas pipeline and the transportation path of the Mississippi River. Sasol's new plant will produce 96,000 barrels a day of diesel fuel and is estimated to cost $10 billion.

Another company you may want to check out in the space is Rentech (NYSE: RTK), which owns the patented Rentech Process. Based on Fischer–Tropsch chemistry, Rentech converts syngas from coal or other biomass into usable hydrocarbons, including jet fuel, diesel, chemicals, and waxes. The stock doubled in 2012 as the market began absorbing new ways for the world to cleanly use its vast coal reserves.

King Coal's Reign Continues

Coal comes in second only to oil in terms of the amount of hydrocarbons used in the world. But it will soon be number one. According to the International Energy Agency (IEA), within ten years coal will eclipse oil as the world's most dominant fuel — despite the extreme environmental concerns. Right now, coal supplies more than 27 percent of global primary energy needs. But it's called King Coal because of how much humans rely on it for electricity production.

Producing the world's electricity

Though coal provides 27 percent of global primary energy, it supplies more than 40 percent of the world's electricity, as seen in Figure 12-1. It became this dominant because coal is so abundant, and it's relatively cheap to build and operate coal-fired power plants compared to other fuel sources. This makes it an easy choice for emerging markets that are moving up the economic chain and need to produce more electricity for their growing middle classes in a hurry.

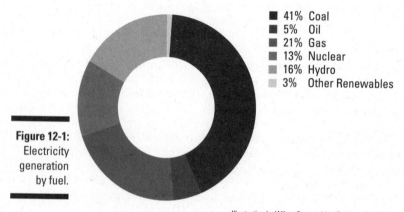

- ■ 41% Coal
- ■ 5% Oil
- ■ 21% Gas
- ■ 13% Nuclear
- ■ 16% Hydro
- ■ 3% Other Renewables

Figure 12-1:
Electricity
generation
by fuel.

Illustration by Wiley, Composition Services Graphics

It takes two to four years to build a coal plant, whereas it takes four to six years to build a natural gas plant. China is dependent on coal because, as of yet, it has not been able to leverage its abundant natural gas fields due to adverse geography. China's ability to leverage its natural gas reserves may improve in the future and is a risk when considering investing in coal.

But at the end of the day, an estimated 1.3 billion people don't have electricity on this planet, and they want the lights on. China produces the most coal of any country in the world and is also the largest consumer and importer of coal.

Going forward, coal demand in China will grow faster than in any other country. Over the next four years, China is building 160 new coal-fired power plants. India, whose population will soon eclipse China's, is building 46 new plants by 2017. You want to keep an eye on coal investment opportunities as these factors combine to make the most widely used fuel on the planet.

Demand forecasts

The backdrop situation for coal is one in which demand has stabilized or is dropping in the United States and Europe at the same time it's increasing in China and India. The expectation is that North American coal will supply Asian demand, which may or may not happen, but it will take a few years in any event. Coal exports from the United States run into port capacity bottle-necks. Right now, the United States supplies roughly 10 percent of global coal demand with most of it being consumed domestically.

U.S. export terminals have a total capacity of 173 million tonnes per year, or just 16 percent of the nation's total output. There are efforts to increase West Coast coal terminals, but there are severe political headwinds in Washington State. Don't look for U.S. exports to fill the global need in the short term.

China will drive the sea-born demand for coal over for the foreseeable future. Chinese energy consumption grew more than 12-fold between 1980 and 2009. India's electricity demand increased by more than 650 percent. By compari-son, the United States increased electricity demand by a mere 78 percent over the same two decades. That's not to say China doesn't have room to grow. On a per capita basis, China's electricity demand would have to increase by 500 percent to match the United States. The International Energy Agency expects China to add 75 percent to its current electric base by 2035.

Though China leads global demand, India is growing faster in terms of coal imports. This growth stems from the fact that India has a less abundant supply, and what it does have is restricted by nebulous government and cul-tural restrictions on land use.

Looking forward, much of the global coal demand will be supplied by Indonesia and Australia. Today, the two nations supply 45 percent of the global seaborne trade. Australia, in particular, is pushing hard to expand its ports to meet China's needs. Indonesia has ramped up its coal exports in recent years due to the inexpensive and low-tech nature of its surface mines, which are located near ports and waterways. The downside for Indonesia is that the country is booming and has an increasing appetite for domestic coal consumption, leading it to use up its reserves. New government policies aim to protect its manufacturing base and keep the energy source at home.

Colombia, Russia, South Africa, and Mongolia are also players in the global export coal game. Increased amounts of coal will flow from Mongolia to China because they share a border, and rail-lines are being built.

The bottom line is that coal use is slated to rise, and you'd be well-served to take advantage of it by making strategic investments in the sector. The official forecast from the IEA is for global coal use to reach 8.6 billion tonnes in 2017, more than 13 percent higher than the 7.6 billion tonnes consumed in 2012, as seen in Figure 12-2. At that point, coal will rival oil as the most widely used fuel on the planet.

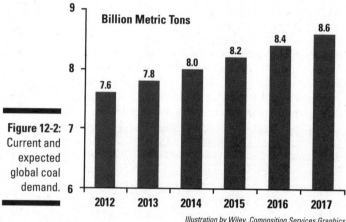

Figure 12-2: Current and expected global coal demand.

Illustration by Wiley, Composition Services Graphics

Chapter 13

Coal: Mining for Profits

• •

In This Chapter

▶ Investing in coal companies and funds

▶ Identifying major coal miners

▶ Seeing how coal trades as a commodity

• •

*Y*ou don't have to have insider knowledge or a geology degree from an Ivy League school to make money from coal. No, you just need to have some common sense and a little bit of knowledge about how the game works.

Investing in coal is a lot like real estate in that people base how much they're willing to pay on various factors. No two houses are the same, but every house has similar features. Likewise with coal deposits. A three-bedroom home with a view is worth more than a four-bedroom house next to the dump. With coal, the only difference is that instead of great rooms and three-car garages, you're comparing coal reserves and cash flow. Instead of half an acre in a great school district, you're buying proximity to transport and insider transactions.

In this chapter I give you an in-depth look into coal-mining investments. I sort through the large caps and give you a few of the long shots in various coal-mining countries, and I cover how to invest in coal via funds and futures.

Turning Fundamentals into Decisions

In the great game of coal, knowing what moves a stock price can be the difference between retiring early and being stuck in a losing stock for years. One of the worst feelings for a commodity investor is being stuck in a stock because you know it's too late to sell. But it happens even to the best investors.

Figure 13-1 shows the price of thermal coal for export from Australia over the past 30 years. As you can see, the price of coal is in a long-term uptrend. The Australian export price for thermal coal is the most important to track in today's market because it exports more than 80 percent of its coal output to bustling markets like China and India.

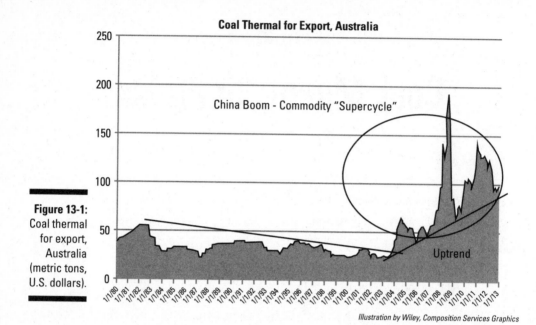

Coal Thermal for Export, Australia

China Boom - Commodity "Supercycle"

Uptrend

Figure 13-1:
Coal thermal
for export,
Australia
(metric tons,
U.S. dollars).

Illustration by Wiley, Composition Services Graphics

From the post–oil embargo years in 1974, the price of coal went down in a steady and predictable way. In the 1980s and 1990s, you could buy and sell coal in a predictable range-bound pattern. You bought low and sold high.

The great thing about coal is that, although it's not sexy, it's simple to understand. The reason why the price of coal fell was because companies got much better at blasting the stuff out of the ground. In other words, technology improved. (Today, you see the same sort of trend with falling natural gas prices and fracking technology; check out Chapter 7 for details.)

Real coal prices for Central Appalachian coal, which is traded on the NYMEX, fell from a high of more than $62 per ton in 1979 to less than $28 per ton in 2000, where they found a bottom. (See the later section "Investing in Coal Futures" for more info on Central Appalachian coal.) Then something strange happened. The price of coal broke out of its 30-year slump and doubled over the next decade — spiking to more than $54 by 2010, as seen in Figure 13-2.

You can find a similar chart on all basic commodities. In 2003, there was a surge of demand from China as well as a construction boom in places as diverse as Dubai, Madrid, and Miami. The global economy was booming. Companies needed both electricity and steel. Coal was in demand, and the price reflected that.

Coal Prices, 1949-2011 (Dollars per Short Ton), Bituminous Coal Real

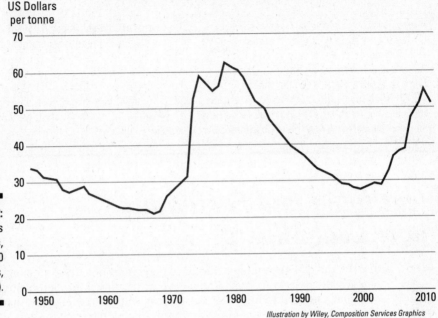

Figure 13-2: Bituminous coal prices, 1949–2010 (short tons, U.S. dollars).

Illustration by Wiley, Composition Services Graphics

Since that time, the Chinese economy has had a series of ups and downs as it adjusts to the Great Recession and falling demand, leaving investors uncertain about the coal market. Most of the major coal miners lost money in 2012.

But investing in the past is a fool's game. The questions you have to ask yourself are:

- ✔ What will happen in the future?
- ✔ What will the market look like six months or a year from now?
- ✔ Will China work down its stockpiles of coal?
- ✔ Will more coal miners close down like Patriot Coal did in 2012?
- ✔ Will there be mergers and acquisitions that boost select share prices?

In the next section, I take a look at some of these questions, getting into the nitty-gritty of coal investing and mentioning some specific coal companies.

Use a stock screener

A great way to find quality investments is through the use of a stock screener. They're available on most brokerage websites like TD Ameritrade, Scottrade, E*Trade, and so on. You can use various metrics to filter stocks, including P/E ratio, peg ratio, float, and share price. Back in 2002, after the dot-com bust, I was running screens by using high revenue growth, low P/E, low debt, low share price, lots of cash, and insider buying. For months I got nothing but coal companies and steel mills — the same companies that had been through a 30-year investment grinder. These industries had been written off to the point that they had become bad jokes on TV and in the movies. That, of course, was the time to buy.

Identifying and Evaluating Major Coal Miners

In 2013, the global economy started to emerge from a five-year slump. Inflation worries and over-building in China have driven down the cost of steel and the coal that's needed to make it. Coal companies that formerly had market values of $20 billion or more are flirting with the $5 billion line. Still, these companies will be the survivors of this market cycle. They will be the buyers, rather than the ones being bought, and you should know their names. In this section, I present the strongest coal companies in the United States, China, and Russia.

United States

America is the country that made coal king. Coal from Southern and Midwestern states is what helped build the strongest economy in the world. Some of the companies that made that possible are still around and are still solid investments.

> ✔ **Peabody Energy** (NYSE: BTU) is a large blue chip coal miner with a $5.9 billion market cap and revenue of $8 billion. Sales fell 9.5 percent in 2012 over 2011. Peabody mines both thermal coal and metallurgical coal and has majority interests in 28 coal projects in the United States and Australia. It also trades and brokers coal, serving clients in almost 30 countries on 6 continents. At the end of 2012, Peabody had around 9 billion tons of proven and probable reserves and was well positioned for high-growth Asian markets with sales volumes for thermal and metallurgical coal from Australia both breaking records.

✔ **CONSOL Energy** (NYSE: CNX) is a blue chip coal miner with headquarters in Pittsburgh, Pennsylvania. Consol has a $7.7 billion market cap and revenue of $5.4 billion. Sales were down 12.6 percent in 2011. The company produces Appalachian coal for sale to electric utilities and steel makers worldwide and is also a leading natural gas producer in the Marcellus and Utica Shales. Its coal division mines and processes both metallurgical and thermal coal. It's not a pure play on coal, however, as a substantial percent of its revenue comes from its gas division, which explores for unconventional gas, including coal bed methane. At the end of 2012, it owned more coal reserves than any other U.S. company, controlling 4.5 billion tons. CONSOL also controls 4 trillion cubic feet of proven natural gas reserves.

✔ **Alpha Natural Resources** (NYSE: ANR) is a mid-cap coal miner with a market value of $1.8 billion. In 2012, the company had revenue of $7 billion, which was down 19.8 percent from the year before. Alpha Natural Resources is the world's sixth largest producer of thermal coal and the third largest producer of metallurgical coal. Its operations are located in West Virginia, Virginia, Pennsylvania, Kentucky, and Wyoming, and it shops to customers on five continents. It can export from multiple terminals on the East and Gulf coasts, and it has a 41 percent interest in Dominion Terminal Associates in Newport News, Virginia. The company has 145 mines and controls 4.7 billion tons of coal reserves.

✔ **Arch Coal** (NYSE: ACI) has $1.2 billion market cap on $4.1 billion in sales. Revenue for 2012 fell 27.1 percent over 2011. Arch Coal produces and sells both types of coal from surface and underground mines in the United States. It has mines in every major U.S. basin, including Powder River, Appalachia, Western Bituminous, and Illinois. Arch controls 5.5 billion tons of coal reserves.

✔ **Walter Energy** (NYSE: WLT) is a mid-major with $1.9 billion market cap on sales of $2.4 billion. Walter saw its revenues drop 33.1 percent in 2012 over 2011. It operates surface and underground mines in the United States, Canada, and the United Kingdom and controls more than 330 million tons of reserves. Walter also has a subsidiary specializing in specialized blends of coking coal as well as a coal-bed methane gas division with more than 1,700 wells that produced 18.1 billion cubic feet in 2012.

American coal miners have been through a tough slog. Cheap natural gas and oppressive EPA regulations made most investors sell U.S. coal over the past few years, with the major players down more than 50 percent since 2008, as seen in Figure 13-3. Since late 2012, some of those stocks have shown signs of appreciation.

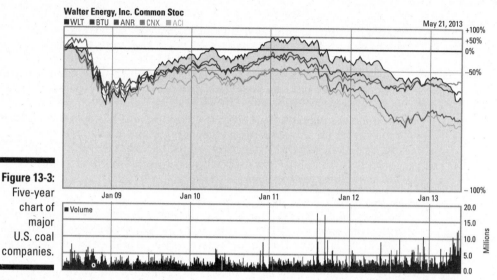

Figure 13-3:
Five-year
chart of
major
U.S. coal
companies.

Illustration by Wiley, Composition Services Graphics

In the final quarter of 2012, Peabody, Alpha Natural Resources, CONSOL Energy, and Arch Coal all beat the earnings expectations of analysts. And other than Arch Coal, the other companies registered better-than-expected revenue for the quarter. Table 13-1 shows earnings per share (EPS) and revenue beat for these companies for the fourth quarter (4Q) of 2012.

Table 13-1	EPS and Revenue Beat for Four U.S. Coal Companies (Fourth Quarter 2012)			
Company	4Q 2012 Actual EPS ($)	4Q 2012 Est. EPS ($)	Earnings Surprise %	Revenue Beat %
Peabody Energy (BTU)	0.36	0.25	44%	4%
Alpha Natural Resources (ANR)	(0.19)	(0.55)	65%	3%
CONSOL Energy (CNX)	0.43	0.24	80%	6.5%
Arch Coal (ACI)	(0.14)	(0.15)	6.7%	(3%)

China

China is slowly working off stockpiles of coal that it built up during the Great Recession. But longer-term expansion of coal-powered plants in China and India will boost demand over the next three or four years. China's power consumption is expected to increase by 8.5 percent in 2013, and it's expected to add 75 gigawatts of coal-fired production in the next two years.

Many Chinese coal companies are state-owned, and only a few are listed for public investment. The ones worthy of a closer look are

- ✔ **Yanzhou Coal Mining** (NYSE: YZC) is China's largest coal miner with a $7.2 billion market cap on $8.9 billion in revenue. The company saw revenue growth of 6.7 percent year-over-year from 2011 to 2012, and in early 2013 it had a forward price to earnings of 15.7. Yanzhou mines and sells coal in China, Japan, South Korea, and Australia. The company deals with both metallurgical coal and thermal coal, as well as their byproducts. Yanzhou runs six coal mines, including the Xinglongzhuang, Baodian, Nantun, Dongtan, Jining II, and Jining III. It's not just a coal company, however, because it also generates revenue from methanol, electricity, railways, and acetic acid.

- ✔ **China Coal Energy Company Limited** (OTC: CCOZY) is a subsidiary of China National Coal Group Corp., the third largest state-owned coal company in the world. It operates coal mines and coking plants and manufactures coal mining equipment. In 2012, it earned $1.3 billion on revenues of $13.6 billion.

- ✔ **China Shenhua Energy Co. Ltd.** (OTC: CSUAY) is the largest coal-mining operation in the world with more than 15 billion tonnes of recoverable reserves. It also owns related businesses, including ports, shipping, railroads, and utilities. It also runs Mongolia's largest coal project through a joint venture with a Russian syndicate and Peabody Energy. It earned $7.8 billion in 2012 on revenues of $39.9 billion.

- ✔ **Hidili Industry International Development Limited** (OTC: HIIDY) operates in the coal-mining and washing sectors, operating more than 40 mines, 10 coal washing plants, and 6 rail yards. Its value has been dwindling since early 2012, as revenues fell by 62 percent and the company posted a $23.5 million annual loss.

Russia

Russia produced 336.3 million tons of coal in 2011, which was 4 percent more than the prior year and a record for the post-Soviet era. Russia is the third-largest exporter of coal with 11 percent of the global market. Despite the fact that 80 percent of its coal is located in Siberia, most of its coal (73 percent) goes to the European Union. This trend is starting to change. Russian and Chinese leaders met in the first quarter of 2013 and worked out loans and trade deals to develop coal resources in eastern Siberia for export to China.

Like China, many of Russia's coal companies are state-owned, with only one listing its shares on a major exchange.

Mechel OAO (NYSE: MTL) is a mid-sized company with a $2.2 billion market cap. Mechel had sales in 2012 of $11.7 billion, which was down 15.4 percent from the previous year. The company also lost $428 million in 2012. Mechel has mines in Russian, Europe, the Middle East, and the United States. The company has four segments: mining, steel, ferroalloys, and power. The company produces both types of coal from open pit and underground mining. The company also produces iron ore and sells finished steel products like wire, stampings, and forgings. Mechel is also involved in nickel, chrome, and silicon. The power segment produces electricity.

Investing in Coal Funds

You can use coal funds to gain diversified exposure to the industry and generate income with a single purchase. Master limited partnerships (MLPs) own coal resources and lease them to mining companies, passing on the proceeds directly to investors. Exchange-traded funds (ETFs) track the combined performance of several companies whose main operations are in the coal sector.

Additionally, you can use coal indexes to get an overall gauge of how the industry is performing. The two most-watched indexes for the coal sector are the Stowe Global Coal Index (COAL) and the Dow Jones U.S. Coal Index (DJUSCL).

The COAL tracks 36 companies with a total market cap of $196.2 billion, with the average being $5.5 billion. You can see its top ten constituents in Table 13-2.

Table 13-2 Stowe Global Coal Index's Top Ten Constituents

Company	Ticker	Country	Weight (Percentage)
China Shenhua Energy	HK: 1088	China	8.4%
Joy Global	NYSE: JOY	United States	8.3%
China Coal Energy	HK: 1898	China	8.2%
Peabody Energy	NYSE: BTU	United States	7.6%
Consol Energy	NYSE: CNX	United States	7.5%
Yanzhou Coal Mining	NYSE: YZC	China	4.6%
Alpha Natural Resources	NYSE: ANR	United States	4.6%
Inner Mongolia Yitai	HK: 3948	China	4.5%
Adaro Energy	Jakarta: ADRO	Indonesia	4.4%
Walter Energy	NYSE: WLT	United States	4.4%

Coal master limited partnerships (MLPs)

A *master limited partnership* (MLP) is a type of publicly traded investment vehicle. It combines the tax benefits of a limited partnership with the liquidity of a publicly traded company. If you like dividends, you'll love MLPs because they pass a percentage of their profits directly to investors.

MLPs were set up by Congress to give average investors a way to play natural resources like the big boys. They are, however, limited by United States code to apply only to enterprises involved in the natural resource sector, such as petroleum and natural gas extraction and transportation. To qualify, an MLP must generate at least 90 percent of its income from oil, natural gas, and coal. What makes them attractive is that, as a partnership, they have to pay out most of their earnings as dividends. And these earnings can be quite substantial. Coal-related MLPs include:

✔ **Alliance Resource Partners** (NASDAQ: ARLP) is a $2.4 billion company in terms of market cap. It had sales of $2 billion in 2012, which were up 15.8 percent over 2011. The company pays a solid dividend of 6.9 percent and is expected to pay $4.43 per share for 2013. Alliance is the third-largest coal producer in the eastern United States and has ten underground mines in five states with more than 911 million tons of reserves. Its quarterly cash distributions have increased 103 percent since 2008.

✔ **Alliance Holdings Group** (NASDAQ: AHGP) is a $3.1 billion company in terms of market cap. It expects to pay a $3.05 per share forward annual dividend, which would be a 5 percent dividend yield. It owns and controls Alliance Resource Management, which is the managing general partner of Alliance Resource Partners (see the preceding bullet), helping it execute its strategy of expanding operations, making productivity improvements, and offering a broad range of coal qualities.

✔ **Natural Resource Partners** (NYSE: NRP) is a $2.5 billion company with revenue of $365 million, which was up 1.6 percent in 2012 over 2011. The company pays a hefty dividend of $2.20 per share, which should result in a 9.8 percent yield for 2013. NRP owns and manages 2.4 billion tons of coal reserves located in West Virginia, Kentucky, Maryland, Indiana, Alabama, Montana, Illinois, and Virginia. Production from its properties accounts for 25 percent of U.S. metallurgical coal production and 5 percent of total coal production. The company doesn't engage in mining but rather leases its properties in exchange for royalty payments that are passed on to investors.

✔ **Penn Virginia Resource Partners** (NYSE: PVR) is a $2.1 billion company in terms of market value. The company had sales of $987 million in 2012, which was down 3.7 percent from the prior year. Penn Virginia expects to pay $2.20 per share in 2013, which would result in a dividend yield of 9.8 percent. PVR gathers and processes natural gas and manages coal resources in the United States. The company operates 4,758 miles of pipelines for natural gas and controls 871 million tons of coal reserves located in 11 states.

Coal exchange-traded fund(s)

Exchange-traded funds (ETFs) give investors a way to have broad exposure to an industry or sector. Instead of marrying your fortunes with one company, or buying five or six companies individually, you can diversify within a sector with one trade.

The only major coal ETF traded in the United States is the Market Vectors Coal ETF (NYSE: KOL), which is designed to replicate the performance of the

Market Vectors Global Coal Index. It has more than $220 million in assets, 58 percent of which are concentrated in its top ten holdings, as outlined in Table 13-3.

Table 13-3	Top Ten Holdings of Market Vectors Coal ETF	
Company	*Ticker*	*Percent of Assets*
Consol Energy	NYSE: CNX	9.1%
China Shenhua Energy	HK: 1088	8.2%
Aurizon	ASX: AZJ	6.9%
Joy Global	NYSE: JOY	6.7%
Peabody Energy	NYSE: BTU	6.0%
China Coal Energy	HK: 1898	5.4%
Yanzhou Coal Mining	NYSE: YZC	4.9%
Banpu	SET: BANPU (Thailand)	4.5%
Walter Energy	NYSE: WLT	3.3%
Alpha Natural Resources	NYSE: ANR	3.2%

The ETF holds dozens of other international coal companies as a lesser percentage of its total assets. Because each company must derive at least 50 percent of its revenue from coal, this fund is probably the easiest and most diversified way to play the sector.

Investing in Coal Futures

You can trade coal futures on the New York Mercantile Exchange (NYMEX). NYMEX coal futures are quoted in dollars and cents per ton, and are traded in contracts of 1550 tons. The coal futures contract tracks the price of the high-quality Central Appalachian coal (CAPP), or *Big Sandy* as it's known in the pits because of the terminals where it's delivered at the confluence of the Big Sandy and Ohio rivers.

Consumers and producers of coal use futures to manage coal price risk. Coal producers need to know that at the end of the year they'll make money, even if the price of coal takes a dive. By using futures, they can lock in their sell price by using what's known as a short hedge. If you're a utility that uses coal, you can lock in the price by using a long hedge. This way, utilities know their fuel costs for the year and can budget accordingly despite the fluctuations in coal prices.

Coal futures are also traded by speculators who assume the price risk that hedgers try to avoid in return for a chance to profit from favorable coal price movement. Traders buy coal futures when they believe that coal prices will go up. On the other side, traders sell coal futures when they think that coal prices will drop.

The coal futures contract trades under the ticker symbol QL, and you can buy and sell for every month going out three years. That said, it's not for the little guy. Coal futures are traded by the companies that have a significant interest in the price of coal. The futures are used as a means of trade between these companies and are moved in large blocks requiring a great deal of capital. The initial margin for trading coal futures is 16 percent of the contract, which at early 2013 prices of $57 per ton equates to more than $14,000.

No major indexes are designed to track coal's price as a commodity because there are so many different types of coal to track. To quickly check coal prices, go to one of these websites:

✔ www.cmegroup.com/trading/energy

✔ www.eia.gov/coal/nymex

Part IV
The Nuclear Option

Coal Prices, 1949-2011 (Dollars per Short Ton), Bituminous Coal Real

US Dollars
per tonne

Real

In this part . . .

- ✔ Understand nuclear energy fundamentals, such as how much electricity it produces, where the reactors are, and how much it costs.

- ✔ See the many sides of the nuclear safety debate.

- ✔ Get to know some uranium basics, including its fuel cycle, reserve figures, and how it's mined.

- ✔ Invest in nuclear energy via uranium and reactor companies, funds, and futures.

Chapter 14

Nuclear Energy Basics

· ·

· ·

Nothing is as cosmically cool as nuclear power. Just step back and revel in the fact that human beings split the atom and unleashed the power of the universe. The fact that this power could both destroy and create is the perfect metaphor for the most basic primordial myths. As Hindus will tell you, Kali the destroyer is also Bhavatarini the redeemer. So too is nuclear energy a destroyer and creator.

I had an early and odd association with nuclear energy as a child of the 1970s. My father worked as an engineer on a nuclear submarine in the U.S. Navy. He worked for Admiral Hyman G. Rickover, the first man who put nuclear reactors on ships — an insane idea if you think about it.

Anyway, my father would come home and put his stuff on the table in the hallway. One of his mysterious items of adulthood was a black, bullet shaped item that clipped to his belt. This item was to measure radiation, he told me. Every week he turned it in and they told him whether it was safe to continue to work. Needless to say, I learned at an early age about the power and risks of nuclear energy.

In this chapter, I cover the basics of nuclear power, including how much of the world's power is derived from nuclear energy, what countries have reactors, as well as where the growth is coming from. This information will lay the groundwork for you to start profiting from nuclear power investments, and you will have plenty of opportunities to invest in this growing field.

Nuclear Fundamentals

The world's demand for energy continues to climb, and all expectations are that it will continue this upward trajectory in demand for decades to come, as you can see in Figure 14-1. Currently, fossil fuels meet some 90 percent of that demand.

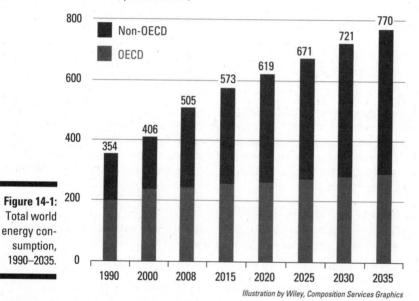

World Energy Consumption, 1990-2035
(quadrillion Btu)

- Non-OECD
- OECD

800 — 770
671 721
619
573
505
406
354
600
400
200
0
1990 2000 2008 2015 2020 2025 2030 2035

Figure 14-1: Total world energy consumption, 1990–2035.

Illustration by Wiley, Composition Services Graphics

Not only will energy demand grow nearly 50 percent by 2035 but the growth will also come from countries outside the Organisation for Economic Co-operation and Development (OECD), which are more commonly known as emerging markets.

For a number of reasons — including political, environmental, and high oil prices — a large portion of energy demand growth will have to be met by sources other than fossil fuels. There has been a strong push for alternatives such as wind and solar, which are covered in Part V of this book. But nuclear energy is still a go-to source of baseload capacity without the emissions associated with carbon-based fuels.

The most common form of nuclear reaction used for power generation is nuclear fission. This process splits the atom into parts. In fission, the mass of total resulting parts is less than the starting mass. In other words, mass is lost due to the creation of heat and radiation, which produces a great deal of energy that can be transformed into electricity. Heat boils water, which creates steam that spins a turbine to make electricity.

Fission produces neutrons that are captured by other atoms in a chain reaction. When the reaction reaches critical mass, it becomes a self-sustaining phenomenon. The risk is that too many neutrons are created, and the reaction gets out of hand. Then you have what's technically known as an explosion. Engineers solved this problem by mixing in control rods with the fuel rods to absorb the extra neutrons. Uranium-235 is the most commonly used nuclear fuel for this process.

The second type of reactor is a fusion reactor. This system uses two light elements like tritium and deuterium. These elements are fused and form helium and a neutron. This reaction is the same reaction used by the sun and other stars. The downside of fusion is that it produces less heat. The upside is that the components are more abundant and cheaper than uranium. But as of yet, fusion hasn't been developed enough to use as a reliable source of nuclear energy.

Percent of electricity generation

Nuclear energy is used primarily for electricity. As with coal, nuclear demand is growing as people in places such as China and India want modern conveniences like turning the lights on and running the dishwasher. In Malaysia, for example, the total number of households with television sets is expected to rise by more than 30 percent over the next ten years as the electric grid expands.

For the past 50 years, the three cornerstones of electricity production have been fossil, hydro, and nuclear. Nuclear power is growing — not only overall but also as a percentage of the electricity fuel source. According to the Nuclear Energy Institute, 31 countries worldwide are operating 437 nuclear reactors for electricity generation, and 71 nuclear plants are now under construction in 14 countries.

Nuclear energy produced at least 12.3 percent of global electricity needs in 2011 (I've seen estimates as high as 17 percent). Thirty countries currently use nuclear power, but only three of them — France, Slovakia, and Belgium — use nuclear as the prime source of electricity. Thirteen countries rely on nuclear energy to supply at least 30 percent of their total electricity. I list the countries that are most dependent on nuclear power in Table 14-1.

Table 14-1	Countries That Are Most Reliant on Nuclear Energy
Country	*Percent of Generated Electricity, 2011*
France	77.7%
Slovakia	54.0%
Belgium	54.0%
Ukraine	47.2%
Hungary	43.3%
Slovenia	41.7%
Switzerland	40.9%
Sweden	39.6%
South Korea	34.6%
Armenia	33.2%
Czech Republic	33.0%
Bulgaria	32.6%
Finland	31.6%

Countries with reactors

While 31 countries have reactors, the bulk of nuclear electricity is generated in the United States, France, and Japan. These are also the countries with the most sound nuclear investment opportunities, which I cover in Chapter 16. Companies based in these countries — like GE, Areva, and Hitachi — also provide planning and construction for many nuclear reactors in other countries. South Korea, through the Korea Electric Power Corporation (NYSE: KEP), is expanding its domestic nuclear capacity and beginning to win contracts in other countries.

Just because a country has a nuclear reactor doesn't mean there's an investment opportunity. Most of Russia's reactors, for example, are built by state-owned companies like Rosenergoatom, in which you can't invest. And Sweden's reactors were built by Westinghouse and the General Swedish Electric Company, which only exist today as units of Toshiba and ABB, respectively.

Table 14-2 lists the countries that consume the most nuclear electricity, along with the world total. The thermal power produced by reactors to make steam is calculated as megawatt thermal (MW(t)), while the electricity created by that steam is measured in megawatt electrical (MW(e)). You can determine which countries are most efficient at producing nuclear electricity by dividing the MW(e) by the number of units they have. By this measure, the French and Germans are most efficient at generating nuclear power.

Table 14-2	Ten Largest Consumers of Nuclear Power	
Country	*Number of Units*	*Total MW(e)*
United States	109	99,784
France	56	58,493
Japan	59	38,875
Germany	21	22,657
Russian Federation	29	19,843
Canada	22	15,755
Ukraine	15	12,679
United Kingdom	12	11,720
Sweden	12	10,002
South Korea	10	8,170
Total	345	297,978
World	432	340,347

Globally, 167 nuclear reactors have been planned, and another 317 have been proposed. These numbers are high historically and point to countries making long-term plans to stably provide electricity as demand grows. Planned reactors alone indicate 40 percent growth in the nuclear industry, while proposed reactors would boost the industry by almost 75 percent.

Table 14-3 shows the countries with the highest nuclear ambitions, including the number of reactors under construction, and the number planned and proposed. Planned reactors already have approval or funding, and are expected to come online in eight to ten years. Proposed reactors have reactor and site proposals and are expected to come online within 15 years.

China's plan to have 60 GW of nuclear capacity by 2020 would make it the second largest nuclear market in today's terms. Its plan to have 200 GW by 2030 and 400 GW by 2050 would make it by far the largest in the world. The nuclear expansion plans of South Korea and India would make those countries top five nuclear energy producers.

The number of planned and proposed reactors becomes more important when I get into uranium investments in Chapter 16, as the countries with the most new reactors will require the most uranium.

Table 14-3	Countries with Highest Nuclear Ambitions			
Country	Operable Reactors	Reactors Under Construction	Planned Reactors	Proposed Reactors
China	17	29	51	120
France	58	1	1	1
India	20	7	18	29
Japan	50	3	9	3
South Korea	23	4	5	0
Russia	33	10	17	20
Saudi Arabia	0	0	0	16
Ukraine	15	0	2	11
UAE	0	1	3	10
United States	103	3	11	13

The United States and Russia are making significant additions, but most new reactors that are planned or on order are in Asia and the Middle East. The plans of countries like Saudi Arabia are pretty transparent: They want to produce nuclear electricity at home instead of burning precious oil that can be exported.

Constant Debate

Many people have written many words about the benefits and costs of employing nuclear energy for both civilian and military purposes. Those of a certain age can remember the battle of the "No Nukes" versus "Know Nukes" bumper stickers. Although there aren't many picket lines in front of nuclear power plants anymore, the debates of safety versus community benefits and no greenhouse gas emissions versus radioactive waste continue unabated.

The people who are in favor of nuclear energy argue that it's a sustainable energy source that reduces greenhouse emissions and can increase energy security by reducing dependence on oil from the Middle East. This "Know Nukes" crowd cites the fact that nuclear power plants produce virtually no emission in contrast to coal- or oil-based electricity.

For many countries that must import hydrocarbons — like France, Japan, and China — nuclear power is the only means to achieve energy independence. Nuclear proponents go on to argue that the safety record is strong, new technology limits risk, and that the perils of storing waste are small and can be further reduced with the proper engineering.

There have been more than 14,000 cumulative reactor years from nuclear power plant operation. A reactor year is the total number of reactors multiplied by the total years they've been in operation. During this time, only three major reactor accidents have occurred, with fewer deaths than associated with other forms of electricity production on a per unit of electricity produced basis.

The three major reactor accidents that have occurred are as follows:

- ✔ Three Mile Island was contained without harm after a partial meltdown occurred in 1979. Despite no deaths and no cancer links, it is considered the worst nuclear accident in U.S. history because of the uncertainty it caused and the decision to release 40,000 gallons of radioactive waste water into the Susquehanna River.

- ✔ In 1986, Chernobyl saw the destruction of the reactor by a steam explosion, which killed more than 35 people and had significant health and environmental consequences, but it was due to poor workmanship and low oversight.

- ✔ In 2011, the Fukushima Daiichi nuclear disaster was caused by an earthquake-induced tsunami coupled with ancient technology. Still, the three cores that melted down were contained. Despite media reports, no deaths were directly attributable to the nuclear power plant. Two workers drowned in the flooding.

Pro-nuclear groups point out that this accident rate compares favorably to accidents in other forms of energy production. Nuclear has few fatalities per unit of electricity generated than hydro, coal, or natural gas. In recent years, some high-profile environmentalists have switched over to pro-nuke as the lesser of evils due to its greenhouse gas benefits over hydrocarbons.

Opponents of nuclear power argue that it poses abundant threats to people and to the environment. There are obvious health risks related to radiation leaks, in addition to uranium mining, processing, and transport. They also point to the risks of nuclear weapons getting into the wrong hands, sabotage, and dirty-bombs, and the unresolved problem of what to do with the waste products.

They go on to point out that nuclear power plants are heavily engineered and complex machines in which many things can and do go wrong. The fact that China, with its reputation for shoddy workmanship, corruption, and abysmal environmental policies, is the largest builder of new power plants puts the safety of the technology and engineering into doubt.

Furthermore, this "No Nukes" faction claims that when the whole chain of nuclear power is considered, from mining to production to waste disposal, nuclear power isn't a low-carbon electricity source.

In addition to the safety debate, there is also the concern of hostile nations getting access to radioactive material. The Middle East gets less of its electricity from nuclear power than any other region (1.8 percent). But the UAE, Iran, Turkey, Jordan, and Saudi Arabia are considering nuclear power as they continue to use up their petroleum assets. An aggressive Iran has been refining uranium, which it claims is for peaceful electricity production, but the West fears it's for a nuclear weapon. The pursuit of nuclear energy in the Middle East has raised military concerns in Israel, the United States, and elsewhere.

This debate will likely continue forever. But the future of nuclear power is solid (see the following section for details). You can't put the genie back in the bottle. After Fukushima and the development of cheap natural gas, the drive to build new plants has diminished in Germany and Japan, yet remains strong in many other countries.

Avoiding greenhouse emissions

Five decades of increasing nuclear use has helped reduce carbon emissions worldwide. If people used coal to generate the amount of electricity produced by nuclear energy every year, the International Atomic Energy Agency estimates annual additional emissions of 1,600 million tonnes of carbon dioxide.

That means that without nuclear energy, global carbon emissions would be 8 percent higher every year than they are today.

Although the goal of most governments in developed nations is to reduce emissions from energy generation, the countries with the most nuclear in their portfolio are proving to have the easiest time doing so. France, Japan, India, South Korea, and Sweden have all reduced carbon dioxide emissions from energy by 30 percent over the past three decades. Countries without nuclear energy have seen only a 10 percent drop. As an investor, be sure to keep an eye out for nuclear as a possible solution to climate change.

Future Plans

The future of nuclear power in the world is one of growth, even if that growth is delayed due to the slowdown in the aftermath of the Fukushima disaster. Thirty countries worldwide are operating 437 nuclear reactors for electricity generation. This number is only 7 fewer than the record of 444 running reactors reached in 2002.

Since 2002, 26 units have been added, and 33 have been deactivated. The total number of gigawatts has increased, however, because more powerful plants replaced older, smaller units. Currently, 167 nuclear reactors have been planned, and another 317 have been proposed.

In 2011, before the Fukushima nuclear accident, the World Energy Outlook estimated that nuclear energy would increase by 90 percent by 2035. After Fukushima, this estimated growth number has dropped to a 60 percent increase. That said, as time passes and the newest generation of plants promise more safety, the fears caused by the Japanese disaster have diminished.

Despite new net nuclear capacity being added over the past few years, total electricity usage in the United States and Europe slowed down while emerging markets continued to outperform.

The cost of building a nuclear power plant has a much longer cycle than coal or natural gas because permits must be met, hearings are held, and funding must be made available. The tremendous upfront cost is amortized over the life of the power plant. These upfront costs have traditionally been guaranteed by governments.

Funding is the central factor when deciding whether a nuclear plant can be economically competitive. Because costs are fixed upfront, the price the utility can charge for electricity is of critical importance. In the now more common liberalized electricity markets, nuclear power becomes less attractive because price fluctuations in hydrocarbons can make power plants unprofitable over the short to medium term.

Costs vary by geography. In China, the cost of building a nuclear power plant is much less because of mass production and lower labor costs. For example, in April 2008, the U.S. company Georgia Power contracted two AP1000 reactors to be built at an estimated cost of $7,000 per kilowatt of electrical output. In 2010, the Chinese nuclear commission started 20 similar plants that will cost $1,000 per KWe.

Table 14-4 shows the relative cost of electricity production from non-carbon resources based on location and hypothetical interest rates for capital funding. As you can see, nuclear is more economic in most cases, which is bullish for future nuclear investments.

Table 14-4		Cost of Non-Carbon Electricity	
Technology	Region or Country	At 10% Discount Rate (Cents/kWh)	At 5% Discount Rate (Cents/kWh)
Nuclear	OECD Europe	8.3–13.7	5.0–8.2
Nuclear	China	4.4–5.5	3.0–3.6
Large hydroelectric	OECD Europe	14.0–45.9	7.4–23.1
Large hydroelectric	China: 3 Gorges	5.2	2.9
Onshore wind	OECD Europe	12.2–23.0	9.0–14.6
Onshore wind	China	7.2–12.6	5.1–8.9
Solar photovoltaic	OECD Europe	38.8–61.6	28.7–41.0
Solar Photovoltaic	China	18.7–28.3	12.3–18.6

Obviously, nuclear energy is cost competitive, but the future of nuclear power is still complicated and to be determined. As Yogi Berra once said, "It's tough to make predictions, especially about the future." Some countries are stepping back from nuclear while others are pushing forward.

In May 2011, Germany publicly stated that it will end nuclear power within 11 years. This statement was a big deal because Germany got 17 percent of its power from nuclear at that time. Japan has also announced plans to end its reliance on nuclear power within 20 years, despite still having planned and proposed reactors on the books. The Swiss also joined in, saying they would phase out their power plants as they reach the end of their life cycles in 2019 and 2034. As time passes and new leaders are elected, these projections may change.

China, on the other hand, has a different set of problems. Instead of fearing the possibility of an environmental disaster from nuclear energy, the country is currently undergoing an environmental disaster stemming from coal-burning power plants. China currently has 13 nuke plants in operation and another 20 under construction. Its last five-year plan called for 11.4 percent of its energy to come from nuclear by 2015. That said, China isn't immune to nuclear fear and it halted the issue of new building permits for almost two years. In December 2012, China ended this ban and started building again.

Other countries are also forging ahead. In March 2013, the UK approved a next generation plant to be built in Somerset. France recently invested more than a billion euros in R&D for its fourth generation nuclear power plants. India plans to build seven in the near future.

To stay up to date on nuclear basics, including prices, safety, and reactor plans, check in frequently with the World Nuclear Association at `http://world-nuclear.org`.

Chapter 15

Uranium in Your Cranium

*W*riting about uranium is exciting because at this particular time in the commodity cycle, uranium is undervalued to the point of being despised (a hated sector raises my contrarian spirits). Uranium is not only undervalued, but also due for a supply cut, which will take some 17 percent of the supply off the market in 2013. This supply cut is due to former Soviet nuclear bomb uranium going off the market.

Due to the Fukushima disaster in 2011 and the global recession, mines have been shuttered or delayed, which further cuts supply. At the same time, demand for uranium will continue to go up as new power plants go online. After the Fukushima nuclear power plant in Japan suffered a core meltdown, many people speculated that it would take ten years for the nuclear power industry to recover. I must admit that I was one of them. However, time has proven that this simply isn't the case.

The Japanese failure has fallen rapidly into the rearview mirror. It's old news. Yes, outdated reactors such as those in Germany will be shut down. But the foundation for new, fourth-generation reactors are being literally poured in places as varied as Saudi Arabia and Vietnam. The end of the nuclear weapon repurposing program, coupled with a major expansion of nuclear capacity in Asia, will lead to a surge in demand for uranium. Select uranium miners, the survivors, will be teed up to profit.

In this chapter, I discuss where uranium comes from, how much is left, how it's mined, and what to do with the waste products. Uranium investments are covered in Chapter 16.

Explaining Uranium

Uranium is used to produce nuclear power, bombs, and uranium glass. Depleted uranium is also used for hardened, armor-piercing tank shells.

Uranium can be formed naturally only in a supernova. The decay of uranium and other elements in the earth's mantle is thought to be the source of heat responsible for the movement of the earth's tectonic plates.

Uranium is a silvery-gray metallic chemical element with atomic number 92. It has the highest atomic weight of all naturally occurring elements. When refined, it's slightly softer than steel.

You can find uranium just about everywhere. It's a naturally occurring element that's found in small quantities in rocks, soil, and water, but these sources aren't viable for mining because the concentrations are too low. Instead, uranium is mined commercially from more concentrated sources found in underground mineral formations.

To find uranium, you first must find the ore, or the rock formations that have minerals containing graphite. More than 99 percent of naturally occurring uranium is uranium-238. But that isotope is not fissile, meaning it can't sustain the reaction needed to produce electricity. Less than 1 percent is uranium-235, which can sustain the chain reaction necessary for energy production. As a result, mined uranium must be enriched to increase the percentage of uranium-235 it contains.

Uranium is used to produce nuclear power, bombs, and uranium glass. Depleted uranium is also used for hardened, armor-piercing tank shells. After the nuclear bombing of Japan during World War II, a Cold War standoff led to the production of thousands of weapons containing highly enriched uranium by the United States and Soviet Union. I cover what happened to this uranium later in this chapter. In the civilian world, uranium is used to fuel nuclear-powered electric plants. One kilogram of uranium-235 can produce about 20 trillion joules of energy, or as much as 1,500 tonnes of coal.

The steps in the process (discovering, mining, and enriching) are where the investment opportunities in the uranium market can be found.

Circling around the uranium fuel cycle

The production of fuel to generate nuclear energy consists of multiple industrial processes that mine, refine, and supply uranium. And it all starts with ore. Though uranium is an abundant element, found in a number of countries around the world, it exists in low concentrations and requires a great deal of refining upgrades before it can be used as a power source. As a bonus, spent fuel removed from a reactor after reaching the end of its profitable life can be processed again into new fuel. This reused uranium accounts for about 30 percent of energy production in a nuclear power plant.

All these systems or processes taken together are called the *nuclear fuel cycle,* beginning with mining exploration and ending with the handling of nuclear waste. Each step adds to the cost of nuclear power generation; those steps include the following:

- ✔ **Mining:** Extracting the uranium ore from underground sources.

- ✔ **Milling:** Crushing the ore and leaching out the uranium with chemicals to produce "yellow cake."

- ✔ **Conversion:** Turning the yellow cake into pure uranium gas, which is then pressurized and cooled into liquid, and then further cooled into a solid compound that must be enriched.

- ✔ **Enrichment:** Concentrating the percentage of uranium-235 by removing other isotopes.

- ✔ **Fuel fabrication:** Turning the enriched uranium back into a gas that is processed into a powder, pressed into pellets, and loaded into tubes called fuel rods.

In the industry, this series of steps is known as of the front end of the fuel cycle. The cost of uranium accounts for 40 percent of the nuclear fuel cycle. Uranium prices are also the most variable, with milling, conversion, enrichment, and fuel fabrication costs being relatively fixed. As a result, you want to invest in uranium miners when the price is high and companies involved in the steps when the price is so, since their margins will be higher.

Nuclear fission

Civilians use nuclear power to generate electricity. Electricity is generated by heating water until it turns to steam. This steam rises and pushes a fan or turbine, which in turn generates electricity.

In a nuclear power plant, the water is heated though a process known as *nuclear fission,* in which atoms (the basic building block of matter) are split in two. This split releases a tremendous amount of energy without the need to combust a fuel.

With growing pressure to reduce emissions thought to cause climate change, nuclear energy could find new love from former foes. Despite a few headline-grabbing incidents, nuclear actually has a pretty safe track record. And more than a few environmentalists have now come to embrace nuclear over coal, which could translate into profits as the world decides how to fuel its future.

Uranium is used for roughly three years as an active fuel source. After that, the remaining fuel may be reprocessed and recycled for further use, or put in storage. This phase is called the *back end* of the fuel cycle. Flip to Chapter 16 to read about the investment opportunities in each of these steps. Figure 15-1 shows the nuclear fuel cycle necessary to produce the 30 tonnes of material required to run a typical 1 gigawatt power plant for one year. You can use this information to visualize the fuel cycle, figure out how much uranium new plants will require, and determine how much usable product a mine has based on its resource estimate.

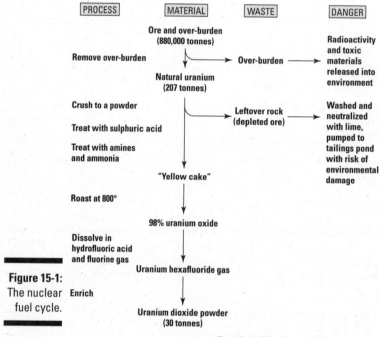

Figure 15-1:
The nuclear
fuel cycle.

Illustration by Wiley, Composition Services Graphics

Gathering information on reserves and production

Although uranium is found in every country on earth, it isn't found in mine-able concentrations. And luckily for anyone who's worried about nuclear proliferation, most of the concentrations are located in friendly nations. Australia leads the list in known reserves, but Kazakhstan leads the world in production. Table 15-1 shows the top ten global countries in terms of uranium reserves.

Table 15-1	Top Ten Countries for Known Uranium Reserves, 2011	
Country	*Tonnes*	*Percent of Global Reserves*
Australia	1,661,000	31%
Kazakhstan	629,000	12%
Russia	487,200	9%
Canada	468,700	9%
Niger	421,000	8%
South Africa	279,100	5%
Brazil	276,700	5%
Namibia	261,000	5%
United States	207,400	4%
China	166,100	3%

Turning Russian warheads into fuel

In the 1990s, after the Cold War ended and nuclear weapons stockpiles were decreased in both the United States and Russia, a deal was struck to turn this highly enriched uranium into fuel for nuclear reactors.

It was a true swords-into-plowshares moment, as military uranium was converted to civilian use through a program called Megatons to Megawatts. Since that time, 50 percent of U.S. uranium demand has been met from Russian military reserves. Globally, around 17 percent of nuclear fuel has been provided from the same supply. Weapons-grade uranium is too pure for civilian power plants and must first be diluted with depleted uranium by three to four percent.

After the Soviet Union fell and the Cold War ended, a large supply of unsecured highly-enriched uranium was still in Russia. This deal reduced the chances of this material being sold to terrorists on the black market.

Russia now sells this fuel for use in U.S. power plants. USEC (NYSE: USU), through its subsidiary, the United States Enrichment Corporation, and Russia's Techsnabexport (TENEX) were the principal parties. USEC agreed to buy 500 tonnes of weapons-grade uranium at a rate of 20 tonnes per year starting in 1999. This supply has put a near-11,000-tonne-per-year overhang on the uranium market, but the agreement comes to an end in 2013, which could be a boon for uranium miners when they fill the gap.

USEC stock is now trading as a penny stock because its main business is coming to an end. Figure 15-2 is the five-year USEC Price Chart. It's not pretty, and I wouldn't recommend you buying it. Instead, check out the miners I discuss in Chapter 16.

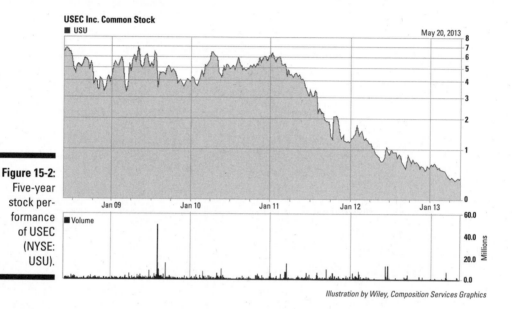

Figure 15-2:
Five-year
stock per-
formance
of USEC
(NYSE:
USU).

Illustration by Wiley, Composition Services Graphics

Mining Uranium

The two types of uranium mining are as follows:

- **Excavation:** Excavation may be further broken down into *open pit* and *underground* mining.

  - **Open pit mining:** The open pit mining technique is used when the ore is located close to the surface and is dug out by using large cranes and dump trucks. Underground mining is used when the deposit is 120 meters or more below the surface, and it requires building tunnels and shafts.

    The negatives of open pit mining are that it moves large amounts of material. A lot of earth must be dug out to get to a relatively small amount of usable uranium. Open pit mining leaves long-lasting scars on the landscape as well as highly toxic tailings, which is the radioactive sludge remaining after the ore is crushed and the uranium is removed.

Obviously, people living near new uranium mines don't want them. This problem is a large barrier to entry in western democratic countries like the United States, Australia, and Canada. The not-in-my-backyard (NIMBY) philosophy means that new mines can't be started quickly even with a spike in the uranium price.

- **Underground mining:** Underground mines leave less of a footprint, and the quantity of material that must be removed to access the ore is considerably less than in the case of an open pit mine. But they cost more than open pit mining and require safety precautions such as increased ventilation to protect against airborne radiation.

✔ **In situ:** The future of uranium mining will see an increase in the use of the *in situ leach mining* technique. This process uses oxygenated groundwater that's circulated through a porous underground ore body to dissolve the uranium oxide and bring it to the surface. In situ leaching uses acidic or alkaline solutions to keep the uranium in liquid form. The uranium oxide is then recovered from the solution. This process historically has taken place in a conventional mill, which consolidates the process and saves costs.

The Cigar Lake Mine disaster spikes uranium prices

The world's second largest undeveloped, high-grade uranium deposit is Cigar Lake in Saskatchewan, Canada. Cigar Lake, operated by Cameco Corp. (TSX: CCO), holds 537,100 tonnes of U3O8 at a grade of 17 percent, compared to the world average grade of 1 percent. It's the proverbial mother lode.

Production from Cigar Lake was scheduled to begin in early 2007. At its peak, Cigar Lake was supposed to provide 17 percent of the world's uranium supply.

Full-scale construction on Cigar Lake started back in the boom-boom commodity days of 2005. Production was geared up for a 2007 launch — and then disaster struck.

In 2006, bitter cold water flowed into the mines, shutting down all operations. After expensive repairs, bailing, and redigging, a second flood hit in 2008 and again shut down operations. The frozen wilds of Canada weren't to be easily tamed. Repairs continued and were successfully completed in 2010. But production has been delayed multiple times and is now slated for 2013.

I was lucky enough to be investing in uranium in 2006. The Cigar Lake Mine flood was the final catalyst that pushed the uranium spot price to a high of $137 per pound up from $20 in 2000. Many uranium miners share prices went up 1,000 percent. It was a lot of fun. Today, the spot price of uranium is below $75, and many of those boom-time miners are now out of business.

Mulling over milling, enrichment, and fuel fabrication

Milling generally occurs at the site of the mine. This process extracts the uranium from the ore by crushing it and turning it into a slurry by adding water. The uranium is dissolved from the solution with sulfuric acid. Milling produces a uranium oxide concentrate commonly called *yellowcake,* which is 70 percent to 90 percent triuranium oxide, or U_3O_8. After drying, it's heated and packed in 200-liter drums for shipping. The highly toxic waste product is then isolated and put back into a former mine along with the tailings, and the mine is sealed.

The uranium is further refined at an enrichment facility, where the proportion of the U-235 isotope is upgraded from below 1 percent to between 3.5 and 5 percent. The enriched uranium is then converted into a powder, pressed into pellets, and inserted in metal tubes to become fuel rods. It takes a couple hundred of these fuel rods to make up a reactor core. One-third of the spent fuel is removed every 12 to 18 months and replaced with fresh fuel.

One tonne of natural uranium produces 44 million kilowatt-hours of electricity. This is equal to 20,000 tonnes of black coal or 8.5 million cubic meters of natural gas.

Poring over uranium production figures

Here are a few things to remember about uranium production:

- Two-thirds of the world's production of uranium comes from mines in Kazakhstan, Canada, and Australia.

- More and more uranium production is coming from in situ leaching, which represents 45 percent of all production.

- Uranium mine production now meets about 85 percent of demand for electrical power plants.

You'll usually want to invest in companies that operate in locations with a history of successful uranium production, since the infrastructure and regulatory framework is already in place. Increasingly, you'll also want to look for companies that are pursuing in situ techniques, since this type of mining is quickly gaining market share.

Table 15-2 shows a list of the ten countries with the largest production in 2010 and 2011.

Table 15-2	Top Uranium-Producing Countries, 2010 and 2011	
Country	**2010 (Tonnes U)**	**2011 (Tonnes U)**
Kazakhstan	17,803	19,451
Canada	9,783	9,145
Australia	5,900	5,983
Niger	4,198	4,351
Namibia	4,496	3,258
Uzbekistan	2,874	3,000
Russia	3,562	2,993
United States	1,660	1,537
China	1,350	1,500
Ukraine	850	890

Lately, the makeup and processing of mines has been changing. Twenty-five years ago, more than half of global production came from underground mines. Underground mines now make up only 30 percent of the total, while in situ leach mining has increased its market share to 46 percent, led by Kazakhstan.

In 2011, in situ production was the most dominant uranium mining method. Judging from its quick ascension, in situ uranium mining will soon account for at least half of annual uranium and likely much more. The trend, which you can see in Table 15-3, is a preview of what's to come and an indication that you should look for companies using and perfecting this technique.

Table 15-3	Distribution of Various Uranium Mine Types, 2011	
Method	**Tonnes**	**Percent of Production**
Conventional underground	16,059	30%
Conventional open pit	9,268	17%
In situ leach (ISL)	25,296	46%
Byproduct	3,987	7%

Kazakhstan was the primary source of Soviet era uranium. As you can see in Table 15-4, it remains one of the largest uranium producers in the world. The table also shows top mines that are in other counties. You can use this information to determine whether a prospective investment is exploring or operating near an already successful mine.

Table 15-4		Top Ten Uranium Mines in the World			
Mine	**Country**	**Main Owner**	**Type**	**Production (Tonnes)**	**% of World**
McArthur River	Canada	Cameco	Underground	7,686	14%
Olympic Dam	Australia	BHP Billiton	Underground	3,353	6%
Arlit	Niger	Somair/Areva	Open pit	2,726	5%
Tortkuduk	Kazakhstan	Katco JV/ Areva	In situ	2,608	5%
Ranger	Australia	ERA (Rio Tinto 68%)	Open pit	2,240	4%
Krasnokamensk	Russia	ARMZ	Underground	2,191	4%
Budenovskoye 2	Kazakhstan	Karatau JV/ Kazatomprom-Uranium One	In situ	2,175	4%
Rossing	Namibia	Rio Tinto (69%)	Open pit	1,822	3%
Inkai	Kazakhstan	Inkai JV/ Cameco	In situ	1,602	3%
South Inkai	Kazakhstan	Betpak Dala JV/ Uranium One	In situ	1,548	3%
Top ten total				27,951	51%

Mines provide about 85 percent of global uranium demand. The remainder is made up of Soviet-era weapons-grade uranium. This supply will come to an end in 2013. The World Nuclear Association projects that world uranium demand will be about 72,680 tonnes in 2015, and most of this supply will need to come directly from mines (in 2010, 22 percent came from secondary sources). A uranium supply shortfall is projected, going forward to 2030. Figure 15-3 shows the uranium supply/demand curve.

Looking ahead to new mines

Understanding this shortfall in supply, many countries started planning new mines. Table 15-5 shows some of the new mines that are expected to reach substantial production over the next few years.

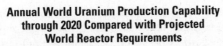

**Annual World Uranium Production Capability
through 2020 Compared with Projected
World Reactor Requirements**

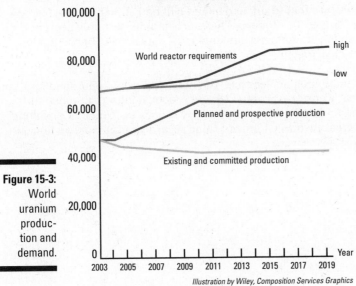

Figure 15-3:
World
uranium
produc-
tion and
demand.

Illustration by Wiley, Composition Services Graphics

Table 15-5	Expected New Uranium Mines	
Mine Name	**Country**	**Expected Start Date**
Four Mile	Australia	2013
Cigar Lake	Canada	2013
Imouraren	Niger	2014
Husab	Namibia	2014
Valencia	Namibia	2015
Omahola	Namibia	2015
Trekkopje	Namibia	2017
Morocco (phosphate byproduct)	Morocco	2017
Dornod	Mongolia	2018

Time will tell whether these start date projections are met. And even if they are met, it won't be enough. Estimated future production from existing mines plus new mines won't be sufficient to meet demand requirements. In 2030, projections are that uranium demand will be 137,000 tonnes, but production will be only 97,000 tonnes. These projections certainly present a bullish scenario for uranium investments in all categories of production, from mining to enrichment.

For more information on nuclear fuel, the Energy Information Administration (EIA) has a great website with detailed and practical information on this sector. You can find it at www.eia.doe.gov/nuclear. The Ux Consulting Company is a great resource for everything regarding uranium and nuclear power. Its website is www.uxc.com.

Chapter 16

Harnessing Nuclear Power for Profit

. . . .

In This Chapter

▶ Trading uranium as a commodity

▶ Investing in uranium companies

▶ Putting your money in power plants and utility firms

▶ Discovering nuclear funds and indexes

. . . .

The nuclear industry has several moving parts. Uranium fuel must be explored for, mined, and refined. Nuclear reactors must be built. And spent fuel must be dealt with. Each of these stages has investable opportunities, all of which are covered in this chapter.

Investing in Uranium

Like all the energy fuels covered so far in this book — oil, gas, and coal — uranium can be traded as a commodity. Uranium, though, is primarily used for one thing, as opposed to the many end uses for other energy commodities. As such, its price is determined by the balance of supply and demand in the nuclear fuel market.

Uranium is a metal whose price is determined by its primary use as fuel for nuclear power plants. When investing in uranium as a commodity, keep in mind that

✔ The uranium price is dictated by long-term private contracts between suppliers and utilities.

✔ Uranium is a commodity, and like all commodities, it has a history of volatility.

✔ Longer-term uranium prices move with the slower-changing philosophy of green movements.

✔ Spikes and busts are driven by geopolitical black swan events, such as the Cigar Lake mining flood and the Fukushima power plant meltdown in Japan.

Exchanges

Unlike other metals like copper or tin, uranium isn't traded on an organized commodity exchange, such as the London Metal Exchange. Historically, uranium prices were set through contracts negotiated directly between a buyer and a seller.

But in 2007, at the height of the uranium bubble, the New York Mercantile Exchange teamed up with Ux Consulting to create a futures contract that trades under the symbol UX. You can trade it on or off exchange in contracts of 250 pounds apiece. This exchange was created to offer a transparent price mechanism to miners, utilities, governments, and banks.

Individual investors can trade uranium futures, but given the volatility of pricing and the 250 pound minimum, which would be more than $10,000 at the 2013 uranium prices of more than $48 per pound, the risks outweigh the benefits.

Due to the small number of global producers and buyers of uranium and the heavily regulated nature of the market, the form of uranium supply contracts vary a great deal when they're negotiated without an exchange. A buyer can lock in a fixed price, have prices based on points in the mining and milling process, or add in insurance based on economic corrections.

A nuclear power plant incurs high upfront costs based on long-term financing coupled with a 30- to 40-year life expectancy. Nuclear power plants can't be turned off and on based on the short-term fluctuations of uranium prices. Therefore, a utility seeks to ensure long-term supply at a fixed cost. Contracts traditionally specify a base price, such as the uranium spot price, and rules for escalation. In base-escalated contracts, the buyer and seller agree on a price that increases over the contract's life on the basis of an agreed-upon formula, which may take economic data points, such as gross domestic product (GDP) or inflation factors, into consideration.

Obviously, due to uranium's uniqueness, it differs from other commodities like gold and silver. You can't own physical uranium, for example, although a fund does exist that does the owning for you, which I cover later in this chapter.

The uranium sector is different in other ways. Utilities want low prices for their fuel, but they also want stability and guaranteed supply. So the market has evolved such that the buyer makes a purchase at various points in the supply cycle. The buyer may purchase enriched uranium, which is the end product, or buy the product underground, in the milling process, or in core form.

In this way, the utilities gain greater control over supply and lower the price for uranium. They also spread the contract out over multiple producers in case one runs into a supply problem and can't fulfill its contract. The suppliers also seek long-term commitments because mining is a cash-intensive business. As in any market, there are brokers and traders.

Markets and pricing

Two separate uranium marketplaces have developed in the world. The first is the one that operates in the Western world, made up of the Americas, Western Europe, and Australia.

The former Soviet Union, Eastern Europe, and China operate a second uranium market. The majority of uranium used by these former communist countries comes from within its own borders, most notably from Kazakhstan. This isn't set in stone, however, and uranium trade occurs between both groups.

Most companies in the industry, including major Canadian miner Cameco (NYSE: CCJ), say they track uranium prices based on data put out by independent market consultants like Ux Consulting and TradeTech. You can see these prices at www.uxc.com. Figure 16-1 shows the price of uranium going back to 1995.

Uranium prices reached an all-time low in 2001, at $7 per pound. This was a low period for all commodities. Oil, for example, traded at $12 per barrel. After the dot-com bust, the global economy was re-inflated, which produced a slow rise in the price of uranium up until a bubble formed around 2005. This was popularly known as the *commodity super cycle* and was fueled by robust growth in China and housing worldwide.

The bubble burst in 2007, with the price of uranium peaking around $137 per pound. This was the highest price in a quarter century. High prices during the bubble created new mines and restarted production in defunct mines.

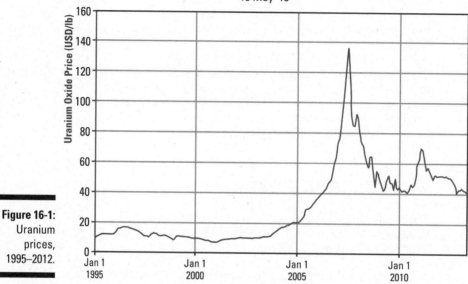

Uranium Oxide Price
40.70 USD/lb
13 May '13

Figure 16-1:
Uranium prices, 1995–2012.

Illustration by Wiley, Composition Services Graphics

Checking Out Uranium Mining Companies

The economic bust, coupled with the Fukushima disaster, restricted financing and shuttered many of the riskier uranium mines. Some strong candidates exist among the survivors. Table 16-1 shows the largest uranium producers by volume and percent of total in 2011.

Table 16-1	World Uranium Production by Producer, 2011	
Producer	**Tonnes U**	**Percent of World**
KazAtomProm	8,884	17%
AREVA (OTC: ARVCF)	8,790	16%
Cameco (NYSE: CCJ)	8,630	16%
Uranium One (TSX: UUU)	7,088	13%
Rio Tinto (NYSE: RIO)	4,061	8%
BHP Billiton (NYSE: BHP)	3,353	6%
Navoi Mining	3,000	5%
Paladin Energy (TSX: PDN)	2,282	4%

Not all the largest producers have access to the largest deposits of uranium, as you can see in Table 16-2, which shows the largest uranium companies by deposits.

Table 16-2	Largest Uranium Companies by Deposits
Company	*Reserves & Resources (Measured, Indicated, & Inferred) in Millions of Pounds*
Cameco (NYSE: CCJ)	1,007.6
Paladin Energy (TSX: PDN)	654.3
Rio Tinto (NYSE: RIO)	601.6
AngloGold Ashanti (NYSE: AU)	257.1
Berkeley Resources (OTC: BKLRF)	206.5

Two major uranium plays worthy of consideration are

✔ **Cameco (NYSE: CCJ):** This corporation operates as a uranium producer, supplier of conversion services, and fuel manufacturer. The company explores, mines, mills, buys, and sells uranium concentrate. It has working properties at McArthur River and Key Lake, Cigar Lake, and Rabbit Lake, located in Saskatchewan, Canada. It also has the Crow Butte property located in Nebraska and the Smith Ranch-Highland located in Wyoming. Its Inkai uranium deposit is located in Kazakhstan. The company's fuel services segment refines and fabricates uranium concentrate. Its products include uranium trioxide, uranium hexafluoride, and uranium dioxide. Cameco also operates four nuclear reactors. The company was founded in 1987 and is headquartered in Saskatoon, Canada. Cameco has a $7.3 billion market capitalization and a price to earnings ratio of 14. Revenue was $2.4 billion in 2012. The stock pays a 2.1 percent dividend.

✔ **Areva SA (OTC: ARVCF):** This French public multinational conglomerate, headquartered in Courbevoie, Paris, was founded in 1958. The company offers technological solutions for nuclear power generation and electricity transmission and distribution. It also manufactures nuclear measurement equipment and transportation safety systems, along with the recycling and reprocessing nuclear fuel. The company has a market capitalization of 4.3 million EUR and a price to earnings ratio of 14.9. Revenue grew 25 percent in the fourth quarter of 2012.

Rio Tinto and BHP Billiton aren't pure plays in the uranium sector but instead are vast mining conglomerates with interests across all metal sectors.

Many of the smaller miners have been wiped out by the great recession. Some are hanging on by a thread, though you could make the case for a high-risk high-reward investment. Two of these are Paladin Energy and Berkeley Resources:

- **Paladin Energy (TSX: PDN):** This company explores, produces, and sells uranium. It owns a 100 percent interest in the Langer Heinrich mine covering 4,375 hectares and located in the Namib Naukluft Desert in Namibia. The company also has 100 percent interests in the Kayelekera mine, located in Malawi, southern Africa; the Aurora project, located in Labrador, Canada; the Manyingee project, located in western Pilbara, western Australia; and the Oobagooma project, located in west Kimberley, western Australia. In addition, it holds a 91 percent interest in the Valhalla Skal & Odin deposits, located in Queensland, Australia; a 41.7 percent interest in the Bigrlyi deposit, located in Northern Territory, Australia; and a 50 percent interest in the Angela deposit, also located in Northern Territory, Australia. The company was founded in 1993 and is headquartered in Subiaco, Australia. Paladin Energy has a market capitalization of $690 million. Revenues were up 90 percent in the fourth quarter of 2012. Net income fell $246 million, however. The company has $104 million in cash and $817 million in debt. The stock price has fallen to $0.82 in 2013. With its high burn rate and low cash, it will have to dilute shares through a secondary offering, gain new financing, go bankrupt, or find a buyer for its assets.

- **Berkeley Resources (OTC: BKLRF):** Berkeley has a market capitalization of $53.8 million and revenue of just $2.2 million on negative earnings. It's too small to be considered as anything other than a possible buyout candidate.

Considering Uranium Waste and Reprocessing

In 2009, the Obama administration effectively ended the possibility that the United States could store its nuclear waste in Yucca Mountain, thus bringing an end to the much-debated and long-held plan. This action begged the question of what to do with spent nuclear material.

The current method of storing the radioactive material in concrete casks at nuclear power plants is widely considered a poor solution. For the record, only about 10 percent of each fuel rod is consumed before it's spent. It's possible to reprocess this unused fuel to cut down on waste and new uranium demand. That said, this method is very expensive (six times the cost of mined uranium) and has nasty problems associated with it. Just one example is that reprocessing uranium produces plutonium, which is a security concern. Plutonium is also used as mixed oxide nuclear fuel for thermal reactors.

Still, the nuclear power industry does recover fissile material from spent fuel for reuse in nuclear power plants. Several European countries, Russia, and Japan have policies to reprocess used nuclear fuel. This recycling can add up to 30 percent more energy from the same amount of uranium. Uranium security is increased, and high-level waste is reduced by about 20 percent. Furthermore, the radioactivity in the waste is smaller and diminishes more rapidly after 100 years than in non-reprocessed waste.

But there is lots of it. The uranium material available for recycling could run the U.S. reactor fleet for almost 30 years with no new uranium input.

As of May 2012, almost 90,000 tonnes of used fuel from commercial power reactors has been reprocessed. Reprocessing capacity has now reached 4,000 tonnes per year for uranium oxide fuels. According to the World Nuclear Association, between now and 2030, some 400,000 tonnes of used fuel is expected to be generated worldwide, including 60,000 tonnes in North America and 69,000 tonnes in Europe.

One potential play on nuclear cleanup is Jacobs Engineering Group Inc. (NYSE: JEC), a large engineering and consulting group based out of Pasadena, California. Founded in 1947, the company serves many needs in the environmental services space. Not a pure play on nuclear cleanup by any means, Jacobs provides consulting services related to scientific testing and analysis, as well as information technology. In other words, it's a large multinational that works with governments and other large multinationals in everything from chemicals and polymers to environmental cleanup to nuclear reprocessing. It has 200 offices worldwide and a market capitalization of $6.4 billion on $388 million in income. It has a price to earnings ratio of 13.2, $1.2 billion in cash, and only $518.2 million in debt. Revenue growth was 4.7 percent in the first quarter of 2013.

Getting a Reaction: Investing in Nuclear Power Plants

More than 60 nuclear reactors were under construction during the first half of 2013. Uranium demand is projected to grow by 3 percent annually through 2022.

Since the mid-1990s, about 18 percent of the global uranium supply has been provided by former Russian warheads being sold to the United States and converted for civilian use in electric power stations. This supply — which is equal to more than Cameco's *entire production* in 2012 — is now shrinking and will come off market by the end of 2013.

Furthermore, the delays of new projects due to the Fukushima disaster, which took one-fifth of demand off the market overnight, are ending. New power plants are being built in India, China, Vietnam, Saudi Arabia, the UK, and the United States, among other places.

The price of uranium is near decade lows — around $40 per pound. This unique circumstance sets up a possible supply shock when demand starts to pick up at the margins.

Since uranium is a highly regulated industry with a complicated supply chain, it can be a volatile, and therefore risky, investment. One way to avoid that risk would be to buy the companies that are building the power plants or to own the historically safe utility companies that operate them.

Nuclear construction plays

Because uranium is a highly regulated industry with a complicated supply chain, it can be a volatile, and therefore risky, investment. One way to avoid that risk is to buy the companies that are building the power plants or to own the historically safe utility companies that operate them.

✔ **Babcock & Wilcox (NYSE: BWC):** This company makes nuclear components for power and steam-using industries worldwide. Its Power Generation segment designs, engineers, manufactures, supplies, constructs, and services utility and industrial power generation systems. The company's Nuclear Operations segment manufactures naval nuclear reactors for the U.S. Department of Energy/National Nuclear Security Administration's Naval Nuclear Propulsion Program, which in turn supplies them to the U.S. Navy for use in submarines and aircraft carriers. The company also processes uranium and does environmental site restoration. The company's Nuclear Energy segment fabricates pressure vessels, reactors, steam generators, heat exchangers, and other auxiliary equipment. The company was founded in 1867 and is headquartered in Charlotte, North Carolina. BWC is a $3 billion company by market capitalization. It has a price to earnings ratio of 10.4. Revenue growth was 8.1 percent in the first quarter of 2013. The company has $472 million in cash and only $4.5 million in debt. The dividend yield is 1.2 percent. BWC is a solid company with a fair value, although it may not be the company you want to own in light of government attempts to reign in defense spending.

✔ **General Electric (NYSE: GE):** GE is one of the world's biggest conglomerates. It creates everything from light bulbs to mortgages to airplanes to oil rigs to locomotives to credit cards. Obviously, GE isn't a pure play on anything other than the general state of the economy. It does, however, make systems and hardware for nuclear power plants. GE is a $236 billion company with a price to earnings ratio of 12. Revenue grew 13.4 percent in the first quarter of 2013. The company pays a 3.3 percent dividend yield. GE is a solid company to have in any portfolio, nuclear or not.

✔ **Siemens (NYSE: SI):** This electronics and electrical engineering company operates in the energy, healthcare, industry, and infrastructure and cities sectors worldwide. Like GE, Siemens is a large multinational and not a pure play on nuclear power, but it does make products for the nuclear power industry. Siemens has a market capitalization of $85 billion with a price to earnings ratio of 10.4. In the first quarter of 2013, the company reported 1.5 percent revenue growth, but earnings fell 12.4 percent as financial problems across Europe escalated. The company pays a 2.8 percent dividend.

✔ **Toshiba (OTC: TOSBF):** This company makes and sells electronic products worldwide. It also has a division that makes power generation systems, including thermal, nuclear, hydro, and photovoltaic. Toshiba is a large multinational and not a pure play on nuclear. The company has a $23 billion market capitalization but no price to earnings ratio because it had no profit in 2012. Revenue declined 5.9 percent in the first quarter of 2013. The company has $2.8 billion in cash and is $19.6 billion in debt. Toshiba trades more on the basis of the Japanese yen than on any underlying nuclear fundamentals.

✔ **Hitachi (OTC: HTHIY):** This company manufactures and sells electronic and electrical products primarily in Asia, North America, and Europe. The company's Power Systems segment offers thermal, nuclear, hydroelectric, and wind power–generation systems. Hitachi has a market capitalization of $28 billion and a price to earnings ratio of 10. The company saw sales and revenue decrease in 2012. It has $7.8 billion in cash and $34 billion in debt.

Major nuclear utilities

In the United States, 103 nuclear reactors are running in 31 states. They're operated by 30 different utility companies. In Table 16-3, you can see the utilities that generate the largest portion of their electricity with nuclear power.

Table 16-3	Utilities with Largest Share of Nuclear Energy, 2011	
Company	Percent of Capacity from Nuclear	Nuclear Power Capacity (MW)
Exelon (NYSE: EXC)	67%	17,047
Entergy (NYSE: ETR)	33%	10,219
PG&E (NYSE: PCG)	31%	2,240
First Energy (NYSE: FE)	30%	3,991
PSEG (NYSE: PEG)	27%	3,661

The company most dependent on nuclear power in the United States is Exelon (NYSE: EXC). Nuclear power plants produce more than half of the electricity it sells. It operates 10 nuclear plants containing 17 reactors. Exelon is making a strong push for more nuclear generation, including starting a series of upgrades to its nuclear plants that are designed to increase power generation by 1,300 to 1,500 megawatts, equal to one new nuclear plant. The company has a market capitalization of $31 billion with a price to earnings ratio of 16 and quarterly revenue growth of 44 percent. Earnings, however, fell 37.6 percent in the first quarter of 2013. The company pays a high 5.8 percent dividend.

Outside the United States, Fortum (OTC: FOJCY) owns the Loviisa nuclear power plant in Finland, as well as shares in the Finnish Olkiluoto power plant and in the Swedish Oskarshamn and Forsmark nuclear power plants. The company has a $15.7 billion market capitalization and an attractive price to earnings ratio of 8.6. In 2013's first quarter, revenue was up 10 percent and earnings were up 43 percent. The company has a dividend yield of 7.6 percent.

Japan's policy-based comeback

The global financial crisis saw the Japanese currency rise, as the yen was looked at as a safe haven. This currency increase put tremendous pressure on Japanese exports. In 2013, new leaders in Japan are printing yen in an effort to force its value back down. This approach is working, and Japanese companies are now going up in dollar terms because their exports are now cheaper.

Nuclear Indexes and Funds

Besides miners and utilities, investors can profit from the nuclear industry by buying simple exchange-traded funds or mutual funds. These can track baskets of uranium companies, nuclear energy companies, or both. They include

- ✔ **Global X Uranium ETF (NYSE: URA):** This $140 million ETF is designed to track the price movements in shares of companies that are active in the uranium mining industry. This fund holds uranium stocks from all around the world. Its largest holding is Cameco (NYSE: CCJ), which accounts for 21 percent of the fund's assets. URA is a great way for investors to maintain diverse exposure to the uranium market while earning a 1.9 percent dividend yield.

- ✔ **iShares S&P Global Nuclear Energy Index Fund (NASDAQ: NUCL):** This is the lowest-cost ETF option for gaining exposure to the global nuclear energy industry, charging an expense ratio of just 0.48 percent. Major country allocations for NUCL include the United States (31 percent), Japan (15 percent), Canada (13 percent), and France (10 percent).

- ✔ **Market Vectors Nuclear Energy ETF (NYSE: NLR):** This fund's holdings include uranium miners, nuclear generation firms, and plant infrastructure companies from around the world. NLR has $75 million in assets and pays a 4.5 percent dividend yield. Daily volume is almost 30,000 shares, giving you much more liquidity than the iShares S&P fund.

According to the fact sheet provided by Standard & Poor's, its Global Nuclear Energy Index (Ticker: SPGTNE) tracks the 24 largest publicly traded companies in nuclear energy and related businesses. The index is equally divided among nuclear materials, equipment and services, and nuclear energy generation, with the United States, Japan, and Canada hosting 15 of the 24 companies it tracks.

The World Nuclear Association Nuclear Energy Index (Ticker: WNAI) describes itself as a benchmark for publicly traded stocks that are materially involved in the nuclear industry worldwide. The 56 companies it tracks have a total market capitalization of more than $775 billion, making it the most representative index of all parts of the global nuclear industry.

You can get full information about these indexes and the companies they track at www.standardandpoors.com and www.snetglobalindexes.com.

Part V
Investing in the Future: Modern Energy

Uranium Oxide Price
40.70 USD/lb
13 May '13

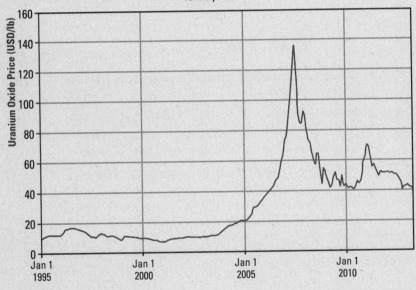

As the world's energy demands continue to grow, new investment opportunities will pop up in unexpected places. Check out www.dummies.com/extras/energy investing for an article on solar energy.

In this part . . .

- ✔ Get acquainted with various solar technologies and discover how to invest in each.

- ✔ See how wind energy is growing and which companies are benefiting the most.

- ✔ Learn about geothermal technologies and how to invest.

- ✔ Discover the future of transportation, including electric vehicles and biofuels.

- ✔ Invest in clean energy via companies, exchange-traded funds, and mutual funds.

Chapter 17

Solar Investing: It's Raining Electrons

In This Chapter

▶ Understanding solar market fundamentals

▶ Identifying the different types of solar technologies

▶ Evaluating solar investment opportunities

The sun gives the earth 970 trillion kilowatt-hours (kWh) of free energy every single day. This amount is more energy than the entire world uses from fossil fuels every year, and enough to supply the United States' demand for energy for a year and a half.

Of course, solar energy is only as good as the technologies used to harness it. This is why, when solar panels gained traction in the 1970s, the technology was still very expensive and very inefficient. But a lot has changed since the days of Jimmy Carter sweaters and bell-bottomed salesmen selling solar power systems in high-income California suburbs. Since the 1970s, technology has advanced dramatically, and costs have fallen so low that in some locations it's actually cheaper to power your home with solar than with conventional fossil fuel–based power generation.

As a result, solar is being installed at a record pace. In 2011, solar accounted for 0.5 percent of global electricity demand. Compare that to 2008, when it was barely an accounting error at 0.02 percent.

And this growth is set to continue well throughout the next couple of decades. By 2050, 22 percent of the world's power generation is expected to come from solar, according to the International Energy Agency. Clearly, this kind of steady and impressive growth is making the solar industry a very attractive one for investors.

In this chapter, I break down the fundamentals of the solar market and identify the various types of solar technologies — photovoltaics, solar heating
and cooling, and concentrating solar power. I also show you how to evaluate
the companies that manufacture these technologies, and even show you how
to invest in the solar industry without having to buy a single stock.

The Three Types of Solar Technology

Solar panels are what come to mind when you think about solar energy. But
the sun's light and heat are actually harvested in multiple ways, all of which
have investable opportunities. The three types of solar technologies in use
today are:

- ✔ Photovoltaics: Using a solar panel with a semiconductor material that
  converts sunlight into electricity
- ✔ Solar heating and cooling: Harnessing the sun's thermal energy to heat
  or cool buildings and water
- ✔ Concentrating solar power: Magnifying the sun's heat to boil water or oil
  for steam to generate electricity

Examining the photovoltaic solution

Of the three types of solar technologies in use today, the most common form
is photovoltaics, or PV for short.

PV is typically what you find on the roofs of homes, buildings, and parking
structures. The technology allows photons of light to be converted into electricity by a semiconductor, much like a computer chip.

Although the PV effect was actually discovered in 1839, the first PV device
capable of producing enough electricity wasn't developed until 1954. In 1958,
PV was tested in real-life situations, and the technology remained largely in
the research phase until the energy crisis of the 1970s.

Unfortunately, at the time, the technology was still very expensive to manufacture on a commercial scale, and the efficiencies of the technology were
quite low.

PV is often measured in terms of efficiency. No PV device can provide a 100
percent conversion of sunlight to electricity. And back in the 1970s, efficiencies of the actual solar cells were quite low. Hardly an economic endeavor

considering the price per watt back in the mid- to late-70s was around $80. By early 2013, it was down to around 70 cents. Figure 17-1 shows the downward trajectory of photovoltaic costs, which have fallen more than 99 percent since the late 1970s.

Price of Crystalline Silicon Photovoltaic Cells, $ per watt

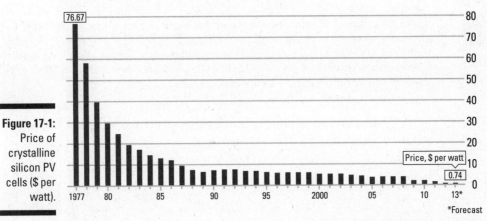

Figure 17-1: Price of crystalline silicon PV cells ($ per watt).

Illustration by Wiley, Composition Services Graphics

Part of this massive price drop is the direct result of advanced technologies and economies of scale. During the solar boom of the early 2000s, however, PV manufacturers were popping up left and right — and so were silicon suppliers.

Traditional PV modules require silicon. And with the run on PV manufacturing came a run on silicon supplies. In 2000, silicon was $9 per kilogram. But by early 2008, after silicon supplies were moving faster than ever just to keep pace with demand, the price got as high as $475 per kilogram.

As a result, silicon suppliers were expanding production in an effort to keep up with demand. But the timing couldn't have been worse.

A few months into 2008, the global economy imploded — right around the time fresh silicon supplies were being produced at record rates. After the global economic meltdown, demand for solar, along with pretty much everything else, fell off. And almost overnight, the PV industry was sitting on a major glut of product. By 2011, the spot price for silicon had fallen below $30 per kilogram.

Meanwhile, for PV manufacturers, margins were shrinking, factories were closing, consolidations were beginning to pick up, and investor sentiment turned bearish.

Governments around the world that once poured hundreds of millions of dollars into solar incentives were pulling back, exacerbating the demand shortfall. And in the United States, high-profile bankruptcies like Solyndra left a scar on the industry that made investors wary of all that they were told solar could offer.

Of course, the solar industry doesn't live and die by a company called Solyndra (see the sidebar later in this chapter for more info). And despite fewer government incentives — on a global scale — technologies continue to advance, production costs continue to fall, and demand continues to be quite impressive, despite continued economic uncertainty. Figure 17-2 shows the 6,700 percent growth in global solar installations between 2000 and 2013, and the 200 percent growth that's expected by 2020.

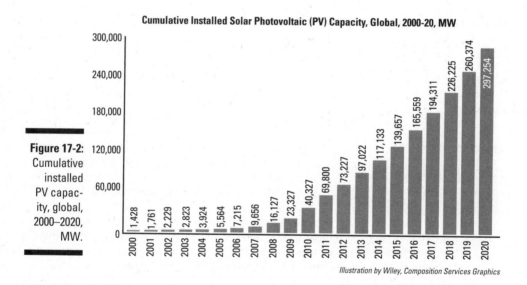

Cumulative Installed Solar Photovoltaic (PV) Capacity, Global, 2000-20, MW

Figure 17-2: Cumulative installed PV capacity, global, 2000–2020, MW.

Illustration by Wiley, Composition Services Graphics

Truth be told, the global economic meltdown that put the kibosh on the PV rush was actually a good thing for the long-term viability of the industry. It essentially cleared out the laggards, forced the industry to expedite cost reductions, and left only the strong to survive. Today, the result is a leaner, meaner solar industry that has both the technological prowess and capital to continue its ascent, leading well-diversified energy investors back to the solar space.

Evaluating solar photovoltaic companies

When trying to identify a quality PV company, look for the following:

- ✔ Technological advantages that offer long-term efficiency gains and the ability to consistently reduce production costs.

- ✔ Marketing flexibility that allows for quick transitions to regions that offer significant government incentives. That doesn't mean all regions lacking incentives are absent a PV market. A successful PV company, however, must be able to concentrate its marketing and sales efforts where PV support is strongest. Reliance on government incentives isn't a static strategy, because most countries will find PV costs competitive with coal, natural gas, and nuclear by around 2030 — without additional subsidies. But for at least the next eight to ten years, easy exposure to countries with strong government support offers PV manufacturers a somewhat stable market that can be counted on for a specific period of time.

- ✔ Quality management with experience in the energy space — not just solar.

- ✔ Minimal debt or at least the evidence that debt is being strategically eliminated in a safe and fiscally responsible manner.

- ✔ Access to capital that allows the company to expand and grow without diluting shareholder value.

Considering specific solar photovoltaic stocks

In this section I show you a list of the top six publicly-traded photovoltaic stocks based on market share. Four of these stocks are based in China.

Today, China is the largest manufacturer of PV, and is also the largest consumer. All these China-based companies, however, are dangerously reliant upon very generous subsidies from the Chinese government. If those subsidies disappear, it's very likely that many of these companies will consolidate or simply cease to exist. So the best way to monitor this situation — after all, this list is likely to change from year to year — is to pay close attention to analysts that have a long history of focusing on PV markets, like those who write for investment letters such as *Energy & Capital* (www.energyandcapital.com) and *Green Chip Stocks* (www.greenchipstocks.com). Here are the largest publicly-traded PV companies by market share:

- ✔ First Solar (NASDAQ: FSLR): U.S.-based

- ✔ Yingli Green Energy (NYSE: YGE): China-based

- ✔ Trina Solar (NYSE: TSL): China-based

- ✔ SunPower Corporation (NASDAQ: SPWR): U.S.-based

- ✔ Hanwha SolarOne (NASDAQ: HSOL): China-based

- ✔ JinkoSolar Holding Co. (NYSE: JKS): China-based

Why Solyndra failed

Solyndra will go down as one of the worst failures of the U.S. Energy Department loan guarantee programs. The company failed because it lacked a very important element of what makes a quality solar company: It had no technological advantage that offered long-term gains.

The company put all its eggs in one basket, betting on a technology called copper indium gallium selenide, or CIGS. It received a $535 million loan guarantee from the government to aid in its development.

From 2005, when the company was founded, through 2009 this seemed like a good idea since polysilicon prices had climbed so high.

CIGS was able to compete at that time. But in the wake of a global recession and a solar glut brought on my cheap Chinese panels, the price of polysilicon fell sharply, and CIGS was no longer competitive.

As a result, Solyndra had no way to compete, and no backup plan. It began announcing layoffs in late 2010 and filed for bankruptcy in August 2011.

Solyndra wasn't the only solar firm to fall in this manner, but it was the most highly publicized one and served to lessen the credibility of the entire industry.

Going thermal with solar heating and cooling

Solar heating and cooling mechanisms "collect" thermal energy provided by the sun. That energy is then used for a variety of things, such as space heating, cooling, hot water, and even providing heat for swimming pools.

Although solar heating and cooling isn't as well-known or popular as PV, it's actually quite efficient and affordable. In fact, the return on investment can be as fast as three years. Read on for some basics on the technology and thermal investments.

Knowing solar heating and cooling basics

The average life of a solar heating and cooling system is about 20 years — which means if you use a solar heating and cooling system for hot water, you could essentially end up getting about 17 years of "free" hot water. Minus the cost of the actual water, of course. And consider that conventional, non-solar water heaters tend to account for between 15 and 25 percent of the energy consumed by a family of four. So the economic advantages of solar heating and cooling can be quite impressive. And because this is a book about energy investing, it's worth noting that a solar heating and cooling system can actually be a very savvy investment.

The different types of solar heating and cooling technologies include:

- Flat plate
- Evacuated tube
- Thermosiphon
- Concentrating
- Integral collector storage

The two most common are flat plate collectors and evacuated tube collectors.

Flat plate collectors use copper pipes that attach to what's called an absorber plate. And evacuated tube collectors are built by using a series of glass tubes. It's called "evacuated" because air has been evacuated from the tubes. This process results in a very efficient heat insulator, which is necessary for the fluid that's used in the tube.

Making solar heating and cooling investments

There's only one publicly-traded pure play solar heating and cooling company. It's called Sunrain, and it trades only in Shanghai, under the symbol (SHA: 603366).

Some analysts suggest that if you want exposure to the solar heating and cooling space that you invest in the companies that supply things like aluminum tubes and specialty glass. Although this strategy does provide an indirect way to play the space, it's rarely enough to move the needle.

You can also look to a company like GE (NYSE: GE), which has invested in smaller solar thermal startups. But if you're looking for the most bang for your solar buck, your best bet will be with PV and concentrating solar (see the previous section for details on PV and the following section for more on concentrating solar).

 If you truly want to invest in solar heating and cooling, look into getting one installed in your own home. That could prove to be the wisest solar heating and cooling investment you can make.

Concentrating on concentrating solar power

Concentrating solar power, or CSP, is actually the oldest form of operational solar, tracing its roots back to the 1870s, when CSP systems were used to drive steam engines. These steam engines were often used to pump water. Of course, today's modern CSP plants are far more advanced than those 19th-century contraptions.

Using a series of specially designed lenses or mirrors, sunlight is concentrated to the point where temperatures get hot enough to drive turbines that create electricity. CSP plants are used primarily as utility-scale power plants. In other words, they generate enough power to send to the grid, just like a coal-fired, natural gas or nuclear power plant would.

The four types of CSP plants, all of which are very large and can occupy miles of land, are as follows:

- **Parabolic trough:** Uses curved mirrors that center the sun onto a receiver. This tube-like structure holds a transfer fluid that absorbs the heat and runs through a heat exchanger.

- **Power tower:** Uses flat mirrors that track the sun and focus the energy onto a receiver that sits on top of a very high tower. Power towers use a transfer fluid as a heat-trapping catalyst for the generation of power. The flat mirrors used in power tower projects are called *heliostats*.

- **Compact linear Fresnel reflector:** Somewhat of a combination of the parabolic trough and the power tower in that it uses flat mirrors that are lined up and tilted to utilize the principles of a trough system.

- **Dish engine:** Instead of relying on steam to move a turbine, like you see in the other three CSP technologies, dish engines use working fluids to drive an engine. The dishes are capable of tracking the sun because they aren't static and can rotate. The dishes themselves are covered in mirrors that, like the other three, focus the sun onto a receiver.

Although CSP does allow for "cheaper" solar power when you break it down to the price per kWh, continued growth is limited by such factors as cheap natural gas in the United States, availability of usable land within close distance of transmission and distribution, and the high upfront capital costs that often come with these types of projects.

That's not to say CSP projects aren't profitable. In fact, billionaire Warren Buffett has purchased a couple over the past few years and has indicated he could be looking for more. But at least in the United States, until natural gas prices get back up to around $6 per Mcf, it'll be hard to convince developers to begin construction on new CSP plants. You have a couple of ways to play CSP — the developers and the companies that produce CSP equipment and technology. These companies include:

✔ Abengoa (Pink Sheets: ABGOY)

✔ NextEra (NYSE: NEE)

✔ ABB (NYSE: ABB)

✔ Siemens (NYSE: SI)

✔ General Electric (NYSE: GE)

Abengoa is the most pure play in this space as it manufactures components of CSP systems, and develops and operates entire CSP installations. It is a world leader in the field, operating 631 megawatts of CSP plants in Europe, the United States, Africa, and Asia. NextEra is an electric utility that owns CSP assets, and is the largest producer of electricity from CSP in the United States. While ABB, Siemens, and GE all make CSP components, as global conglomerates this industry only accounts for a portion of their revenue.

The Future Is Organic: Organic Photovoltaics

Imagine spraying a clear solar film on your windows or covering your entire roof with a sort of solar plastic wrap. Or better yet, imagine covering your home with a solar paint. This scene isn't science fiction, my friend. It's potentially the future of solar.

Conventional solar cells rely on inorganic semiconductors — like silicon. But in a next-generation solar technology called *organic photovoltaics* (OPV), organic solar cells rely not on inorganic semiconductors, but instead on small, conductive carbon-based materials.

Now I'm not going to turn this into a big science lesson, because this is a book about energy investing, not chemistry. If, however, you want to read more about the science behind organic photovoltaics, you can check out a book that was released out of the University of Hong Kong called *Organic Solar Cells: Materials and Device Physics* (Springer).

For the sake of this book, just think of organic PV as a technology that essentially transforms large, bulky solar panels into easily manipulated structures that can be used in a variety of forms — from ultra-thin plastics to liquid sprays to multipurpose outdoor and indoor paint.

One of the advantages of OPV is that it can work with relatively low light. Even under the glow of a hanging chandelier, OPV can suck that light in and produce power. Other benefits of OPV include:

- **Cost:** OPV is very inexpensive to manufacture. The materials needed for the production of OPV are much cheaper than materials required for conventional PV.
- **Flexibility:** OPV materials are flexible and form-fitting.
- **Installation:** OPV can be installed on virtually any surface.

Of course, because OPV technology is still relatively new, there are also a number of disadvantages that researchers are working hard to overcome. These include:

- **Extremely low efficiencies:** OPV efficiencies hit a record of 12 percent in 2013, thereby making OPV incapable of competing with low-cost, conventional PV.
- **Degradation:** Prolonged exposure to sunlight results in rapid degradation.
- **Nascence:** Still very reliant upon research grants and subsidies to further advance the technology. As a young technology, it is still more expensive than other forms of solar, so costs must be brought down and economies of scale created before it can compete on a broad level.

No pure play OPV companies exist today. And if they did, they'd be extremely risky. However, some larger public companies have made significant OPV investments. These companies include:

- BASF (Pink Sheets: BASFY)
- DOW Chemical Company (NYSE: DOW)
- E.I. DuPont (NYSE: DD)

There's really not much here for investors, but it's important that you understand that this technology exists, and is being advanced. OPV potentially represents some very serious future competition for the leading PV manufacturers today. In fact, as OPV technology advances, it's likely that the major PV players will acquire much of this technology.

Installation Nation

While solar PV manufacturing maintains a steady pace, across the globe, especially in the United States, the installation market is booming.

With lower selling prices from the PV manufacturers, installers have been able to offer some pretty amazing deals to consumers. And through solar leasing programs, some installation companies are now pulling in hundreds of millions of dollars a year. Check out Figure 17-3 to see the forecast growth of photovoltaic installations through 2016 by region.

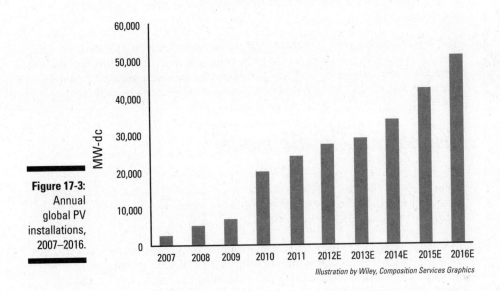

Annual Global PV Installations, 2007 - 2016E

Figure 17-3:
Annual global PV installations, 2007–2016.

Leasing profits

Solar leases haven't been around long, but they're proving to be wildly successful.

With a leasing model, a homeowner can lease a solar power system with little or no money down, reducing the electric bill while allowing the sun to produce much of the needed electricity. The leasing company takes care of pretty much everything: It covers the materials, panels, the installation, the inverters, the insurance, even cleaning and maintenance.

Solar leasing has really given the solar industry a shot of steroids. In fact, in 2011, solar leasing accounted for about 60 percent of residential installations in California — the hottest solar market in the United States. The leasing models have also proven to be quite profitable in Arizona, Hawaii, Maryland, Colorado, New York, and Pennsylvania.

The three largest companies that provide this leasing model are:

> ✔ SunRun
>
> ✔ Sungevity
>
> ✔ SolarCity (NASDAQ: SCTY)

The latter is a publicly-traded company in which regular investors can invest, and it doubled in value in the first six months following its initial public offering in late 2012.

The solar leasing model is certain to grow and develop going forward, and it's likely that some of the other installation companies that offer the solar leasing option will also go public. So keep an eye out for those companies, because the solar installation and solar leasing markets are extremely lucrative.

Trying the Mosaic model

Through the Mosaic model, New York and California residents can invest in solar projects that are installed on affordable housing apartments for low-income residents. These investments offer as much as a 4.5 percent annual return with terms of about nine years.

Mosaic launched in January 2013. Early funding opportunities sold out within 24 hours. So there's clearly a market for this type of solar investment. A few other solar crowdfunding operations are looking to launch over the next few years. Keep an eye on those opportunities, because they may prove to be some of the safest and steadiest gains available for solar investors. You can read more about how it works and how to invest at https://joinmosaic.com.

Chapter 18

When the Winds Change Direction

Wind can provide 5,800 quadrillion BTUs of energy every single year, which is roughly 15 times what today's world requires.

But like solar, wind energy is only as good as the technologies used to harness it. This is why, especially over the past few decades, wind turbine sizes and efficiencies have improved dramatically.

In fact, the largest single turbine in development today will be able to generate enough energy to power more than 5,700 European households. Compare that to the earliest uses of wind power back in 200 BCE, when it was used to pump water and grind grain in the Middle East and China.

In this chapter, I break down the fundamentals of the wind power market and identify the various types of wind power technologies. I also show you how to evaluate the companies that manufacture these technologies, and share with you some of the top wind power players in the industry.

The Rise of Wind: Evaluating Wind Turbine Manufacturing Companies

Today, more than 200,000 wind turbines generate power all across the globe.

In 2011, wind power accounted for more than 6 percent of new installed global energy capacity at 238 gigawatts. Compare that to the 6 gigawatts installed in 1996, which barely registered any meaningful contribution to global energy installations. Figure 18-1 shows global cumulative installed wind capacity between 1996 and 2012, in which time the market grew 4,530 percent. That's faster growth than any fossil-based energy source.

Figure 18-1:
Global cumulative installed wind capacity, 1996–2012.

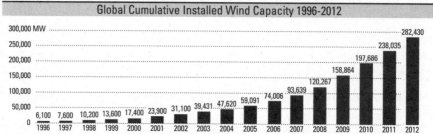

Illustration by Wiley, Composition Services Graphics

Check out Table 18-1 to see the ten largest wind energy markets today, as they are the prime regions for investment. While many of the turbines are manufactured by European corporations, the bulk of them end up installed in the United States and China.

Table 18-1	Top Ten Global Wind Markets
Country	*Total Installed Wind Capacity (MW)*
China	75,564
United States	60,007
Germany	31,332
Spain	22,796
India	18,421
United Kingdom	8,445
Italy	8,144
France	7,196
Canada	6,200
Portugal	4,525
Rest of world	39,852
Total	282,482

To further break down the U.S. market, Table 18-2 shows the top five wind-producing states in the nation, based on percentage of electricity generation by wind in 2011.

Table 18-2	Top Five Wind-Producing States, 2011
State	*Percent of Electricity from Wind, 2011*
South Dakota	22.3%
Iowa	18.8%
North Dakota	14.7%
Minnesota	12.7%
Wyoming	10.1%

By 2020, wind power is expected to supply up to 12 percent of global electricity needs, and by 2030, more than 20 percent. In the United States, wind power is expected to supply 20 percent of total power generation by 2030. Today, it supplies around 3.5 percent, so plenty of growth is ahead. When investing in wind, the turbine manufacturers see most of the action. After all, without wind turbines, you have no wind power.

But similar to what happened with the solar market (see Chapter 17), after the global economy imploded, it took the wind out of the wind energy's sails. The result was devastating for wind turbine manufacturers. Many either went bankrupt or sold their assets to the highest bidder.

However, despite an economic downturn that weighed heavily on the industry across the globe, the number of wind turbine manufacturers has actually grown — especially those installing turbines in the United States.

In 2007, the United States had only eight major wind turbine providers. By 2011, that number grew to 23. Figure 18-2 shows which companies were manufacturing in the United States for each year between 2007 and 2011. The list is also a good starting point for researching turbine companies for potential investment.

Of course, with less government support available for the U.S. wind energy industry, some of those 23 are likely to lose out on market share to a handful of companies that continue to maintain very competitive advantages. As an investor, use these advantages (which I discuss in the following sections) to evaluate wind turbine companies as possible investments.

Wind Turbine Manufacturers Installing Turbines in the U.S., by Year

2007	2008	2009	2010	2011
GE Energy	GE Energy	GE Energy	GE Energy	GE Energy
Vestas	Vestas	Vestas	Siemens	Vestas
Siemens	Siemens	Siemens	Gamesa	Siemens
Gamesa	Suzion	Mitsubishi	Suzion	Suzion
Mitsubishi	Gamesa	Suzion	Mitsubishi	Mitsubishi
Suzion	Mitsubishi	Clipper	Vestas	Nordex
Clipper	Clipper	Gamesa	Acciona WP	Clipper
Nordex	Acciona WP	REpower	Clipper	REpower
	REpower	Acciona WP	REpower	Gamesa
	Fuhrlander	Nordex	DeWind	Alstom
	DeWind	DeWind	Nordex	Sany
	AWE	AAER/Pioneer	Samsung	VENSYS
	DES	Goldwind	Northern Power	Samsung
	Northern Power	Northern Power	Nordic	Goldwind
	VENSYS	Fuhrlander	AAER/Pioneer	Hyundai
		VENSYS	EWT Americas	Nordtank (refurbished)
		EWT Americas	Turbowinds	Kenersys
			PowerWind	Northern Power
			Elecon	Unison
				Sinovel
				Nordic
				PowerWind
				Aeronautica

Figure 18-2: Wind turbine manufacturers installing turbines in the United States, by year.

Illustration by Wiley, Composition Services Graphics

Bottom line: When you're looking at any wind turbine manufacturer as an investment, you must make sure that it boasts a first-mover advantage, technological superiority, and plenty of diversification.

Today, the wind turbine manufacturers that maintain all these advantages are:

✔ GE (NYSE: GE)

✔ Siemens (NYSE: SI)

✔ Mitsubishi Heavy Industries (Pink Sheets: MHVYF)

That's not to say all wind turbine manufacturers that don't meet these requirements will fail. But just know that without those three requirements, you definitely take on more risk.

You should also be aware of up-and-coming Chinese turbine providers, because China is now the largest wind market in the world. Here are a few publicly-traded wind turbine companies based in China:

✔ Xinjiang Goldwind Science & Technology (Pink Sheets: XJNGF)

✔ China Ming Yang Wind Power Group (NYSE: MY)

✔ Sinovel Wind Group (SHA: 601558)

First mover advantage

The first company to a market enjoys first mover advantage. That is, its product is the first to be used by consumers and has a higher likelihood of being more widely adopted as a result.

For me, this was confirmed years ago when I went to visit a few wind farms in the Tehachapi region of California. It's here where I found a booming wind energy industry. During my tour, I spoke with a number of engineers who all had one thing in common — they weren't fond of change when it came to trying out new turbines. As one seasoned wind energy veteran told me, "If these blades stop turnin', we stop earnin'." Certain companies have been supplying turbines for these guys for decades. They know them inside and out, and they know which perform the best. Most simply don't want to risk trying out a new multimillion-dollar turbine when their other turbine manufacturers have a solid history of success. They simply don't want to take on the risk. And who can blame them? A lot of money is at stake here.

So it's no surprise that some companies will continue to expand and grow, simply due to their first mover advantage. These companies include:

- GE (NYSE: GE)
- Vestas Wind Systems (Pink Sheets: VWDRY)
- Mitsubishi Heavy Industries (Pink Sheets: MHVYF)
- Siemens (NYSE: SI)
- Gamesa (Pink Sheets: GCTAY)
- Suzlon (NSE: SUZLON)
- United Technologies Corporation (NYSE: UTX) — by way of acquisition of Clipper Windpower in 2010
- Nordex (Pink Sheets: NRDXF)

Of course, the technology these manufacturers develop must also keep pace with the demands of the global market.

Technological superiority

Although the development of wind turbine technology doesn't advance as quickly as the solar space, it still evolves at a pace that enables wind farm developers to pressure turbine manufacturers for the next big thing. And when it comes to wind turbines, the key word is *big*.

In the late 1970s, wind turbines weren't even producing power in megawatts. But by the height of the wind boom in the 2000s, many of the newer turbines in operation were rated between one megawatt and three megawatts apiece.

And these things are just going to keep getting bigger. In development today are wind turbines being planned and built on a scale ranging from eight to ten megawatts.

Manufacturers are also being forced to improve the reliability of their turbines in an effort to allow for far less damage in high winds, and to lower operation and maintenance costs. The companies that don't continue to further develop these technologies are sure to fail over the long-term, and should be avoided as potential investments.

Diversification

With the United States threatening to end the production tax credit for the wind industry in 2012, wind turbine manufacturers began idling shops. They pared back production but kept all the equipment. This ordeal dealt a major blow to the industry.

Still in place, in tough times, these incentives tend to get watered down or disappear altogether. At this point, wind turbine manufacturers that are well-diversified show they can weather the storm, while most pure plays get crushed.

Having the ability to continue operations, even during lean times, is what separates the solid players from the higher-risk manufacturers. This is why companies like GE and Siemens can continue to pump out turbines, even without the assistance of government incentives.

Going Offshore

In an effort to seek out more consistent winds than one would find in land-locked regions, wind farm developers continue to work toward developing more wind farms offshore where winds tend to be relatively constant and steady. Oceans actually make excellent locations for wind turbines.

The cost to develop offshore wind farms is significantly more than that of onshore wind farms. However, with steady and consistent winds, offshore wind can deliver much more electricity to the grid. So much, in fact, that a recent Stanford University study found that the East Coast of the United

States, from Maine to Florida, could run solely on wind power generated from offshore wind farms along the coast.

So far, the United States has no operational offshore wind farms. Most of today's operational offshore wind farms are in Europe, where in 2012, the EU installed more than one offshore wind turbine per working day.

But offshore wind isn't exclusive to Europe. In fact, following the Fukushima disaster in Japan, Japanese officials announced that Japan would build a one-gigawatt wind farm by 2020. This project would make Japan the home to one of the largest offshore wind farms on the planet, powering about 700,000 homes.

China is also actively developing offshore wind farms, and it's likely that the United States will begin to see wind farm construction off the East Coast by around 2020.

The point is that offshore wind farm development is underway. Research and consulting firm GlobalData projects that the global offshore wind power market will grow from a cumulative installed capacity of 5.1 gigawatts in 2012 to 54.9 gigawatts by 2020. That's a compound annual growth rate of 34.5 percent. Not bad!

In the offshore wind space, the two main opportunities are:

- ✔ Turbine manufacturing (I tell you more about it in the next section.)
- ✔ Electricity transmission (See the later section "Additional offshore wind opportunities" for details.)

Evaluating offshore wind turbine manufacturers

When looking for potential investment opportunities, you should employ the same three indicators for offshore turbine manufacturers as you do for onshore turbine manufacturers — a first-mover advantage, technological superiority, and diversification (see the earlier section "The Rise of Wind: Evaluating Wind Turbine Manufacturing Companies" for details).

The leader, based on this criteria, is Siemens (NYSE: SI), which maintains a leadership role in the offshore wind space, particularly in Germany where plans are in place to replace nuclear reactors with renewable sources. Offshore wind has been singled out as one of the most important replacements for nuclear. The country has ponied up more than $700 billion to make this happen.

Other leading offshore wind turbine manufacturers include:

- ✔ Vestas Wind Systems (Pink Sheets: VWDRY)
- ✔ Suzlon (NSE: SUZLON)
- ✔ Areva (Pink Sheets: ARVCF)
- ✔ Gamesa (Pink Sheets: GCTAF)

Additional offshore wind opportunities

Beyond offshore turbine manufacturers, offshore wind opportunities can also be found in the companies that provide subsea power transmission. After all, when connecting offshore wind farms to the grid, specialized transmission technology must be employed.

The leader in this space is undoubtedly ABB (NYSE: ABB).

Also worth noting is that in 2011, Northrop Grumman (NYSE: NOC), along with Gamesa, launched the Offshore Wind Technology Center in Chesapeake, Virginia. Representatives from Northrop Grumman said they were getting into the offshore wind business because it could create a new market for the company's shipbuilding arm.

And finally, Google (NASDAQ: GOOG) signed on to invest in a new offshore wind power grid that will eventually serve as the transmission backbone for a string of offshore wind farms along the U.S. East Coast. Dubbed the Atlantic Wind Connection, it will be located about ten miles offshore, stretch 350 miles from New Jersey to Virginia, and connect 6,000 megawatts of capacity — enough to power about two million homes.

Wind Farm Developers

Although most of the opportunities associated with wind energy investing are found in turbine manufacturers, you can also play the wind farm developers. Wind farm developers are actually a bit safer to play because the indicators of success tend to be glaringly obvious. The following are the three things to look for in a quality wind farm developer:

- ✔ **Access to capital:** Wind farms can be quite expensive to develop. At more than a million dollars per megawatt, the costs for turbines alone can add up pretty quickly on a 300 megawatt wind farm.

✔ **Lucrative locations:** Wind farm developers often locate their projects in close proximity to existing power transmission or in an area where transmission is actively being constructed. The further away the project is from transmission, the more it costs to build. Also keep an eye on environmental delays. Sometimes a wind farm developer can find his project held up due to environmental impact studies that weren't done prior to the planning stages.

✔ **Power purchase agreements:** The sweet spot for developers is the power purchase agreement. A power purchase agreement guarantees revenue. Without a power purchase agreement in place, the construction of the wind farm isn't guaranteed.

Here are some of the top wind developers from across the globe:

✔ Acciona Energia (Pink Sheets: ACXIF)

✔ Duke Energy (NYSE: DUK)

✔ E.ON (Pink Sheets: EONGY)

✔ EDF (EPA: EDF)

✔ Exelon (NYSE: EXC)

✔ Gamesa Corp. (Pink Sheets: GCTAF)

✔ Iberdrola Renewables (Pink Sheets: IBDRY)

✔ NextEra Energy (NYSE: NEE)

Note that many of these top wind developers are utility companies that generate only a portion of their revenues from developing and operating wind farms.

Winds of Change: The Future of Wind Energy

Although today's wind farms pump power to the grid by using the most cutting edge turbines currently available, it isn't unlikely that in about 20 years these farms will be seen as relics of the past, utilizing outdated technologies that simply can't match the superior efficiencies and cost structures of the latest technologies.

You can get a glimpse of what's to come, even though some of it is still in the lab or just beginning some very long testing phases. The companies that advance new technologies and get them deployed on a commercial scale will have a very strong competitive advantage. The following sections give you a few to keep a lookout for.

Floating turbines

Floating turbines are essentially wind turbines affixed to a floating structure. The advantage of a floating turbine is that it can utilize strong wind resources in waters that are too deep for towers.

In 2009, Norwegian oil and gas player Statoil ASA (NYSE: STO) teamed up with Siemens to build the first floating wind turbines for deepwater use. In 2010, the UK's industry economic valuation report predicted that floating wind turbines would eventually offer the most power generating potential in the wind industry. And in 2012, a consortium of Japanese companies finalized a new deal to build a 12 megawatt floating wind farm.

Direct-drive turbines

Traditional gear-driven systems require three stages of gears, each with its own bearings and structures. These gears are prone to problems and require regular maintenance. So some companies are seeking to remove those extraneous moving parts and replace them with one direct-drive system. The result is a turbine that significantly increases reliability while making turbines safer for maintenance workers. Some direct-drive turbines are actually in use today, and are expected to grow rapidly after a few years of solid "in-the-field" data.

The two companies leading the way in direct-drive turbine technology are GE (NYSE: GE) and Siemens (NYSE: SI).

New designs

Nearly every turbine in commercial operation is based on a similar design — three spinning blades mounted on a very tall tower. But tomorrow's turbines may look a bit different. Many of these new designs offer increased efficiencies, lower production costs, smaller geographic footprints, quieter operations, and more practical applications.

To stay on top of the latest technologies and wind energy data, make sure to check in frequently with the Global Wind Energy Council at http://www.gwec.com.

Chapter 19

Geothermal: The Devil's Hot Tub

In This Chapter

▶ Understanding geothermal market fundamentals

▶ Identifying the different types of geothermal power generation and technologies

▶ Evaluating geothermal investment opportunities

According to the Massachusetts Institute of Technology, more than 100 million quads of accessible geothermal energy are available worldwide. The world consumes only 400 quads.

Despite the enormous amount of geothermal energy bubbling below your feet, the geothermal industry hasn't had nearly as much recent success as solar and wind. The reasons are mostly due to the high level of risk associated with developing new geothermal wells and the enormous amount of time and capital it takes to construct a geothermal power plant.

The advantage of geothermal over solar and wind is that it produces *baseload power*. In other words, it runs consistently, 24/7. And once operational, geothermal is actually the cheapest of all forms of renewable energy.

In this chapter, I break down the fundamentals of the geothermal market and identify the various types of geothermal technologies. I also share some of the companies that are leading the way in geothermal power production.

Drilling for Heat, Drilling for Profits

Two types of geothermal power are in use today:

- **Utility-scale:** Utility-scale geothermal power involves steam or super-heated water from deep inside the earth used to drive a turbine and generate electricity.

- **Heat pumps:** Geothermal heat pumps are basically HVAC systems used for heating and cooling in homes and office buildings.

Although heat pump systems are efficient and cost-effective in new construction, they offer very few opportunities for investors. But investors have plenty of opportunities in the utility-scale space.

Considering geothermal-based electricity production

Unlike solar and wind, the geothermal industry in the United States has been growing at a slow but modest pace since 2005, as you can see in Figure 19-1.

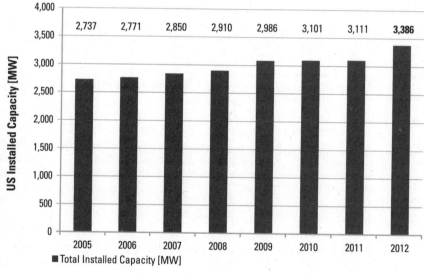

Figure 19-1: Annual U.S. installed geothermal capacity growth, 2005–2012.

Illustration by Wiley, Composition Services Graphics

But on a global scale, geothermal growth has actually outpaced that of the United States, moving significantly from 2010 to 2012, as seen in Figure 19-2.

In the United States, the Department of Energy has forecast that geothermal will triple its capacity by 2035, providing up to 6 percent of total U.S. renewable power. And in the global marketplace, the International Energy Agency is forecasting that by 2050, geothermal will provide about 3.5 percent of total global electricity production, with Asia providing the biggest gains, as you can see in Figure 19-3.

Of course, even as the global market has shown impressive growth, and data suggests continued growth over the next 30 to 40 years, geothermal is still far behind solar and wind in terms of growth, energy market penetration, and power generation. But that doesn't mean there aren't any opportunities. It just means you have fewer from which to choose. Before taking a closer look at those opportunities, I show you how to evaluate geothermal companies.

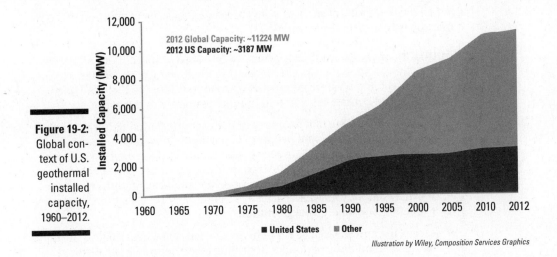

Figure 19-2: Global context of U.S. geothermal installed capacity, 1960–2012.

Illustration by Wiley, Composition Services Graphics

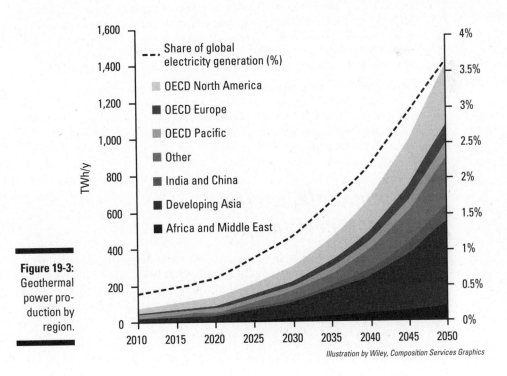

Figure 19-3: Geothermal power production by region.

Illustration by Wiley, Composition Services Graphics

Evaluating geothermal-based electricity production companies

I've had a fair amount of success over the years investing in geothermal companies by focusing on three things:

- ✔ **Quality of geothermal properties:** Geothermal resources are all across the globe. And in the United States, they're abundant, particularly in the southwest and western regions of the country. Most of the U.S.-based geothermal companies you find operate primarily in the west.

  The mere existence of a property in the western United States doesn't mean a company's actual property is particularly valuable. Certainly there have been many instances of companies drilling expensive holes only to come up with a resource that doesn't produce as expected. And it's not cheap to drill these things. So when analyzing a particular geothermal company, always make sure that it can prove that its resource is meeting or exceeding expectations.

- ✔ **Access to capital:** Drilling isn't cheap. I've witnessed companies burning through millions of dollars in drilling costs before finally hitting a resource that produces. And geothermal power plants don't go up like shopping malls; they take a long time to build and are quite expensive. So access to capital is key. If a particular company is low on cash and it doesn't have access to capital, it's likely to dilute shareholder value to raise funds. That's not a geothermal company you want exposure to.

- ✔ **Power purchase agreements:** If a geothermal company can't lock in a long-term power purchase agreement with a utility company, then it's of no value. The ability to sell its power is critical. I absolutely never invest in a geothermal company unless it has power purchase agreements locked in for its projects.

Geothermal electricity production companies

Because drilling deep wells may or may not hit a viable geothermal resource, there are only two pure play companies to mention here. A few smaller companies are trying to establish projects, but they've run into funding problems, and many of them are defunct or going out of business. So it's wise to stick with companies that have a track record of success and access to capital.

A century of geothermal

The first modern geothermal plant was constructed in 1904 in Lardarello, Italy, although the existing plant didn't begin operations until 1913. It remained the only large-scale geothermal electricity plant in the world until 1958.

That plant is still operational today and provides 10 percent of the world's geothermal electricity — enough to power around 1 million homes. Geothermal is so reliable that the plant has gone off-line only one time in more than a century. And that was because of an interruption caused by a World War II bomb.

When the plant was first installed, it had a capacity of 250 kilowatts. It was upgraded to 12.5 megawatts by 1930 and had a capacity of 132 MW when it was destroyed in 1944. It was then rebuilt and had a capacity of 300 MW by 1950. Over the years, plants have been added and upgraded, and Lardarello now has a capacity of nearly 800 MW.

The plant is now operated by Enel Green Power, a unit of Enel, which trades on the Milan stock exchange.

Additionally, Chevron is one of the largest geothermal operators in the world, but geothermal accounts for only a tiny portion of its business.

✔ **Calpine Corp.** (NYSE: CPN) isn't a pure play geothermal company, but it is the largest supplier of geothermal power in the United States. It's also one of the safest, because its portfolio is diversified with strong natural gas projects.

✔ **Ormat Technologies** (NYSE: ORA) is a major developer of geothermal power plants across the globe and is the only one that's vertically integrated. The company also develops recovered energy power generation systems (REG). These systems work by capturing unused residual heat from industrial operations and converting it into electricity.

It's also worth noting that, just like in the wind and solar space, General Electric and Siemens provide various technologies and systems for the geothermal industry. Mitsubishi Heavy Industries (Pink Sheets: MHVYF) also operates in this space.

Enhancing the Heat: The Future of Geothermal

The future of geothermal can be described in three words: enhanced geothermal systems (EGS).

EGS is the holy grail for the geothermal industry. It's basically fracking for geothermal. But because you're simply talking about heat — and not a dedicated spot holding a finite resource — with EGS, geothermal power plants could be set up practically anywhere. You can't do that with wind or nuclear. And the best part is that with EGS, you can produce electricity more cheaply than nearly anything else produced today, and the resource is nearly inexhaustible. In fact, an MIT report found that accessible geothermal resources in the United States are 130,000 times greater than the country's total annual energy consumption.

Continue to closely watch enhanced geothermal companies, because EGS could be a real game-changer. The two publicly traded companies currently testing EGS in the United States are Ormat Technologies (see the earlier section, "Geothermal electricity production companies," for details) and a small geothermal development company called U.S. Geothermal (AMEX: HTM). U.S. Geothermal is actually a very aggressive geothermal company, and it's one of the few in the United States that currently generates revenue from its operations. It has a strong management team, and it continues to expand rapidly. It's also very thinly traded and somewhat risky. Conservative investors should avoid it.

Chapter 20

Transportation:
Plugged-In and Corn-Fed

In This Chapter

▶ Understanding electric car and biofuel fundamentals

▶ Identifying the different electric vehicle and biofuel technologies

▶ Evaluating electric vehicle and biofuel investment opportunities

*H*ere's an interesting fact: More than 90 percent of the energy people use for transportation comes from oil, a resource that's now being consumed faster than it's being produced.

Although the fracking boom in the United States has unleashed record levels of American oil back into the market, every investor must be aware of one undeniable truth: This wealth of oil production will never keep pace with global demand.

Sure, domestically produced oil provides a certain buffer against oil imports, particularly from the Organization of the Petroleum Exporting Countries (OPEC). But no matter how you slice it, the demand for oil that's fueling the growth of emerging economies far exceeds what the world produces. And for this reason, alternative transportation fuels are paramount to the continued growth of the global economy.

Three forms of alternative fuels are now starting to take a bit of market share in the transportation sector, albeit at a snail's pace: natural gas, electricity, and biofuels. Chapter 7 has information about natural gas as a transportation fuel, so in this chapter I focus on electricity and biofuels.

Investing in the Electric Car

Today's electric cars aren't the glorified golf carts of the past. Instead, they look just like any other modern-day car but offer the advantages of economic and environmental sustainability. With all-electric ranges of commercially available electric cars running as high as 300 miles per charge, more than 70 percent of the daily U.S. commuting population can use an electric car without the need to buy a single drop of gasoline.

As the price of gasoline continues to creep up, rest assured, the economic case for electric cars becomes greater and greater. Which is why nearly every major car maker on the planet now has an electric vehicle in showrooms or in production.

By 2020, electric cars are expected to represent at least 2 percent of the total U.S. car market. And globally, electric vehicle sales are expected to hit 3.8 million annually, according to Navigant Research (see Figure 20-1).

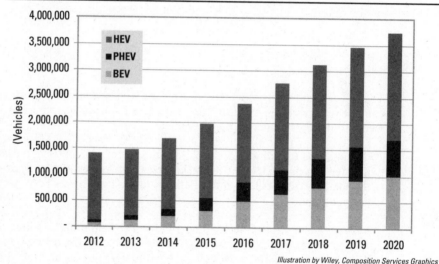

Annual Electric Vehicle Sales by Vehicle Type, World Markets: 2012-2020

Figure 20-1:
Annual electric vehicle sales, globally: 2012–2020.

Illustration by Wiley, Composition Services Graphics

Electric vehicle technologies

Three main types of vehicles rely on batteries either for "fuel" or to assist in the powering of the vehicle. These are

- **Hybrid electric vehicles:** Combine internal combustion with an electric propulsion system. Examples: Toyota Prius, Honda Insight, Ford Fusion Hybrid.

- **Plug-in hybrid electric vehicles:** Contain both an internal combustion engine and an electric motor. The electric motor can provide all-electric driving for short distances, typically between 30 and 40 miles. When the electric motor is nearly depleted, the internal combustion engine kicks

> in. Various types of PHEV technologies exist, but all provide the same basic driving capabilities. Examples: Chevy Volt, Toyota Prius Plug-In.
>
> ✔ **Battery-electric vehicles:** Powered exclusively by rechargeable batteries. Mileage ranges vary from around 60 to 300, depending on the vehicle. Examples: Nissan LEAF, Mitsubishi i, Tesla Model S.

Electric vehicle investments

You can get in on the burgeoning electric vehicle market by investing in five areas:

> ✔ Electric car manufacturers
>
> ✔ Electric motor companies
>
> ✔ Battery manufacturers
>
> ✔ Battery materials providers
>
> ✔ Charging station companies

Electric car manufacturers

Today, there's only one pure play on electric vehicles, and that's Tesla Motors (NASDAQ: TSLA). Although Tesla is still a young company, its vehicles have proven thus far to be the safest, most reliable electric cars on the market. The company went public in 2010 and was cofounded by Elon Musk, the cofounder of PayPal. Tesla's two mains models are the Roadster and the Model S.

Besides Tesla, which only manufactures electric cars, a handful of major automakers also have electric cars on the roads today. These include

> ✔ Ford (NYSE: F)
>
> ✔ General Motors (NYSE: GM)
>
> ✔ Honda (NYSE: HMC)
>
> ✔ Mitsubishi (OTC: MMTOF)
>
> ✔ Nissan (OTC: NSANY)
>
> ✔ Toyota (NYSE: TM)

However, playing any of these automakers is not the way to get exposure to the electric vehicle market. Although most are quite bullish on electric vehicle development, electric vehicles represent a very small fraction of their overall production. For investment exposure to electric vehicles, you want to check out companies that make vital components of the cars like motors and batteries, which I cover later in this chapter.

Electric motor companies

The trend for most electric car makers is to manufacture their own electric motors. However, there are still a couple of electric motor companies regularly doing deals with automakers looking to pump out electric cars.

Siemens (NYSE: SI) is one, although it's not a pure play because electric motors are not its primary business.

If you're looking for a pure electric motor play, you can check out a company called UQM Technologies (AMEX: UQM), which has been providing electric motors, generators, and power controllers for the auto industry for years. It is, however, a fairly risky stock to own.

Battery manufacturers

Most automakers are looking to supply their own batteries. Some are well on their way, and others will likely be there soon. Still, a few battery manufacturers still supply the major automakers, including

- Johnson Controls (NYSE: JCI)
- LG Chem (KOREA: 051910)
- NEC Corporation (OTC: NIPNF)

Battery materials providers

Most of the batteries used for electric vehicles today are lithium-ion batteries. In fact, according to Navigant Research, the market for lithium-ion batteries in light-duty transportation is expected to grow from $1.6 billion in 2012 to nearly $22 billion by 2020, as you can see in Figure 20-2.

However, as technology advances, lithium will be used in various combinations with other materials, such as graphite, vanadium, and zinc.

Some of the major players in these materials include

- Chemical & Mining Company of Chile (NYSE: SQM): Lithium
- Flinders Resources (TSX-V: FDR): Graphite
- FMC Corp. (NYSE: FMC): Lithium
- GrafTech International Ltd. (NYSE: GTI): Graphite

- Northern Graphite Corp. (TSX-V: NGC): Graphite
- Rockwood Holdings (NYSE: ROC): Lithium
- Syrah Resources (ASX: SYR): Graphite

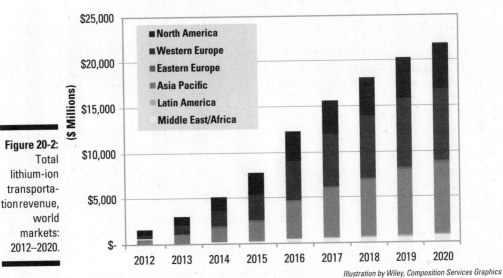

Total Lithium Ion Transportation Battery Revenue by Region, World Markets: 2012–2020

Figure 20-2:
Total
lithium-ion
transporta-
tion revenue,
world
markets:
2012–2020.

Illustration by Wiley, Composition Services Graphics

WARNING!

Many of the mining companies traded on the Toronto Stock Exchange Venture Exchange (TSXV) have small market caps and are thinly traded. Make sure to do your due diligence before investing.

Alternatively, you can invest in the Global X Lithium ETF (NYSE: LIT), which holds Chemical & Mining Company of Chile, FMC Corp., Rockwood Holdings, and several other foreign and domestic players in the lithium sector, on both the mining and battery production sides of the market.

Charging station companies

One of the big opportunities in the electric vehicle space is infrastructure, particularly private and public charging stations.

According to Navigant Research, the global market for electric vehicle chargers is expected to grow to $3.8 billion by 2020, representing a 27.1 percent compound annual growth rate (CAGR) from 2013. And Navigant Research has predicted electric vehicle equipment sales to grow from fewer than 200,000 units sold in 2012 to nearly 2.4 million units sold in 2020. You can see this coming growth in Figure 20-3.

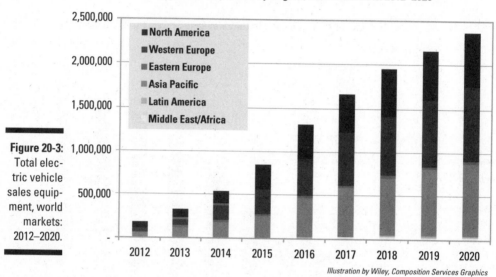

Total EVSE Unit Sales by Region, World Markets: 2012–2020

Legend:
- North America
- Western Europe
- Eastern Europe
- Asia Pacific
- Latin America
- Middle East/Africa

Figure 20-3: Total electric vehicle sales equipment, world markets: 2012–2020.

Illustration by Wiley, Composition Services Graphics

Although there are one or two pure play electric car charging station stocks, I only focus on the leaders here. These aren't pure plays, although they do allow you some exposure to this sector while also delivering a fair amount of safety through diversification. These include

- AeroVironment (NASDAQ: AVAV)
- Eaton (NYSE: ETN)
- General Electric (NYSE: GE)
- Siemens (NYSE: SI)

Can the grid handle millions of electric cars?

According to the U.S. Department of Energy (DOE), off-peak electricity production and transmission capacity could fuel 184.8 million plug-in hybrid electric vehicles. This represents about 80 percent of all U.S vehicles. And because most commuters would typically plug in at night, during off-peak hours, the utilities would actually end up getting a new market for their product.

Sugar in Your Gas Tank: Investing in Biofuels

In 2005, with the introduction of the government-mandated Renewable Fuels Standard, 7.5 billion gallons of renewable fuel were to be blended into gasoline by 2012. Then, through the Energy Independence and Security Act of 2007, the U.S. government mandated that 36 billion gallons of renewable fuel be blended into gasoline by 2022.

Investors have had an opportunity to profit from the biofuel sector primarily because of these government actions. Without the government mandate, biofuel production, particularly corn-based ethanol, would barely register as an accounting error. But because of the government mandate, ethanol production in the United States has grown 240 percent since 2005, as you can see in Table 20-1.

Table 20-1	U.S. Ethanol Production by Gallons, 2005–2012
Year	*Millions of Gallons*
2005	3,904
2006	4,855
2007	6,500
2008	9,000
2009	10,600
2010	13,230
2011	13,900
2012	13,300

Identifying biofuels

Biofuels can be broken down into two segments: ethanol and biodiesel.

Ethanol
Ethanol is a type of alcohol that can be used in three concentrations:

- Pure ethanol: Only usable in specially modified engines.

- E10: A mix of 10 percent ethanol and 90 percent gasoline. You typically find this in most gas stations in the United States today.

✔ E85: A mix of 85 percent ethanol and 15 percent gasoline. A standard engine must be modified to run on both regular gasoline and E85.

Vehicles that can run on E85 are labeled as *flex fuel* vehicles.

A number of different feedstocks can be used to produce ethanol. Sugar is one of the most popular, and the most efficient. It's used mostly in Brazil, where an ethanol fuel program has been in place for nearly 40 years. Brazil is the second largest producer of ethanol in the world, and it actually sells more ethanol than gasoline.

Corn is also an extremely popular feedstock, particularly in the United States, where large agricultural giants produce massive corn yields, thanks in part to extremely generous corn subsidies. However, corn is a much less efficient feedstock than sugar.

In an effort to further diversify the United States' ethanol feedstocks, the government has been very aggressive in pushing new standards that will require the use of non-corn feedstocks, such as agricultural waste and perennial grasses, also known as cellulosic feedstocks.

The potential for cellulosic ethanol is massive because it helps provide a hedge against using food crops for fuel. However, to date, little headway has been made on improving the economics of cellulosic ethanol production. Therefore, it remains only a niche player.

Biodiesel

Biodiesel is similar to diesel from petroleum and is made from vegetable oils or animal fats. The fuel is just as effective as diesel and can be used in a standard diesel engine, typically without modification. Biodiesel primarily comes in two concentrations:

✔ B100: 100 percent biodiesel.

✔ B20: A mix of 20 percent biodiesel and 80 percent petroleum-based diesel. B20 works better than B100 in colder climates.

Like ethanol, a number of different feedstocks can be used to produce biodiesel. The two most popular are soy and palm. However, jatropha and algae are being touted as the biodiesel feedstocks of the future because of their heavy oil contents and the potentially better economics they offer for growing and harvesting.

Evaluating biofuel investment opportunities

You have two ways to play the biofuel market: biofuel production companies and the big ag and biotech companies that help grow and increase the yields of biofuel feedstocks. Because the biofuel industry is so directly tied to government support, particularly in the United States, you should focus primarily on the major players, as well as the well-diversified companies that count the biofuel industry as only one of their many profit centers.

Biofuel production companies

Since 2008, Cosan has delivered by far the best return in the biofuel field, nearly doubling in price, because it's Brazilian-based and enjoys the better economics that sugar offers as a fuel feedstock. The following companies count biofuel production as their main business:

- The Andersons, Inc. (NASDAQ: ANDE)

- Cosan, Ltd. (NYSE: CZZ)

- Green Plains Renewable Energy, Inc. (NASDAQ: GPRE)

- Rex American Resources Corporation (NYSE: REX)

Big ag and biotech companies

Other companies help improve the economics of biofuels by increasing crop yields or genetically modifying plants to produce more sugars or oils. These include

- Archer Daniels Midland Company (NYSE: ADM)

- Bunge, Limited (NYSE: BG)

- DuPont (NYSE: DD)

- Monsanto (NYSE: MON)

- Syngenta (NYSE: SYT)

You can stay up to date on alternative transportation fuels, including production figures and the companies involved, by checking out www.eia.gov/renewable.

Chapter 21

Efficiency: Doing More with Less

....

In This Chapter
▶ Understanding the market for high-performance, energy-efficient buildings
▶ Checking out investment opportunities in the transportation industry

....

Strict energy-efficiency policies enacted in California in the 1970s resulted in Californians consuming 40 percent less energy per person than the national average. This consumption decrease helped prevent the need to build 24 new power plants.

One of the simplest and most cost-effective solutions to high energy prices doesn't involve new power generation at all, but rather using the energy people generate now more efficiently. So this solution is about decreasing consumption instead of increasing generation. This approach has long been considered the low-hanging fruit in the world of energy, and over the past decade, it has become increasingly important as the global community attempts to curb environmental burdens associated with power production while increasing power supplies, particularly in emerging economies.

Energy conservation and efficiency can be broken down into two segments:

✔ Buildings
✔ Transportation

I cover the fundamentals and general investment opportunities for both in this chapter.

High-Performance Building Fundamentals and Investments

The global market for high-performance, energy-efficient buildings is expected to grow from $77.8 billion in 2011 to $103.4 billion by 2017. You can see the trajectory this growth is expected to take in Figure 21-1.

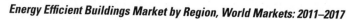

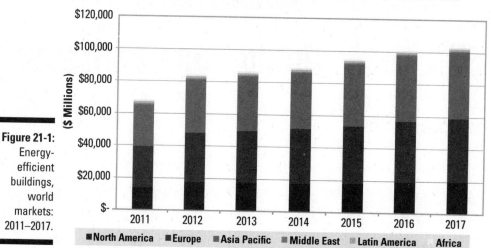

Figure 21-1: Energy-efficient buildings, world markets: 2011–2017.

This growth presents a huge opportunity for those who invest in high-performance buildings, known as *green buildings,* and the materials that make them possible.

Green buildings are designed to be ecologically mindful. That means using sustainable materials and being built so the structure consumes as few resources as possible — during construction and throughout its life. Green Buildings are extremely energy efficient, and there are many materials that make it possible.

The primary areas of investment in this sector include:

✔ Lighting

✔ Windows

✔ Motors

✔ Energy intelligence

✔ Design

Lighting

Nearly 20 percent of the total energy used in the United States is for lighting, at a cost of roughly $50 billion per year. However, with the advent and utilization of more efficient lighting technologies, this cost, as well as the percentage of overall energy used to power these lights, is expected to fall dramatically.

The most common replacement for incandescent light bulbs today is the compact fluorescent lamp, or CFL. But while CFLs are significantly more efficient than common incandescent light bulbs, they're actually inferior to the efficiency gains and cost reductions associated with a new generation of light-emitting diodes, or LEDs. You can see a comparison of these three types of bulbs in Table 21-1.

Table 21-1	Light Bulb Efficiency Comparison Based on 10 Hours per Day, 365 Days		
Bulb/Feature	**LED**	**CFL**	**Incandescent**
Life span	25,000+ hours	8,000 hours	1,200 hours
Watts used	8–12 watts	13–15 watts	60 watts
Kilowatts used	44 kilowatt hours/year	55 kilowatt hours/year	219 kilowatt hours/year
Carbon dioxide emissions	45 pounds/year	56 pounds/year	225 pounds/year

LEDs are rugged, boast a very long life, produce no ultraviolet radiation and very little heat, and offer superior design flexibility. LEDs, plain and simple, represent the future of lighting. In fact, Navigant Research has predicted that LEDs will account for nearly half of the $4.4 billion commercial lighting business by 2021.

Many large construction projects these days use LEDs. Local and state governments also use LEDs for road and transportation infrastructure lighting. LEDs are commonly found in today's modern vehicles, and the military is one of the largest consumers of LEDs on the planet.

Some of the big names in LEDs include

- ✔ General Electric (NYSE: GE)
- ✔ Siemens (NYSE: SI)
- ✔ Koninklijke Philips Electronics NV (NYSE: PHG)
- ✔ Sharp Corp. (OTC: SHCAY)
- ✔ Cree, Inc. (NASDAQ: CREE)
- ✔ Toshiba Corp. (OTC: TOSYY)
- ✔ Veeco Instruments, Inc. (NASDAQ: VECO)
- ✔ Universal Display Corp. (NASDAQ: PANL)

Windows

It's nearly impossible to find new construction these days that doesn't include energy-efficient windows. And window replacements are now big business as well. With the ability to cut energy costs by as much as 25 percent, replacing old, drafty windows with technologically superior energy-efficient windows can serve as an excellent investment.

All kinds of different energy-efficient windows and window frames are available. Though the most efficient tend to be triple-pane and triple-glazed, with pockets of air or gas separating each piece of glass, you can find various levels of efficiency.

You don't have any direct way to play any of these window companies. However, a company called Ameresco, Inc. (NYSE: AMRC) provides all kinds of energy efficiency and conservation solutions. Among those are projects that require the procurement and installation of energy-efficient windows.

Or, for a more direct way to invest in this sector, consider upgrading your old, energy-siphoning windows for new, energy-efficient windows. Over the long haul, you may end up saving a small fortune in energy costs, and the new windows will add resale value to your home as well.

Motors

Space conditioning and ventilation in the commercial sector is responsible for about 20 percent of motor energy consumption in the United States. That's why a number of companies today are upgrading to high-efficiency motors and motor management systems. One of the more well-documented cases is Eastman Kodak, which conducted a 600 motor retrofit many years ago. By upgrading to premium-efficiency motors, the company saved $664,000 annually and realized full payback in 2.3 years.

When Eastman Kodak moved forward on that particular upgrade, these types of concerns about motor management weren't particularly popular. Today, not only are outdated motors being replaced, but nearly all new construction calls for high-efficiency systems that require high-efficiency motors. And a sizable portion of these motors are supplied by only a handful of companies, including

- ✔ General Electric (NYSE: GE)
- ✔ Siemens (NYSE: SI)
- ✔ Toshiba Corp. (OTC: TOSYY)

Energy management systems

Perhaps you've already heard the term *smart grid*. As the U.S. Department of Energy (DOE) points out, the current electric grid was built in the 1890s and was improved upon as technology advanced along the way. But today, it's being stretched beyond what it was initially intended to handle. Thus, the need for a new smart grid.

A smart grid is essentially the next evolution of energy transmission and distribution. It allows for

✔ More efficient transmission of electricity

✔ Quicker restoration of electricity after power disturbances

✔ Reduced operations and management costs for utilities, and ultimately lower power costs for consumers

✔ Increased integration of large-scale renewable energy systems

✔ Better integration of customer-owner power generation systems, including renewable energy systems

✔ Improved security

According to Navigant Research, smart grid technology revenues will grow from $33 billion in 2012 to $73 billion in 2020, as you can see in Figure 21-2.

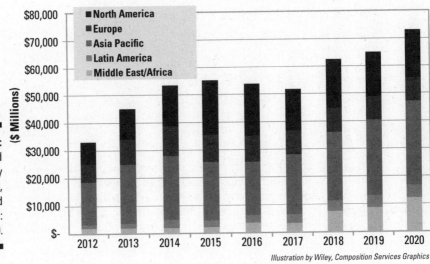

Smart Grid Technology Revenue by Region, World Markets: 2012–2020

Figure 21-2: Smart grid technology revenue, world markets: 2012–2020.

Illustration by Wiley, Composition Services Graphics

Smart grids have many components, one of which is the smart energy management system.

Energy management systems can be broken down into two segments: smart meters and smart appliances.

Smart meters

As the DOE explains, *smart meters* provide the smart grid interface between consumers and energy providers. Installed in place of old, mechanical meters, smart meters operate digitally and allow for automated and complex transfers of information between one's home and one's energy provider.

Smart appliances

Smart appliances are appliances that are networked together, allowing consumers to access and operate them through an energy management system. This system allows one to turn on a heater or air conditioner from work or on the way home from work. It can also keep track of energy use.

Here are a few leaders in the energy management game:

- ABB Ltd. (NYSE: ABB)
- Cisco Systems, Inc. (NASDAQ: CSCO)
- EnerNOC, Inc. (NASDAQ: ENOC)
- ESCO Technologies (NYSE: ESE)
- General Cable Corp. (NYSE: BGC)
- Honeywell International (NYSE: HON)
- ITC Holdings Corp. (NYSE: ITC)
- Itron, Inc. (NASDAQ: ITRI)
- MYR Group, Inc. (NASDAQ: MYRG)

Design

Combining a number of different energy-efficiency elements into a single structure with modern energy solutions (such as solar, wind, and geothermal) is paramount for those in the high-performance building sector. Many folks refer to these structures as *net-zero,* meaning the building produces as much energy as it consumes. And quite frankly, this *is* the future of building.

How the Empire State Building saves $4.4 million a year

In 2010, the owner of the Empire State Building approved a $13 million project that included new insulation, various energy-efficiency upgrades, and the retrofitting of the building's 6,514 windows. This resulted in an energy savings of $4.4 million a year, which delivered a three-year payback. Going forward, through energy savings alone, the Empire State Building adds $4.4 million a year to the bottom line, without lifting a finger. This is why high-performance buildings represent an excellent investment opportunity for retail investors, homeowners, and business owners.

Transportation Efficiency

Efficiency plays a major role in the transportation industry, particularly when it comes to personal transportation and mass transit. In this section, I look at how conventional vehicle technology is utilizing more fuel-efficient technologies, how mass transit is changing the landscape of the world's major cities, and how a new network of high-speed rail lines will change the face of long-distance travel forever.

Personal transportation and conventional vehicle efficiency

For decades, fuel efficiency wasn't of particular concern to car makers. Aside from a brief moment during the energy crisis of the 1970s, the fuel economies of internal combustion vehicles have not only remained somewhat stagnant, but in some cases, have actually become worse. The inefficiency of conventional internal combustion engines has certainly helped expedite the global depletion of crude oil.

Most folks don't realize this, but only about 15 percent of the energy from a tank of gasoline actually moves a car. Of course, when the price of oil hit $140 a barrel back in 2008, it was a wake-up call for the world. As George Bush once declared, America is addicted to oil. But it's not just the United States. Truth is, oil continues to be the slippery glue that keeps the global economy moving. And any abrupt shortage can certainly wreak economic havoc on a mass scale.

This is one of the reasons that the automotive industry has become more aggressive with its plans to increase the fuel economy of its vehicles.

National fuel economy standards

On August 28, 2012, the Obama Administration finalized standards to increase fuel economy to the equivalent of 54.5 miles per gallon (mpg) for cars and light-duty trucks by 2025. The new standards are expected to save consumers more than $1.7 trillion dollars in fuel costs.

Initially, there was some push back from car makers, but between bailouts and a business case that supports a model of increased fuel economy standards, most manufacturers ended up supporting the plan. After all, the bottom line on fuel efficiency is that it can serve as a profit motive.

According to a 2009 University of Michigan report, "Fixing Detroit: How Far, How Fast, How Fuel Efficient," researchers noted that the old culture within the domestic auto companies systematically underestimated the value of fuel economy. Researchers for that report found that

- ✔ An industry-wide mandated increase in fuel economy of 30 percent to 50 percent (35 mpg to 40.5 mpg) would increase the Detroit 3's gross profits by roughly $3 billion per year and increase sales by the equivalent of two large assembly plants.

- ✔ The Detroit 3 — Ford, General Motors, and Chrysler — gain profits over base in all scenarios, with the largest profits gained from pursuing more aggressive fuel economy.

- ✔ Japanese automakers' profit gains are smaller than the Detroit 3, with the smallest profits gained from pursuing a 50 percent increase in fuel economy.

- ✔ At a 50 percent increase, the Japanese industry loses sales while the domestics continue to gain in sales and profitability, a result driven by the different starting points.

- ✔ Because Detroit 3 automakers have long underestimated the consumer value of fuel economy, raising fuel economy standards won't cost more than consumers would be willing to pay.

- ✔ In every scenario, the average cost per vehicle is less than what consumers would be willing to pay.

This report built on an earlier University of Michigan Transportation Research Institute study that predicted the Detroit automakers could lose billions in profits and thousands of jobs in the event of an oil spike.

So in an effort to increase fuel economy, automakers are developing and producing hybrid and electric vehicles faster than ever. I cover electric vehicles in Chapter 20, but what about the case to increase the fuel economies of conventional internal combustion vehicles? The improvement in fuel economy standards will no doubt stem primarily from hybrid and electric vehicles, but there's something to be said for a new generation of internal combustion vehicles that are integrating new technologies in an effort to increase miles per gallon. And these technologies, not necessarily the automakers, serve as potential opportunities for investors. Some of the companies leading the way on fuel-efficient technologies for cars and trucks include

✔ BorgWarner (NYSE: BWA): Dual-clutch transmissions and other fuel-saving technologies

✔ Delphi Automotive (NYSE: DLPH): Power-train technologies and electronic distribution systems

✔ Johnson Controls (NYSE: JCI): Start-stop technology

Start-stop systems were initially used in hybrids but are now used in upgraded internal combustion engines. They work to automatically shut down and restart engines, so the engine spends less time idling. This equates to a more fuel-efficient vehicle; fuel economy gains from this technology run at about 5 to 10 percent.

Johnson Controls is the major player in start-stop technology, but a smaller, somewhat riskier play is Exide Technologies (NASDAQ: XIDE).

Mass transit

Mass transit is growing rapidly across the globe to facilitate a transition toward a more efficient transportation system.

Although driving a personal vehicle has certain benefits, efficiency isn't one of them. However, mass transit is one of the most efficient ways for commuters to travel and results in economic benefits that bolster the case for expansion. Which, of course, makes this segment worthy of coverage for investors.

Here are just a few of the benefits that are bolstering the economic case for public transportation, according to the American Public Transportation Association (APTA):

✔ For every dollar communities invest in public transportation, approximately four dollars are generated in economic returns.

✔ Every $10 million in capital investment in public transportation yields $30 million in increased business sales.

✔ The gas savings resulting from public transportation are roughly 4.2 billion gallons per year.

Across the United States, public transportation ridership has been increasing steadily since the 1950s. In fact, in 2012, a record 10.5 billion trips were taken on U.S. public transportation. This was the second highest annual ridership since 1957.

Global mass-transit ridership continues to grow as well, particularly in emerging economies. But the United States is where you find most of the growth opportunities in mass transit. After all, America has long been, and remains, a very car-centric nation. This is unlikely to change in the near-term. But with escalating gas prices and the fallout from a global economic meltdown that will reverberate for at least another decade, leaving middle-class folks in a position where stretching a dollar is paramount, the lure of public transportation will be strong.

In fact, according to the APTA, households that regularly use public transportation can save nearly $10,000 a year.

Bottom line: The business case for expanded mass transit and the economic case for Americans using mass transit are strong enough to make this industry an integral one for energy investors. In this section, I examine the three areas of mass transit that offer the most profit potential for investors:

✔ Buses

✔ Light rail

✔ High-speed rail

Buses

Today's modern, mass-transit buses are a far cry from buses of the past.

Gone are the days of black smoke–belching diesels and exceptionally slow rides. These days, modern mass-transit buses are primarily cleaner hybrid and diesel machines. They're quieter, less pollutive, and more efficient, resulting in lower maintenance and fuel costs.

You can play this angle with the battery and drive train suppliers, like Siemens (NYSE: SI) or Johnson Controls (NYSE: JCI), or the actual makers of buses, like New Flyer Industries (TSX: NFI), for example. For more on battery investments, see Chapter 20.

Also coming on the scene are new fleets of natural gas–powered buses. With a wealth of natural gas now at the world's fingertips, natural gas is being considered a go-to source for transportation fuel, particularly in the truck and bus market. A couple of the companies profiting from this angle are Clean Energy Fuels (NASDAQ: CLNE) and Westport Innovations (NASDAQ: WPRT).

Light rail

Although the days of streetcars are mostly gone, modern-day light-rail systems are making a comeback in the United States.

Already quite common in Europe, light-rail systems offer quick and efficient transportation, primarily for those living within and just outside city borders. And for reasons already discussed, demand for light-rail expansion in the United States is growing. In fact, over the past few years, light rail has led much of the growth in mass-transit ridership.

Some of the major players in the light-rail game include

- ✔ Alstom (OTC: AOMFF)
- ✔ Bombardier (TSX: BBD-A)
- ✔ Siemens (NYSE: SI)

High-speed rail

Perhaps one of the most crucial forms of mass-transit options is high-speed rail (HSR).

Siemens built the first high-speed train in 1903 in Germany, and it ran with a maximum speed of 126 miles per hour. By the 1930s, the German railway inaugurated an HSR system with regular service from all major cities in Germany to Berlin.

And in 1959, the Japanese government approved the construction of the first segment of the first modern high-speed rail, the Shinkansen. In 1964, the Shinkansen began service from Tokyo to Osaka. Today, the latest series of Shinkansen trains runs throughout the country at speeds up to 186 miles per hour.

While the United States continues to lag in the race to build and expand high-speed rail systems, operational fleets on a global scale have actually grown from 1,737 high-speed train sets to nearly 3,000 from 2009 to 2012. About 60 percent of these fleets are in China, France, Germany, Japan, and Spain. And by 2015, that number is expected to hit 4,000. This is the kind of stuff you may not read about in the news, but it's happening, and savvy investors are paying close attention.

In Europe, new high-speed rail lines are in development in France, Germany, Italy, Poland, Spain, Sweden, and Turkey. And China is currently building the most extensive HSR network in the world. By 2020, it will consist of more than 9,940 miles of HSR track with 150 stations. It will cover more than 90 percent of the population in China, while targeting these major city-pairs:

- Beijing to Shanghai: four hours
- Shanghai to Hong Kong: four hours
- Hong Kong to Guangzhou: 48 minutes

Taiwan and South Korea also have HSR networks in place that are currently undergoing expansions.

Brazil has a new HSR system in development, too. As do Argentina, India, Morocco, Portugal, and Russia. Even in the Middle East, an extensive rail line is currently being planned, and some sections are actually under construction right now.

Here are some of the biggest players in the HSR game:

- Alstom (OTC: AOMFF)
- Bombardier (TSX: BBD-A)
- Harsco (NYSE: HSC)
- Mitsubishi Heavy Industries (PK: MHVYF)
- Siemens (NYSE: SI)
- Timken (NYSE: TKR)

Most HSR development in the near-term will be found overseas, but it will eventually be adopted by the United States.

One of the saving graces for HSR in the United States is its ability to offer a viable and economical alternative to short-distance air travel (between 200 and 600 miles). Passenger air travel in the United States gets about 45 passenger-miles per gallon of fuel, whereas HSR systems in Japan and Europe currently deliver efficiency equivalents of about 300 to 500 passenger-miles per gallon.

HSR offers an opportunity to drastically cut a significant chunk of American fuel consumption. And although some people believe the airlines would fight to keep market share, that's simply not the case.

Most airlines don't make money on those short trips; they make their money on longer trips. For the most part, the airline industry has actually been very supportive of HSR development. And in parts of the world where HSR is an option, the data suggest consumers are eager to exchange their boarding passes for HSR tickets.

In Europe, high-speed trains have taken about 50 percent of the air traffic where rail trip times are four and a half hours or less. And on routes where high-speed train times are two hours or less, rail gets about 90 percent over air transportation.

As air travel costs continue to rise — and as air travel becomes more and more of a hassle because of heightened security measures, flight delays, and increased traffic congestion — HSR will become more and more appealing. Truth is, no matter how much politics slows development in the United States, the global market is ripe for continued growth.

The Energy Information Administration offers a full guide to energy efficiency, including state and federal programs, studies on how various industries are adopting efficiency measures, and the companies and organizations that are making it happen. You can find this guide at www.eia.gov/emeu/efficiency/energy_savings.htm.

Additionally, the DOE has an entire office dedicated to energy efficiency, which you can find at www.eere.energy.gov.

Chapter 22

Investing in Modern Energy

*N*ot long ago, modern, renewable energy investing was monopolized by wide-eyed environmentalists and wealthy eccentrics. But faced with the reality of oil supply constraints, growing global populations, and a rapid decline in alternative energy production costs, renewable energy is now the domain of corporate giants like General Electric (NYSE: GE), Siemens (NYSE: SI), and ABB (NYSE: ABB). And some of the world's most powerful people are facilitating renewable energy's growth.

In this chapter, I cover some of the well-known names committed to expanding the use of clean energy, the utilities that are adopting it, and the funds you can invest in to take advantage.

Funding the Modern Energy Revolution

Take a look at Warren Buffett. One of the richest men on the planet, Buffett has invested billions in the modern energy space. In fact, by 2013, Buffett's MidAmerican Energy Holdings Company, a unit of Berkshire Hathaway (NYSE: BRK-A), had invested more than $6 billion in wind and more than $3 billion in solar. And in 2012, MidAmerican announced that it was actually forming a new branch of the company dedicated solely to renewable energy development.

Other billionaires who've already invested or pledged to invest no less than $1 billion in modern energy development include Sun Microsystems cofounder Vinod Khosla, CEO of the Virgin Group Richard Branson, and mega-successful investor George Soros.

The point is, today's renewable energy movement is being led primarily by the rich and powerful, not commune-seeking hippies and well-intentioned environmentalists. And because the economics of renewable and alternative energy integration actually support the rapid expansion of things like solar, wind, geothermal, and electric cars, those who invest appropriately can make an awful lot of money in this space.

But make no mistake, without the ability to make an economic case for renewable energy, opportunities would be nearly nonexistent. So you can certainly thank those who put in the hours and got their hands dirty in the earliest stages of the modern energy revolution, because those folks began the long and arduous journey of making modern, renewable energy cost-effective and competitive.

Modern Energy Developers

In the previous chapters I focus primarily on individual companies operating in various sectors of the clean energy market. But the truth is, the utilities are responsible for the lion's share of modern energy production. From solar to wind to geothermal, the utilities are funding much of the growth in the clean energy space. Here are six utilities that have significant exposure to modern, renewable power generation:

- ✔ **Pacific Gas & Electric (NYSE: PCG):** Thirty-seven percent of PG & E's energy mix is derived from renewable energy (20 percent of which is non-hydro). The company is also the first in the nation to deploy all-electric bucket trucks in the field, as well as 80 electric vehicle charging stations across its service area.

- ✔ **Northeast Utilities (NYSE: NU):** Twenty-two percent of Northern Utilities' energy mix (through its Public Service of New Hampshire division) is derived from renewable energy.

- ✔ **Consolidated Edison (NYSE: ED):** This utility allows customers the option of deriving 100 percent of their power from renewable energy — primarily hydro and wind power.

- ✔ **Sempra Energy (NYSE: SRE):** San Diego Gas & Electric, which Sempra owns, derived more than 20 percent of its power from renewables in 2011. In compliance with California's Renewable Portfolio Standard, the company is expected to derive 33 percent of its power from renewables by 2020.

- ✔ **Edison International (NYSE: EIX):** Southern California Edison, which is owned by Edison International, derives more than 21 percent of its power from renewables. Also in compliance with California's Renewables Portfolio Standard, the company is expected to derive 33 percent of its power from renewables by 2020.

- ✔ **NextEra Energy (NYSE:NEE):** More than 22 percent of NextEra Energy's energy mix is derived from renewables. It's also the largest wind energy provider in the United States.

California: Spearheading the renewable revolution

In 2006, California Senate Bill 107 mandated that 20 percent of the state's electricity retail sales must come from renewable energy sources by 2010. Then, in 2008, Governor Arnold Schwarzenegger issued an executive order that mandated retail sellers of electricity generate no less than 33 percent of their power from renewable energy by 2020. As of the end of 2012, about 20 percent of energy electricity sales for California's three largest investor-owned utilities came from renewables.

Funds for Modern Energy

For those who don't have the time or desire to trade or invest in individual stocks, opportunities are available to invest in modern energy funds. From mutual funds to exchange-traded funds (ETFs), a handful of fund-based investment vehicles are available to individual investors.

Many of these modern, renewable or "clean" energy funds tend to be heavily diversified with holdings that don't fall into the realm of renewable energy. This is because many of these funds look to secure a hedge against the uncertainty and volatility that still exists in the modern energy space today. So when researching these funds, do your due diligence and review the fund's holdings so you know exactly what you're investing in.

Modern energy mutual funds

Here are some of the more well-known modern energy mutual funds and their holdings:

- **New Alternatives Fund (NALFX):** This was the first mutual fund focused primarily on alternative energy. It chooses companies based on efforts in recycling, clean air and water, pollution prevention, and conservation. Its modern energy and modern energy-related holdings include

    - Abengoa (solar, biofuels, and transmission)

    - Brookfield Renewable Energy Partners (wind and hydropower)

    - Gamesa Corporation (wind)

    - Johnson Controls (batteries)

    - Ormat Technologies (geothermal)

- Vestas Wind Systems (wind)
- WaterFurnace Renewable Energy (geothermal)

✔ **Alger Green Fund (SPEGX):** Eighty percent of this fund is dedicated to companies that, according to management, "conduct their business in an environmentally sustainable manner while demonstrating promising growth potential." Its modern energy and modern energy-related holdings include

- Cree, Inc. (LED lighting)
- First Solar (solar)
- General Electric (wind and energy efficiency)
- Covanta Holding Corp. (waste-to-energy)
- Itron, Inc. (smart meters)
- Tesla Motors (electric cars)
- EnerNOC, Inc. (energy management systems)
- Johnson Controls
- Solazyme, Inc. (biofuels)

✔ **Calvert Global Alternative Energy Fund (CGAEX):** This is probably one of the most popular modern energy funds. Its holdings include

- Eaton Corp. (power management systems)
- Johnson Controls
- Cree, Inc.
- Covanta Holding Corp.
- NextEra Energy (power generation)
- Cosan (biofuels)
- Tesla Motors
- Ormat Technologies
- Itron, Inc.
- Ameresco, Inc. (energy management)
- Trina Solar (solar)

✔ **Guinness Atkinson Alternative Energy Fund (GAAEX):** This fund focuses primarily on alternative energy or energy technology companies. Some of these include

- Canada Lithium (lithium)
- Good Energy Group PLC (decentralized power development)
- Boralex (solar)

- SunPower Corp. (solar)

- Ormat Technologies

- WaterFurnace Renewable Energy (geothermal)

- Nordex (wind)

Modern energy ETFs

ETFs serve as an excellent vehicle for those seeking to invest in the modern energy space through dedicated funds. You can choose from both diversified modern energy ETFs and sector-specific modern energy ETFs.

Clean energy funds certainly allow you to just "set it and forget it," but you're likely to get the most bang for your buck by investing in individual clean energy stocks or directly in clean energy upgrades (like solar, energy-efficient windows, and LEDs) for your home or office. In many cases, replacing old windows with modern, energy-efficient windows is a very savvy investment.

Diversified

Diversified clean energy funds hold companies from multiple sectors within the industry. The following funds will give you exposure to all things directly and tangentially related to renewable energy and sustainability, including wind, solar, biofuels, smart grid, efficiency, electric vehicle, and green building plays.

- ✔ **Market Vectors Global Alternative Energy ETF (NYSE: GEX):** This fund's holdings include

  - Cree, Inc.

  - Cosan

  - Enel Green Power SpA (solar, wind, hydropower, geothermal, and biomass)

  - Tesla Motors

  - Covanta Holding Corp.

  - EnerSys (batteries)

  - China Longyuan Power Group (wind)

  - SolarCity Corp. (solar)

  - MEMC Electronic Materials (solar)

  - SunPower Corp.

  - Xinjiang Goldwind Science & Technology (solar)

✔ **PowerShares WilderHill Clean Energy ETF (NYSE: PBW):** This fund's holdings include

- First Solar

- Tesla Motors

- SolarCity Corp.

- Trina Solar

- Maxwell Technologies (ultracapacitors and supercapacitors)

- EnerNOC, Inc.

- Ormat Technologies

✔ **First Trust NASDAQ Clean Edge Green Energy Index Fund (NASDAQ: QCLN):** This fund's holdings include

- Cree, Inc.

- Tesla Motors

- Itron, Inc.

- First Solar

- Veeco Instruments (LED lighting)

- AVX Corporation (electronic components)

Sector-specific

Sector-specific funds are just that: they only hold companies that operate in one segment of the clean energy market. The funds below focus exclusively on solar, wind, or the smart grid.

✔ **Market Vectors Solar Energy ETF (NYSE: KWT):** This fund's holdings include

- First Solar

- Wacker Chemie AG

- GCL-Poly Energy Holdings

- MEMC Electronic Materials

- Hanergy Solar Group

- SunPower Corp.

- Power-One, Inc.

- GT Advanced Technologies

✔ **Claymore/MAC Global Solar Energy ETF (NYSE: TAN):** This fund's holdings include

- First Solar
- GCL-Poly Energy Holdings
- Power-One, Inc.
- MEMC Electronic Materials
- GT Advanced Technologies
- SunPower Corp.
- Trina Solar
- Renewable Energy Corp.

✔ **First Trust Global Wind Energy ETF (NYSE: FAN):** This fund's holdings include

- China Longyuan Power Group
- Nordex AG
- Gamesa Corporation
- Vestas Wind Systems
- Iberdrola
- EDP Renovaveis
- Greentech Energy Systems
- China WindPower Group
- Japan Wind Development Co.

✔ **First Trust NASDAQ Clean Edge Smart Grid Infrastructure Index Fund (NASDAQ: GRID):** This fund's holdings include

- ABB
- Quanta Services
- Schneider Electric
- General Cable Corporation
- Itron, Inc.
- ITC Holdings Corporation
- ESCO Technologies, Inc.
- MYR Group, Inc.

Continuing your modern energy education

Keep in mind that the modern energy industry is still very young, and it continues to grow and develop at light speed. And what you've read in this chapter is only the beginning. It's an introduction, really, to a world of investment opportunities that will become more and more profitable as the world continues to transition to an energy economy that's more diversified and more inclusive of modern energy technologies, such as wind, solar, geothermal, energy efficiency, and alternative transportation fuels.

If you want to stay up to speed on the rapidly changing environment of modern energy, visit websites such as www.greenchip stocks.com and www.energyand capital.com, both of which I contribute to. These two sites have a long history of publishing up-to-the-minute information and intelligence on modern energy investing. They can be your guide to wealth creation in the new energy economy.

Part VI
The Part of Tens

the part of tens

 Enjoy an additional Energy Investing Part of Tens chapter online at www.dummies.com/extras/energyinvesting.

In this part . . .

- ✔ Uncover the top energy investment resources to enhance your energy investment education.

- ✔ Identify which energy-related data and figures are most critical to track.

- ✔ See the top exchange-traded funds (ETFs) for investing in energy.

- ✔ Discover the energy breakthroughs and events that will shape the future.

Chapter 23

Top Ten Energy Investment Resources

*O*ne of the most important factors for success when investing in energy is staying up to date on related data and news. But with the entire Internet at your fingertips, knowing exactly where to get the best information can be difficult.

Over the years, I've put together a short list of trusted sites, outlets, and organizations that offer the most accurate energy figures, the freshest news, and the most insightful analysis. Using these resources, which I present in this chapter, ensures that you're always on top of new and changing themes in the energy sector to make you a better investor.

Energy & Capital

I've been an editor at Energy & Capital since 2007. Together with energy experts Jeff Siegel, Keith Kohl, and Christian DeHaemer — all of whom contributed to this book — I put out a daily newsletter and web content that covers every facet of the energy industry. You can find us at www.energy andcapital.com.

Our website is where we forecast oil's run to more than $145 per barrel long before it happened. We were discussing the coming revolution in fracking four years before it hit the mainstream press. We publish several pieces every day that not only help you understand what's happening with energy around the world but also show you the best ways to invest for profit.

Energy Information Administration

I couldn't do my job without the Energy Information Administration (EIA), which you can find at www.eia.gov. I reference it several times throughout this book for a reason: It's the most comprehensive collection of energy data anywhere. You can find import and export figures, reserve numbers, pricing data, and production rates for every energy source. Read its weekly reviews to keep your finger on the pulse of what's happening in every sector of the market.

You also find reports and analysis that project what the energy scenario will look like in individual states, the entire United States, and countries around the world. Its "Annual Energy Outlook" should be a staple in your energy investment library because it helps you make smart decisions based on coming trends.

International Energy Agency

Founded in response to the oil crisis of the early 1970s, the International Energy Agency (IEA) is online at www.iea.org. It's an independent organization working to ensure affordable and sustainable energy for its 28 member nations. Its analysis, reports, and recommendations are respected the world over.

Its flagship publication is the annual "World Energy Outlook," which projects supply, demand, investment broken down by country, and fuel for the next two decades. That publication costs a couple hundred bucks, but the IEA also offers hundreds of free energy reports that you can find at www.iea.org/publications/freepublications.

The CME Group

The CME Group was formed when the Chicago Mercantile Exchange merged with the Chicago Board of Trade (CBOT) in 2007. It has since purchased the New York Mercantile Exchange (NYMEX), Commodity Exchange, Inc. (COMEX), the Kansas City Board of Trade (KCBOT), and 90 percent of Dow Jones indexes, including the Dow Jones Industrial Average. So as you can imagine, it controls an exorbitant amount of trading information and data.

As it pertains to energy, you can find much of that information at www. cmegroup.com/trading/energy. You can see current prices and get charts for all energy commodities traded on the exchange, look at the contract expiration calendar, learn with simulated trading, and get access to a variety of analytic reports and articles.

The Oil Drum

The Oil Drum (www.theoildrum.com), published by the Institute for the Study of Energy and Our Future, features no-spin analysis of oil data from across the globe. It's run by a team of petroleum geologists and engineers with hundreds of combined years in the oil business.

The posts on the site analyze the projections of major oil companies and global governments and offer proprietary studies and projections about the global oil industry. You won't find a more in-depth cumulative analysis of the global oil industry by high-level thinkers anywhere else on the web.

Greentech Media

Back when my beat was alternative energy, I checked out www.greentech media.com every single day. Its team of contributors post several unique clean energy articles on a daily basis, covering everything from solar and wind to efficiency and corporate sustainability.

It also posts case studies and reports from businesses, universities, and organizations from around the world and publishes in-depth reports on every sector of the clean energy market, complete with production forecasts, policy analysis, and investment totals.

Gregor.us

If you're looking for well-reasoned, well-researched, long-form analysis of macro energy trends, the eponymous Gregor.us is where to find it. Run by journalist Gregor Macdonald, it does a wonderful job of getting you to think about the shape the ongoing energy transition will continue to take. The site isn't just about statistics and figures but about getting you to consider the various implications of providing 7 billion people with energy from finite resources. It takes you out of your comfort zone to think about energy in ways you never have, making you a more sharp-witted investor.

Bloomberg

For daily energy news, you want to stay on top of www.bloomberg.com/ news/energy. On any given day, you'll find most of what you need to know about the energy sector at this site. You can also find information, news, charts, and analysis for energy companies and commodities. The slide shows and videos are a great way to get a maximum amount of information in a minimum amount of time.

Oil & Gas Journal

You won't find a more comprehensive website devoted solely to oil and gas than this site (www.ogj.com), which has dedicated sections for everything from exploration to transportation. If something happens in the oil and gas industry, it's sure to be here. Because it's a trade journal, you'll see oil and gas insights here that you won't find anywhere else, and you can even subscribe to the magazine to get those insights delivered right to your door.

Yahoo! Finance

Other than your broker's website, Yahoo! Finance (www.finance.yahoo. com) is the most comprehensive portal for universal stock information. You can get critical data for individual companies like price, volume, price-to-equity ratios, and share structure information, as well as info on how insiders and institutions have been trading a certain stock. You can also search for companies by sector and see how they stack up against their peers in multiple metrics. Additionally, you can use Yahoo!'s advanced charting feature to see how an individual or group of stocks is performing, or you can see recent news to find out what a company has been up to and what analysts are saying about it.

Chapter 24

Top Ten Energy Data to Track

The world of energy is fast-moving. Prices for key fuels change daily, often by the minute. Supply and demand are also in constant flux. What's more, many macroeconomic factors affect the energy markets, and you must monitor those as well. You certainly have a lot to keep track of, and doing so can be daunting, even for the most seasoned investor. In this chapter, I present a list of the top ten energy-related metrics you should keep tabs on to be a successful energy investor.

Crude Oil Prices

For me, crude oil prices are the most important thing to watch in the energy game because they affect so many things. Of course, oil prices are critical if you trade oil futures or a fund that tracks them, but they also determine how much profit an oil company makes per barrel, after costs are netted out. The price of oil also dictates when other technologies become economically viable. Nobody would want an electric or natural gas vehicle, for example, if crude was still selling for $40 per barrel. And finally, global oil prices have larger implications. High oil prices that put gasoline and related products out of reach for average consumers can lead a country into recession, which would affect all other energy investments.

You should track both West Texas Intermediate and North Sea Brent crude, which are tracked on their exchange websites and quoted on many financial sites on the web.

Natural Gas Prices

Like crude oil prices, global natural gas prices have an impact far beyond just those who trade natural gas futures. Rising and falling prices determine the fuel mix that utilities choose to create electricity; they burn more gas when it's cheaper than coal or nuclear and less gas when it's more expensive.

You should also keep track of natural gas prices in various regional markets because the spread can be quite big. In 2013, for example, gas trading for around $3 per million British thermal units (MMBtu) in the United States was fetching around $15 per MMBtu in Asia. This price difference can affect where natural gas ultimately ends up and is why there's talk of exporting America's newfound gas wealth to Asia, where it commands the highest price.

EIA Reports

Rather than tell you to watch this or that report from the Energy Information Administration, I suggest following all of them. The EIA releases numerous reports that come out on a weekly, monthly, quarterly, and annual basis, and listing them all would take up way more than ten spots in this chapter. In Table 24-1, I list a few that you should pay particularly close attention to and give the frequency of their release.

Table 24-1	EIA Reports, Publishing Schedule	
Report	*Frequency*	*Schedule*
Annual Energy Outlook	Annually	December
Coal Production	Weekly	5 p.m. Thursday
Domestic Uranium Production Report	Quarterly	45 days after the end of the quarter
Electric Power Monthly	Monthly	Last week of the month
International Energy Outlook	Annually	June
Natural Gas Update	Weekly	2:30 p.m. Thursday
Petroleum Status Report	Weekly	10:30 a.m. (EST) Wednesday
Short-Term Energy Outlook	Monthly	First Tuesday after the first Thursday of each month
State Renewable Electricity Profiles	Annually	July

The EIA has a report for every energy sector tracking production, supply/demand, imports/exports, pricing, reserves, forecasts, and more. You can check out the full publishing schedule at www.eia.gov/reports.

World Energy Mix

Knowing the world's energy mix is a prime foundation for being a successful energy investor. It's one of those things you should keep in the back of your mind and take note of annually to see how it's evolving. You can also look at today's mix compared to future forecasts to see which sectors are slated to grow the most. For the record, Table 24-2 shows the world's primary energy mix in 2011, the most recent year for which complete data is available.

Table 24-2	World Energy Mix, 2011
Source	*Percent of Total*
Oil	33%
Coal	30%
Natural gas	24%
Hydro	6%
Nuclear	5%
Renewables	2%

Table 24-2 shows the primary energy mix, meaning the total of all fuels used for all purposes. If you look at just the electricity mix, you'll see a different scenario.

You can find this information from various sources, and all will vary, but the three I use the most are:

✔ EIA's International Energy Outlook

✔ The International Energy Agency's (IEA) World Energy Outlook

✔ BP's Statistical Review of World Energy

OPEC Production

When a single organization supplies over one third of the world's oil, it's important to keep track of it. The Organization of the Petroleum Exporting Countries (OPEC) can raise or lower production quotas at will, affecting global oil prices in the process. Knowing how much oil OPEC is producing is a smart way to avoid unexpected surprises.

OPEC publishes its production info and other important data on its website. I like to check out its Market Indicators report, which comes out monthly. You can find it at www.opec.org/opec_web/en/data_graphs/334.htm.

Gross Domestic Product

Gross domestic product (GDP) is the most closely watched macroeconomic indicator in the world. It's a measure of all goods and services produced by all entities in a given country. A rising GDP is bullish for energy because countries need more energy to produce an expanding amount of goods. Conversely, a falling GDP is bearish for energy.

You can find the GDP for every country, but I like to keep tabs on the United States, China, and total world figures. The United Nations, the International Monetary Fund, and the World Bank all publish this data annually.

U.S. Dollar

As the world's reserve currency, the U.S. dollar is used to price global energy commodities. It also has an impact on the bottom line of U.S. companies that operate in many countries. When the dollar rises compared to other currencies, for example, it takes less of them to buy a barrel of oil, and prices fall. When the dollar is falling, it takes more of them to buy a barrel of oil, and prices rise.

Similarly, if a U.S. oil company has to pay a firm in a foreign country, and the dollar is strong against that country's currency, the U.S. company needs fewer dollars to pay the foreign firm, which boosts the bottom line.

Levelized Cost of New Electricity Generation

The *levelized cost* of electricity generation is the break-even price for a specific fuel source over the life of the project, when all costs are considered. This price ranges from $60 to $300 per megawatt-hour depending on the fuel source, with natural gas being the current cheapest and solar thermal the most expensive.

But that situation is changing, and you need to watch it. By 2018, for example, the EIA is forecasting the levelized cost of electricity from wind to be $86.60 per megawatt-hour, which would be cheaper than electricity from coal, nuclear, and some forms of natural gas. How much a power plant costs over its lifetime is a prime factor for utilities when deciding what kind of energy assets to acquire. And as an investor, you want to know which sources will see increased demand as a result of falling costs.

Forecast Growth Rates

If you knew how fast each energy source would grow in the future, being a successful investor would be much easier. And though you can never know precisely what the future holds, looking at forecast growth rates from various agencies can give you a rough idea. Doing so is extremely beneficial if you're a long-term investor.

Forecasts are available from the EIA, the IEA, many of the major oil companies, and several third-party consulting firms. They vary slightly, so check them all out to arrive at a consensus, and make long-term investments based on the forecast growth trajectory of individual energy sources.

Your Utility Bill

I check out all the various energy data presented in this chapter, but I still find great insights by examining my monthly utility bill. It shows me the current cost of natural gas and electricity in my area; how much I used that month, the previous month, and the same month a year ago; and what the average temperature was in those months. Your utility bill is a great tool to help you identify annual trends that can make you a better investor. Not only that, but paying closer attention to your personal energy consumption can help you make smart, energy-efficient investments for your home.

Chapter 25

Top Ten Energy ETFs

Throughout this book, I present various exchange-traded funds to help you profit from every sector of the energy market. ETFs are a wise choice if you manage your own portfolio because they allow you to gain diversified exposure without making multiple stock purchases and paying multiple fees.

ETFs also allow you to profit from certain strategies without risking a lot of capital, and they give you access to strategies once reserved for sophisticated investors. Rather than trading an oil futures contract (which requires a 1,000-barrel commitment) to profit from rising oil prices, for example, you can simply buy an ETF that's designed to track oil's price. Similarly, instead of trading on margin for leverage or employing risky strategies like shorting, you can buy an ETF that employs a short or leveraged strategy for you.

In this chapter, I cover a wide range of go-to ETFs that allow you to invest in energy from multiple angles.

Energy Select Sector SPDR

Perhaps the most ubiquitous energy ETF, Energy Select Sector SPDR (NYSE: XLE) trades more than 5 million shares per day, on average. It's designed to track the return of the S&P Energy Select Sector Index (INDEX: IXE). Since its inception in December 1998, the fund has delivered more than 10 percent annualized returns. According to its website, $10,000 invested on the day it started trading would be worth nearly $45,000 today.

It offers a 1.75 percent dividend yield while giving you access to 45 of the most well-known stocks in the energy industry by allocating 80 percent of its assets to oil, gas, and consumable fuels and 20 percent to energy equipment and services. A glance at its holdings reveals all the household names, like Exxon, Chevron, Hess, Valero, and more. I suggest considering XLE as a staple of your energy portfolio.

Vanguard Energy

Vanguard has come to be known for low-cost, well-managed funds by investors and advisors alike, and the Vanguard Energy ETF (NYSE: VDE) is no different. At 0.14 percent, its expense ratio is 91 percent lower than other funds with similar holdings. Though it's not as liquid as the Energy Select Sector SPDR discussed in the preceding section, it trades around 100,000 shares per day and tracks the MSCI U.S. Investable Market Energy 25/50 Index. It holds 169 companies for great diversification, including exposure to coal and uranium. Given that Vanguard invented the index fund and is focused on passing savings on to investors, the Vanguard Energy ETF is a top contender if you're looking to carve out a long-term diversified position in energy.

PowerShares Dynamic Energy Sector

The nice thing about the PowerShares Dynamic Energy Sector ETF (NYSE: PXI) is that it's actively managed. It doesn't just track an index, although it's based on the Dynamic Energy Sector Intellidex Index, which the fund says "evaluated companies based on a variety of investment merit criteria." This fund costs a bit more than some others, though, with an expense ratio of 0.66 percent. But it's proving to be worth it. The fund outperformed the S&P 500 Energy Sector Index almost three times over between 2008 and 2013. It is rebalanced and reconstituted quarterly, and it isn't as heavily weighted toward the oil majors as other major energy funds.

iShares S&P Global Energy Sector

The iShares S&P Global Energy Sector fund (NYSE: IXC) is a prime choice to get exposure to major energy companies headquartered outside of the United States. Of the 90 stocks the fund holds, 49 percent of them are international energy players. Though the fund is still heavily weighted with Exxon (14.43 percent of assets) and Chevron (8.59 percent of assets), it also has BP, Royal Dutch Shell, Total, and Eni among its top-ten holdings. With a 0.48

percent expense ratio, it's a bit more expensive than other index funds, but it also boasts a 2.44 percent dividend yield and has delivered more than 12 percent annual returns since 2003.

Market Vectors Uranium+Nuclear Energy

Market Vectors Uranium+Nuclear Energy (NYSE: NLR), which tracks the DAXglobal Nuclear Energy Index, is a one-stop shop for all your nuclear investment needs. It gives you exposure to uranium miners, fuel fabricators, waste handlers, reactor builders, and utilities with nuclear assets. It's also geographically diversified, with 26.7 percent of its assets in Canada, 24.8 percent in Japan, 21.5 percent in the United States, and 12 percent in France. If you're looking to get broad exposure to the global nuclear industry, this fund is definitely the way to go.

Market Vectors Coal

Like the nuclear fund in the preceding section, Market Vectors Coal (NYSE: KOL) is one of the few ways to take a broad stake in a niche energy sector with a single purchase. It holds 34 coal-related stocks that are part of the Market Vectors Global Coal Index, with more than 80 percent of its assets in the United States, China, Australia, and Indonesia — the leading coal-producing nations. This fund is where you want to be as emerging markets continue to fuel their growth with coal.

PowerShares DB Energy

If you want to invest in energy commodity prices but don't want to trade expensive futures contracts, then PowerShares DB Energy (NYSE: DBE) is the way to go. It holds equal weightings in Brent crude, West Texas Intermediate, gasoline, and heating oil futures at 22.5 percent apiece, with the remaining 10 percent in natural gas futures.

Be careful, though: This fund is cheaper than many others because it doesn't have the minimum trading requirements associated with futures, but it's still just as risky because of the speculative nature of the futures contracts it holds.

PowerShares Global Clean Energy

If you want exposure to alternative and renewable energy companies, take a look at the PowerShares Global Clean Energy fund (NYSE: PBD). It invests 90 percent of its assets in stocks that comprise the WilderHill New Energy Global Innovation Index. But you won't find just energy companies in this fund. It has 23.1 percent of its assets in utilities and 5.3 percent in energy, but more than 60 percent in information technology and industrials, giving you access to companies that are driving efficiency or manufacturing the picks and shovels of renewable energy, like LED manufacturer Cree (NASDAQ: CREE) and smart grid pioneer EnerNOC (NASDAQ: ENOC).

Alerian MLP

With a fracking boom underway, the United States is producing more oil and gas than it has in more than a decade. And all that fuel needs to be transported, stored, and distributed, making energy infrastructure a great play. The Alerian MLP ETF (NYSE: AMLP) capitalizes not only on this infrastructure need but also on the dividend payments of master limited partnerships (MLPs). The fund holds 25 energy-related MLPs, like Kinder Morgan Energy, Enterprise Products, and Enbridge Energy.

This fund also yields 5.72 percent (though this can change) and alleviates the tax complications of owning MLPs by allowing you to report with a Form 1099 instead of a Schedule K-1. I think it's smart to use a fund like this to generate income from the toll-road business models of energy infrastructure partnerships as the American oil and gas renaissance continues to play out.

Guggenheim S&P Global Water

As discussed in Chapter 3, the global energy industry requires a lot of water. Whether for nuclear cooling, well injection, or steel production, energy will never be able to escape its dependence on water. Guggenheim S&P Global Water (NYSE: CGW) can help you take financial advantage of this water dependence. It owns 53 companies that are a part of the S&P Global Water Index, with firms from the United States, UK, Switzerland, France, and Brazil among its top holdings. You get access to companies that clean and transport water and companies that make the pipes, valves, and meters that get water where it needs to go.

Chapter 26

Top Ten Energy Developments on the Horizon

*E*nergy investors are always looking for the next big thing. You can see this clearly throughout energy's history, covered in Chapter 2, as conventional energy technologies are perpetually replaced with disruptive ones: horses to cars, gas lamps to electricity, whale oil to petroleum, and so on.

With each of these disruptions come new opportunities for investment. Investing early in a successful new technology is the stuff that makes legends. In this chapter, I cover a few breakthroughs I believe may have major impacts on the energy market in coming years.

But as discussed throughout this book, the world is already in the midst of a massive energy transition. Oil is getting expensive and harder to find, while natural gas should remain relatively cheap for years to come. The developed world is shunning coal and beginning to embrace renewables. The developing world will take whatever it can get.

This transition is ongoing, and this chapter also covers what its implications will be over the coming years.

Demand Growth

Energy is a great sector to invest in because, barring something catastrophic in the macro economy, demand is always growing. The future will be no different; it will usher in myriad opportunities to parlay that demand growth into winning investments.

The Energy Information Administration projects total world energy consumption to be 770 quadrillion Btus in 2035, as you can see in Figure 26-1. That's more than a 50 percent increase in two decades' time.

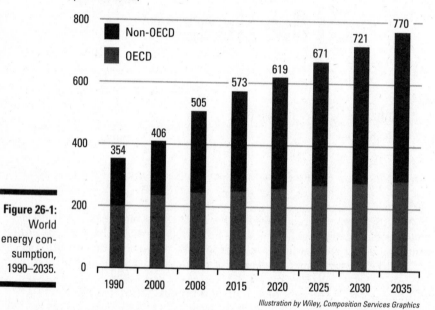

World Energy Consumption, 1990–2035
(quadrillion Btu)

Figure 26-1:
World
energy con-
sumption,
1990–2035.

All available options will be on the table as the world races to meet this surging demand. The world population will need as much oil, natural gas, coal, uranium, and renewables as it can get. And there will be numerous improvements made to how people get these energy options — and how they use them — along the way.

Continued Fracking Expansion

A global expansion of hydraulic fracturing, to extract as much oil and gas from tight formations as possible, is in the offing. In the early 2010s, the United States was the fracking leader. The technology was perfected there and was employed first by U.S. companies to harvest reserves like the Bakken, Barnett, and Marcellus shale formations. As a result, the United States produced more oil in 2012 than it has since 1996 and more natural gas than any other year in history.

Other countries now want to apply that technology to their own fields. Major oil companies from China and Europe are already buying up U.S. fracking assets to learn the ropes. Just look at the deals that have been struck since 2011:

- ✔ China's Sinopec (NYSE: SNP) paid $2.2 billion for a partial stake in some of Devon Energy's (NYSE: DVN) shale plays.

- ✔ PetroChina (NYSE: PTR) paid $1.2 billion to purchase shale acres from Encana (NYSE: ECA).

- ✔ Sinopec paid $1 billion for Oklahoma fields from Chesapeake Energy (NYSE: CHK).

- ✔ CNOOC Limited (NYSE: CEO) paid $15.1 billion to buy out Nexen Inc. (NYSE: NXY).

- ✔ Total (NYSE: TOT) paid $2.3 billion to Chesapeake Energy for 619,000 acres in Ohio's Utica shale.

Be on the lookout for these companies, and the U.S. companies they bought or learned from, to expand fracking to any corner of the globe where they can economically harvest unconventional oil reserves.

IGas Energy (LSE: IGAS) CEO Andrew Austin has said that the production of shale gas in the UK is likely by 2016. The British Geological Survey has said there may be shale reserves there totaling more than 5 trillion cubic feet (TCF). Exploration is also underway in Austria, Bulgaria, Germany, Hungary, Ireland, Poland, and Ukraine.

Falcon Oil & Gas (TSX-V: FO), Shell (NYSE: RDS), Sasol (NYSE: SSL), Chesapeake Energy (NYSE: CHK), and Statoil (NYSE: STO) are obtaining permits in South Africa. Reliance Natural Resources and Vikas are looking into shale gas in India. Australia, New Zealand, and South America also have significant reserves that have yet to be fully quantified and explored.

You want to keep an eye on the companies developing new shale reserves over the coming years.

Methane Hydrates

While fracking is currently underway and will expand in the coming years, a new source of natural gas may also burst onto the scene. Unless you're an oceanic geologist, *methane hydrates* is likely an unfamiliar term. Yet these massive deposits of methane gas may turn into the next major energy source.

Methane hydrates, also called *methane ice,* are basically a form of water ice that contains methane gas, the principal component of natural gas. This ice is produced when methane gas and water are merged at freezing temperatures. Under intense pressure for millions of years, tiny molecules of methane slowly become encased in ice, creating methane hydrates.

Originally, methane hydrates were thought to occur only in the outer regions of the solar system, where temperatures are low and water ice is common. But with recent technology, extremely large deposits of methane hydrates have been found under sediments all across Earth's ocean floors. Today, methane hydrate reservoirs are thought to contain between two and ten times the world's reserves of conventional natural gas.

China is in the middle of a ten-year, $100 million program to study how to economically recover methane hydrates. A recoverable reserve of around 100 billion cubic meters has also been discovered under the Gulf of Mexico.

A joint project by ConocoPhillips (NYSE: COP) and Japan Oil, Gas, and Metals National Corporation (JOGMEC), partially funded by the U.S. Department of Energy, announced it had successfully extracted natural gas from methane hydrates in early 2013 and is currently evaluating the findings' economic viability. Japan estimates that around 1.1 trillion cubic meters of natural gas lie 300 meters under the sea in the Nankai Trough — enough to power the entire country for ten years.

If the technology to locate and extract this gas is perfected, it would go a long way toward bridging the gap to renewables with cleaner-burning natural gas.

Natural Gas Vehicles

With so much natural gas being produced worldwide, using it to power vehicles and machines makes a lot of sense. But currently, less than 1 percent of natural gas goes toward this purpose. As touched on in Chapter 7, many more vehicles, especially fleets, are starting to use natural gas instead of gasoline.

Already, AT&T, UPS, Waste Management, and a number of taxi and public transportation fleets have switched to natural gas–powered trucks and buses. Still, the United States has only a few hundred thousand natural gas vehicles.

This is beginning to change, as Honda, Ford, General Motors, and Chrysler Group have all added natural gas options to their lineup of vehicles. Ford sold four times as many natural gas vehicles in 2012 as it did in 2010, and

Navigant Research is forecasting the market to grow 10 percent per year through 2019.

Westport Innovations (NASDAQ: WPRT), in conjunction with Cummins (NYSE: CMI), is making engines that will replace diesel in heavy trucks and buses. Clean Energy Fuels (NASDAQ: CLNE) and Shell (NYSE: RDS) are building a network of fueling stations. And General Electric (NYSE: GE) is working on a home fueling station that would tie into your local natural gas supply.

Because natural gas is cheaper, burns cleaner, and is more abundant than oil, I'd look for natural gas vehicles to catch on in a big way.

Energy Independence of the United States

In its 2012 World Energy Outlook, the International Energy Agency forecast that the United States could temporarily pass Saudi Arabia as the world's largest oil producer by 2020. But it also said the United States would still be importing 3.4 million barrels of oil per day (nearly 20 percent of current consumption) in 2035.

The idea that the United States will become energy-independent is predicated on a significant increase in natural gas production that may displace oil demand, as well as increased efficiency measures that will decrease overall demand.

If it does occur, I don't see it happening for the next half century. Either way, a country becoming energy-independent has little investment value because energy is a global commodity. Your bottom line would be better served focusing on the companies that are increasing oil and gas production and deploying energy-efficiency technologies rather than whether the United States can provide all its energy needs with domestic resources.

Grid Parity

Grid parity is the point at which alternative energy sources can supply electricity at or below the levelized cost of energy of conventional resources. It's an important threshold because it signifies the point when renewables like solar and wind can compete directly with coal, nuclear, and natural gas without government subsidies.

When grid parity occurs in a certain location, the use of alternative sources of energy covered in Part IV of this book expand much more rapidly, leading to a better investment scenario for that sector.

Many factors affect when grid parity occurs, of course. Commodity prices, government regulation of utility rates, and macroeconomic events can cause a fluctuation in energy prices of all stripes, making an exact date for global grid parity hard to nail down. But many countries and a few U.S. states already enjoy grid parity for solar, including Australia, India, Italy, Spain, and Hawaii.

With fossil fuel prices generally heading higher and the cost of renewables generally falling lower, widespread grid parity is expected between 2015 and 2020. This will be a major catalyst for all companies in the renewable energy space.

Vehicle-to-Grid Technology

Right now your car only consumes energy. But with vehicle-to-grid technology, future electric cars could communicate with the power grid and help quell periods of high demand by selling some of their batteries' juice to the local utility. Because cars are parked the majority of the time, they can easily be used to absorb any excess demand or provide emergency supply.

It's still early, but the Pacific Gas & Electric Company (NYSE: PCG) is already using the Toyota Prius for vehicle-to-grid experiments on Google's Mountain View campus. And Xcel Energy (NYSE: XEL) is conducting similar tests with Ford's Escape Hybrid. In Denmark, IBM (NYSE: IBM), Siemens (NYSE: SI), and DONG Energy are working with several universities to use electric vehicles to help balance the unpredictable amounts of energy produced by the country's numerous wind farms.

You want to keep an eye on utilities, major technology conglomerates, and car and battery manufacturers for potential investment opportunities.

Next-Gen Nuclear Reactors

The world currently uses second and third generation nuclear reactors, most of which are pressurized water reactors (PWR) or boiling water reactors (BWR), with the type of water referring to how the plant is cooled. But a variety of Generation IV reactors are currently being developed, and the U.S. Nuclear Regulatory Commission has said it may approve some of the designs as early as 2013.

Three such reactors are already undergoing pre-application review, with design certification expected for small modular reactors from Westinghouse (87 percent owned by Toshiba — OTC: TOSBF) and Babcock & Wilcox (NYSE: BWC) in 2014.

This coming series of smaller, safer reactors may finally be the spark needed to light off a nuclear renaissance that was supposed to begin a decade ago.

Graphene

Graphene is simply a one-atom-thick layer of graphite. Andre Geim and Konstantin Novoselov discovered it in 2004, earning them both Nobel prizes and knighthoods. Because of its unique characteristics, graphene is being looked to for major advances in medicine, energy, defense, and many other industries.

And it's not hard to see why. Graphene is nearly 1 million times thinner than a human hair, yet it's 200 times stronger than steel and conducts electricity better than copper. Already, researchers are working on graphene electrodes that allow batteries to store 10 times as much energy and charge 10 times faster, solar cells that can produce 10,000 times more energy from a given amount of carbon than any fossil fuel, and tiny sensors that can be injected underground in search of gas and oil.

 Remember, graphene is made of carbon, the fourth most abundant element on Earth. So instead of a resource play, you want to seek out companies that are using graphene to make technological leaps forward.

Hydrogen

No roundup of future energy developments would be complete without mentioning hydrogen, which has been a few years away for the past 40 years. Indeed, the term *hydrogen economy* was coined all the way back in 1970.

There are no large sources of pure hydrogen, so it has to be made from hydrocarbons or water electrolysis, which actually makes it an energy carrier rather than an energy source. And today, more than 90 percent of the world's hydrogen is produced from fossil fuels, meaning the world would still depend on natural gas, oil, and coal to produce the necessary hydrogen to run engines.

Even though using a hydrogen fuel cell and an electric motor to power a car would be two to three times more efficient than a gasoline engine, doing so is still much more expensive. And hydrogen is extremely dangerous to transport and store, as evidenced by the Hindenburg disaster in 1937.

Though many auto companies and countries are testing hydrogen distribution systems, progress has been extremely slow. Iceland, the first country committed to transitioning to a hydrogen economy, doesn't think it will be possible until 2050.

I'm taking a wait-and-see approach to hydrogen investing, allowing more time for developments to be made before taking a stake in any related company.

Index

• **C** •

• N •

About the Authors

Nick Hodge is an investment newsletter publisher based in Baltimore, Maryland. He is the founder and editor of *Outsider Club,* a daily newsletter that covers how retail investors can take control of and manage all their own investments. He's also the investment director of Early Advantage, a fee-based advisory service that researches and recommends investments for thousands of clients.

Though this is his first *For Dummies* book, Nick previously worked with Wiley as the coauthor of *Investing in Renewable Energy: Making Money on Green Chip Stocks.* His insights on energy and other areas of the stock market have also been published in *The Futurist, Renewable Energy World,* and *SFO Magazine.* He's also gotten out from behind the keyboard to be a guest on the Business News Network, Yahoo!'s Daily Ticker, Clean Skies TV, and several radio programs. Hodge has been a featured speaker at the Money Show, the New Orleans Investment Conference, and the Cambridge House International series of conferences.

The author holds a Bachelor of Arts from Loyola University Maryland, where he studied communications after leaving his family's small farm in northeastern Maryland. When he's not writing, investing, or meeting with company executives, Nick can usually be found in a boat on the Chesapeake or on a farm pursuing the outdoor activities he grew up with and continues to love. His pit bull, Denver, is the most handsome dog you'll ever meet. Nick's website is www.outsiderclub.com.

Jeff Siegel is an analyst and writer specializing in energy investing, with a focus on alternative and renewable energy. He is the managing editor of the independent investment advisories *Energy & Capital* and *Wealth Daily,* and he is the lead author of *Investing in Renewable Energy: Making Money on Green Chip Stocks* (Wiley).

Christian DeHaemer is an internationally acclaimed author who has been writing about emerging markets and energy investments since 1996. He is managing editor of the investment newsletter *Crisis & Opportunity,* and he publishes a weekly column in *Energy & Capital.*

Keith Kohl is the analyst and chief investment strategist for the investment advisories *Energy Investor* and *Oil & Gas Trader.* For the better part of a decade, Keith has been reaching out to hundreds of thousands of readers every day, helping them capitalize on the rapidly changing face of the North American energy landscape.

Dedication

For my grandparents, Italo and Antonietta Mazza, who crossed oceans, cultures, languages, and many other barriers to pave the way for a better future for themselves and those who came after them.

Author's Acknowledgments

My gratitude must be extended to Wiley for the opportunity to write this book. I am happy for tackling the task, though it proved challenging to produce an all-encompassing energy investment guide in an easily digestible form. Many of those challenges were eradicated and assuaged by Wiley's top-notch editorial team. I'm thankful for acquisitions editor Stacy Kennedy, who got this project rolling and showed a deft hand while ironing out wrinkles along the way. And I certainly appreciate all the hard work and back-and-forth with editors Tim Gallan, Todd Lothery, and Sarah Faulkner. Our e-mail exchanges numbered in the hundreds but only served to make the book better thanks to their attention to detail and quest for clarity.

Folks at my day job at Angel Publishing must also be commended for their contributions: Brianna Panzica for her research; Jason Azat for his image work; and Jason Freiert for setting up needed web pages and helping to navigate my refusal to purchase Microsoft Word. And thanks to everyone else for putting up with me while I pulled double-duty.

My coauthors — Keith Kohl, Christian DeHaemer, and Jeff Siegel — were also crucial in making sure each energy resource was covered as thoroughly as possible. Keith's oil and gas expertise, Christian's knowledge of coal and emerging markets, and Jeff's insights on all things clean and sustainable were invaluable during the writing process.

Finally, I'd like to thank my parents — John and Giulia Hodge — for instilling in me a passion to succeed and supporting me even when I didn't; my wife-to-be, Lindsay, for endless encouragement and packed lunches; and my dog, Denver, who has taught me not to stress too hard over anything.

Publisher's Acknowledgments

Acquisitions Editor: Stacy Kennedy

Project Editors: Tim Gallan, Sarah Faulkner

Copy Editor: Todd Lothery

Technical Editor: McLean Giles

Project Coordinator: Sheree Montgomery

Cover Image: ©iStockphoto.com/cemkolukisa

e & Mac

For Dummies,
Edition
1-118-49823-1

ne 5 For Dummies,
Edition
8-1-118-35201-4

acBook For Dummies,
h Edition
78-1-118-20920-2

S X Mountain Lion
or Dummies
78-1-118-39418-2

logging & Social Media

acebook For Dummies,
th Edition
78-1-118-09562-1

Mom Blogging
or Dummies
78-1-118-03843-7

interest For Dummies
78-1-118-32800-2

WordPress For Dummies,
th Edition
78-1-118-38318-6

Business

Commodities For Dummies,
nd Edition
78-1-118-01687-9

Investing For Dummies,
th Edition
78-0-470-90545-6

Personal Finance
For Dummies,
7th Edition
978-1-118-11785-9

QuickBooks 2013
For Dummies
978-1-118-35641-8

Small Business Marketing Kit
For Dummies,
3rd Edition
978-1-118-31183-7

Careers

Job Interviews
For Dummies,
4th Edition
978-1-118-11290-8

Job Searching with
Social Media
For Dummies
978-0-470-93072-4

Personal Branding
For Dummies
978-1-118-11792-7

Resumes For Dummies,
6th Edition
978-0-470-87361-8

Success as a Mediator
For Dummies
978-1-118-07862-4

Diet & Nutrition

Belly Fat Diet For Dummies
978-1-118-34585-6

Eating Clean For Dummies
978-1-118-00013-7

Nutrition For Dummies,
5th Edition
978-0-470-93231-5

Digital Photography

Digital Photography
For Dummies,
7th Edition
978-1-118-09203-3

Digital SLR Cameras &
Photography For Dummies,
4th Edition
978-1-118-14489-3

Photoshop Elements 11
For Dummies
978-1-118-40821-6

Gardening

Herb Gardening
For Dummies,
2nd Edition
978-0-470-61778-6

Vegetable Gardening
For Dummies,
2nd Edition
978-0-470-49870-5

Health

Anti-Inflammation Diet
For Dummies
978-1-118-02381-5

Diabetes For Dummies,
3rd Edition
978-0-470-27086-8

Living Paleo For Dummies
978-1-118-29405-5

Hobbies

Beekeeping
For Dummies
978-0-470-43065-1

eBay For Dummies,
7th Edition
978-1-118-09806-6

Raising Chickens
For Dummies
978-0-470-46544-8

Wine For Dummies,
5th Edition
978-1-118-28872-6

Writing Young Adult Fiction
For Dummies
978-0-470-94954-2

Language & Foreign Language

500 Spanish Verbs
For Dummies
978-1-118-02382-2

English Grammar
For Dummies,
2nd Edition
978-0-470-54664-2

French All-in One
For Dummies
978-1-118-22815-9

German Essentials
For Dummies
978-1-118-18422-6

Italian For Dummies
2nd Edition
978-1-118-00465-4

Available in print and e-book formats.

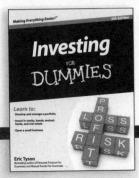

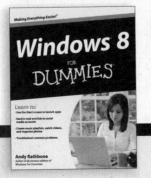

Math & Science

Algebra I For Dummies,
2nd Edition
978-0-470-55964-2

Anatomy and Physiology
For Dummies,
2nd Edition
978-0-470-92326-9

Astronomy For Dummies,
3rd Edition
978-1-118-37697-3

Biology For Dummies,
2nd Edition
978-0-470-59875-7

Chemistry For Dummies,
2nd Edition
978-1-1180-0730-3

Pre-Algebra Essentials
For Dummies
978-0-470-61838-7

Microsoft Office

Excel 2013 For Dummies
978-1-118-51012-4

Office 2013 All-in-One
For Dummies
978-1-118-51636-2

PowerPoint 2013
For Dummies
978-1-118-50253-2

Word 2013 For Dummies
978-1-118-49123-2

Music

Blues Harmonica
For Dummies
978-1-118-25269-7

Guitar For Dummies,
3rd Edition
978-1-118-11554-1

iPod & iTunes
For Dummies,
10th Edition
978-1-118-50864-0

Programming

Android Application
Development For
Dummies, 2nd Edition
978-1-118-38710-8

iOS 6 Application
Development For Dummies
978-1-118-50880-0

Java For Dummies,
5th Edition
978-0-470-37173-2

Religion & Inspiration

The Bible For Dummies
978-0-7645-5296-0

Buddhism For Dummies,
2nd Edition
978-1-118-02379-2

Catholicism For Dummies,
2nd Edition
978-1-118-07778-8

Self-Help & Relationships

Bipolar Disorder
For Dummies,
2nd Edition
978-1-118-33882-7

Meditation For Dummies,
3rd Edition
978-1-118-29144-3

Seniors

Computers For Seniors
For Dummies,
3rd Edition
978-1-118-11553-4

iPad For Seniors
For Dummies,
5th Edition
978-1-118-49708-1

Social Security
For Dummies
978-1-118-20573-0

Smartphones & Tablets

Android Phones
For Dummies
978-1-118-16952-0

Kindle Fire HD
For Dummies
978-1-118-42223-6

NOOK HD For Dummies,
Portable Edition
978-1-118-39498-4

Surface For Dummies
978-1-118-49634-3

Test Prep

ACT For Dummies,
5th Edition
978-1-118-01259-8

ASVAB For Dummies,
3rd Edition
978-0-470-63760-9

GRE For Dummies,
7th Edition
978-0-470-88921-3

Officer Candidate Tests,
For Dummies
978-0-470-59876-4

Physician's Assistant Exam
For Dummies
978-1-118-11556-5

Series 7 Exam
For Dummies
978-0-470-09932-2

Windows 8

Windows 8 For Dummies
978-1-118-13461-0

Windows 8 For Dummies,
Book + DVD Bundle
978-1-118-27167-4

Windows 8 All-in-One
For Dummies
978-1-118-11920-4

Available in print and e-book formats.

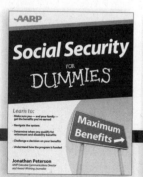

Take Dummies with you everywhere you go!

Whether you're excited about e-books, want more from the web, must have your mobile apps, or swept up in social media, Dummies makes everything easier .

Dummies products make life easie

- DIY
- Consumer Electronics
- Crafts
- Software
- Cookware
- Hobbies
- Videos
- Music
- Games
- and More!

For more information, go to **Dummies.com**® and search the store by category.

FOR DUMMIES

A Wiley Brand